# ON THE RADIO

# ON THE RADIO

## Music radio in Britain

STEPHEN BARNARD

OPEN UNIVERSITY PRESS
Milton Keynes • Philadelphia

*To my mother and father*

Open University Press
Open University Educational Enterprises Limited
12 Cofferidge Close
Stony Stratford
Milton Keynes MK11 1BY

and
242 Cherry Street
Philadelphia, PA 19106, USA

First Published 1989

*British Library Cataloguing in Publication Data*

Barnard, Stephen, *1954–*
   On the radio: music radio in Britain.
   1. Great Britain. Radio broadcasting.
   Role of pop music
   I. Title
   384.54'4

   ISBN 0–335–15284–8
   ISBN 0–335–15130–2 Pbk

*Library of Congress Cataloging-in-Publication Data*

Barnard, Stephen.
   On the radio: music radio in Britain/Stephen Barnard.
     p.      cm.
   Includes index.
   1. Popular music radio stations—Great Britain.    I. Title.
   PN1991.67.P67B37 1988
   302.2'344'0941—dc 19      88–22362   CIP
    ISBN 0–335–15284–8   ISBN 0–335–15130–2 (pbk.)

Printed and bound in Great Britain by
Biddles Limited, Guildford and Kings Lynn

# Contents

# Introduction

'Now everything is Radio GaGa' ran the words of a record by Queen, issued in 1984, that drew unfavourable parallels between contemporary radio and the radio shows of the 1950s and 1960s – the era of Radio Luxembourg and the pirate stations.[1] The record had interest not so much for anything startling in its music and lyrics as for the fact it was probably one of the most truly subversive records ever to find its way on to the airwaves – subversive because it undermined the jolly neutrality of daytime radio fare and put forward a point of view that seemed to demand a response from every presenter who played it. It questioned the very function of contemporary radio (a 'background noise' according to the lyric) prompting several disc jockeys on occasions when I was listening to drop their affable personas and attack what was interpreted as a criticism of their professionalism with some belligerence. That kind of reaction is rarely heard on radio: controversy interferes with the prevailing mood that radio programmes, during the daytime at least, seek to create – which was precisely the point that the song's creator, Queen's drummer Roger Taylor, was trying to make.

But *is* everything Radio GaGa? Radio is the most pervasive, the most readily available, the least escapable of all mass communications media in Britain. Radio entertainment accompanies human activity from dawn to dusk and, in the case of some stations, round the clock; the portability and cheapness of radio sets enables listening in bedroom and bathroom, kitchen and car, garden and garage; it is almost impossible to negotiate shopping, commuting, walking in the park, having an MOT test or football or cricket matches without encountering radio music or chatter at least once. Radio is routine, everyday, a portable pal, a soundtrack to life – but what *kind* of soundtrack does it provide? Does radio punctuate and enliven the lives of listeners, as many of its practitioners would claim, or is it more appropriate to view the medium as an ever-present cushion against silence or loneliness, as an aural tap to be turned on in search of temporary pleasures? Is radio a medium that is taken for granted – and is that its greatest strength, in that it fits in so well with our lives because it does not impose, impinge or demand too much?

These are important questions, but those who complain of radio's vacuousness perhaps miss the point. The medium's post-war evolution from a primary source of entertainment and information into a non-intrusive, companionable utility item, a gap-filler, proved its lifeline in the coming television age, and radio criticism needs to be approached not from the point of view of a nostalgic preoccupation with its passing as a primary medium but from an understanding of its utilitarian nature and the consequences that has had for the message conveyed. Because radio is, for most, a secondary medium (in a double sense: as a source of entertainment and information, as a background to other activities) does not mean that it is basically 'unimportant'. If we take John Downing's point in *The Media Machine* that it is 'the daily operation of media which is at the heart of their role' and not the temporary influence of individual items like a television play or a newspaper story on public consciousness, then radio must be seen as one of the most insidiously impactive mass media of all, its messages and its conventions repeated relentlessly, day in and day out, year after year, by station upon station.[2]

Radio is rarely accorded the critical or academic coverage enjoyed by the visual media, and such radio criticism as does exist – in the radio columns of quality newspapers – seems generally locked in a 1940s timewarp, concentrating almost wholly on the output of BBC Radios 3 and 4, on drama and documentary, and ignoring the much more widely patronized (and more 'popularly' programmed) Radios 1 and 2 and the output of over ninety local radio stations. Where the latter's programmes do provoke critical comment – commonly in the pages of rock music publications – it is usually on the mundane level of listeners' beefs about the lack of coverage of favourite artists or of particular musical areas, with the overall reliance of radio stations on music and the nature of the relationship between broadcasters and music manufacturers left unquestioned. With the notable exception of, among others, the Local Radio Workshop's acerbic accounts of radio in London and essays by Rosalind Coward, Anne Karpf and Dorothy Hobson, even academic studies have mainly centred on the drama and documentary fields, with the utility nature of the radio medium – its use by listeners as a source of background music, information or companionship – acknowledged but rarely discussed in its own terms.[3]

This book is presented with a view to redressing some of the critical and academic neglect that the whole field of 'popular' radio has suffered, but its main concern is a specific one – the treatment of popular music by Britain's radio institutions, past and present, and the key role that music plays in the functioning of the medium. Music (and especially music on record) forms the core of modern radio programming, enabling the medium's utilitarian aspects to function smoothly and effectively – framing the talk and information content, setting a mood conducive to continued listening, providing an environment in which (in the case of commercial radio) advertisements can be heard to most positive effect, matching the very pace of domestic life and the working-day itself. The aim of the book is to consider how music came to assume these functions and how 'music radio' operates, and it attempts to answer some basic questions: why should certain styles of music be favoured over others, why do radio's gatekeepers place such apparent faith in record sales charts, why music should be the prevalent sound in the ether in the first place, why virtually all Britain's music-based stations should favour an almost schizophrenic split between daytime and night-time programming, why there should be a standard acceptance among radio professionals that daytime radio is the province of a listenership of mothers at home. The answers have much to do with tradition and convention but even more with economics, that is with the relative cost-effectiveness of music radio and the onus on radio (even BBC radio) to prove its economic worth in the form of constant and consistent audience patronage.

The book is structured in two sections, the first of which offers an historical overview of the development of music radio in Britain, dwelling at particular length on the circumstances which brought Radios 1 and 2 and Independent Local Radio into existence. My main aim here is to show that the programming patterns prevalent in both BBC radio and ILR – the treatment of so-called minority tastes; the favouring of an artificial middle ground, a supposed consensus in taste, in deciding musical content; the domestic orientation of the programmes – are peculiarly British. Although I refer frequently to American radio, in most cases it is purely in the context of an indirect American influence on already established modes of broadcasting in Britain: though the switch to sequential, pop-based, quasi-American programming in the wake of the 1960s pirate stations has been described as a major stage in the 'Americanization' of British popular culture, I would suggest that radio was the only mass communications medium in which that process was successfully held at bay, checked by the application of a highly parochial (and paternalistically motivated) kind of populism. Even commercial radio in Britain has been unable to escape either the constraints of a BBC-engendered tradition or the consequences of the Corporation's mutually convenient relationship with the music industry: not only was British music radio fashioned in a paternalistic environment, distanced from the commercial factors that determined the shape and prevalence of its counterpart across the Atlantic, the UK music industry's legally won (and zealously enforced) right to charge home-based radio stations for use of commercially recorded music on the air helped fashion that usage in a manner that had few parallels abroad.

The second section is more discursive, isolating and exploring particular aspects of music radio as it exists in the mid-1980s. Whereas in the first section I talk of popular music in a very general sense, here I deal more specifically (though not exclusively) with 'pop radio' – 'pop' being defined, for my purposes, as music of topical appeal marketed at a mainly teenage audience. This change of emphasis is in keeping with the domination of contemporary radio programming by pop, though one of the paradoxes of the UK version of music radio is that pop buyers and pop radio listeners are not necessarily one and the same: because pop is identified by the radio stations as having an appeal *beyond* those who purchase it in record or tape form, it is used by them in a manner that devalues pop's 'meaning' as youth culture – its 'youthful' aspects, in other words, are diluted in pursuit of all-round, cross-generation acceptability. In this section, I elaborate upon these and some of the other themes and tendencies traced in Part One, extending the scope of the study beyond the stations themselves to take in British radio's relationship with the music industry, which uses the medium not only as a promotional vehicle but as an important source of revenue; the process of music selection and the criteria informing it; the uses to which radio's 'gatekeepers' – the producers and programme controllers – put popular music in gearing their programmes to particular audiences, and how daytime programming is fashioned to meet the latter's assumed 'needs'; the consequent marginalization of musics that do not fit with the conventional radio interpretation of daytime suitability, and the direct link between this and the growing pressure for community radio in the 1980s.

Radio in Britain is a medium of public service traditions seeking to survive in a media environment governed largely by commercial concerns. It always was, of course – Reith saw the BBC as a bulwark against capitalism's worst effects, a cultural oasis in a press- and cinema-infested desert – but it is only in the 1980s that the old paternalism has shown signs of breaking down for good, the political will to preserve and foster it no longer prevalent. Radio, and particularly music radio, is increasingly the preserve of the marketing man, its programme content tailor-made for the target audience, the tastes and 'needs' of that audience carefully researched and tirelessly analysed. Even for Radio 1 – adopting a weekend stereo sequence for the compact disc fraternity in apparent imitation of Capital Radio's experiment in single-frequency 'yuppie' radio[4] – such 'life-style' marketing offers the way ahead, while much-awaited government plans for an expansion of radio services cleverly confuse the public service aspect of community radio (as a service for underrepresented minorities) with the concept of market fragmentation, of catering for economically-defined, commercially attractive 'communities'.[5]

Radio, even BBC radio, cannot be understood in isolation from the marketing process, and in this book I have drawn freely on commercial sources and particularly on the business and professional trade press to back up my arguments and elucidate some of the issues. Sources such as these can, of course, be problematic: the interests and functions they serve are those not of the public at large but of an industry whose reason for existence is to capitalize on, perpetuate and even create popular 'needs'. Much of what appears in the trade press is written from the point of view of an implicit industrial consensus, a common ground based on common marketing objectives. Even so, no finer insights can be gained into the world of commercial radio in particular than from a critical reading of the pages of *Marketing* or *Marketing Week*; nowhere are the economic and political pressures on programming better articulated and described than in the pages of *Broadcast*. It is not a question of accepting an 'industry position' at face value, rather a matter of taking what the industry is saying to *itself* as a candid reflection of that industry's ideology. As someone whose own working background is in a marketing rather than an academic environment, I have tried to bring to the text my own practical understanding of how marketing works. The intention, particularly in Part Two, is to explore music radio in practice, and for this reason I have deliberately concentrated on the institutions themselves – the way they work, the philosophies that inform their operation – rather than go deep into areas of semiotics or extended cultural theory. Readers will not find a great deal of theoretical discussion in these pages: the aim is to sketch out patterns, clarify issues, discern trends and provide a critical overview.

I would like, finally, to acknowledge the help of a number of institutions in the research and writing of this book, and particularly those individuals at radio stations who gave freely of their time to answer my questions and discuss at length the various issues I have attempted to confront here. I am especially grateful to Tony Fish at BBC Radio York, Keith Skues and the senior staff at Radio Hallam, Johnny Beerling and Derek Chinnery at Radio 1, David Thomas at Swansea Sound, Tony Gillham at BBC Radio Bedfordshire and Capital's Charlie Gillett. Thanks are also due to Andrew Clifton, Bob Ellis and Preman Sotomayor, and to Richard Middleton and Dave Harker for their valuable comments on the text. But the biggest thanks of all must go to Eril, my wife, who not only undertook some of the interviewing at a moment's notice but was unfailingly helpful in clarifying my sometimes obtuse theorizing. Without her wizardry on the word processor the book would have taken much longer to complete; without her support and encouragement, I could never have undertaken it at all.

# Part one
# Patterns of development

Accounts of the history of popular music on British radio commonly show a post-1950s bias, taking as their starting point the sponsored record programmes of Radio Luxembourg and tracing the story through three distinct but connected phases – the proliferation of 'pirate' radio stations off the coast of the United Kingdom in the mid-1960s, the creation of BBC Radio 1 as a national pop network in 1967, and the establishment and expansion of a system of commercially funded radio stations on land from 1973 onwards. One problem with this approach is that it suggests a degree of symbiosis between the development of British rock music – as a distinct musical style, as a branch of youth culture, as a commercial industry – and that of the British version of 'pop radio', each feeding off and benefiting from the growth of the other. Such parallels are tenuous, as we shall see. Also, the kind of chronology outlined above tends to imply that British music radio developed and exists within a broadcasting tradition – piratical and populist in flavour, commercial in orientation, with antecedents in American rock 'n' roll radio – entirely separate from that of the tradition of public service broadcasting established by the BBC. This is erroneous, for all of Britain's predominantly music-based stations, whether funded by advertising or licence fee, operate within parameters and conventions of music broadcasting that were to a great extent established during the first two decades of the BBC's existence.

In exploring the reasons for the preponderance of popular music in radio schedules and the manner in which that music is programmed and presented, it is necessary to consider not only the nature of these conventions but also the external and institutional constraints that have fashioned broadcast output over the years. Particularly important here is the historical relationship between the broadcasting institutions and the *producers* of popular music – the record companies, music publishers and musicians themselves, who by exercising economic and industrial muscle (most obviously, by requiring payment for the airplay of records and songs) have helped mould the course and character of music on British radio. It is also vital to consider how programme-makers have traditionally perceived the function of music on the radio – initially as a means of relaxation, later as a background sound for both leisure and work activities – and the formulation of policy appropriate to it, the allocation of resources to it, and the place of popular music on a scale of 'cultural' priorities. For all the apparent newness of the records-plus-chat 'strip show' format, British radio in the 1980s remains highly traditional in style and content – which is to say institutionalized, paternalistic, domestically oriented and (as the evening programmes of both BBC and independent stations show) still inclined to elevate certain types of music over others according to questionable notions of intellectual value and cultural importance. To trace the origins of these tendencies, we must begin at the beginning.

# 1 Beginnings: 1923–38

Not only does the broadcasting of some eighty records help listeners choose the best records with the least trouble to themselves; but expert advice on the choice and care of gramophones is at the disposal of anyone who writes to ask for it. In other countries the risk of allowing this feature to degenerate into a form of mere advertisement might be considerable; but the BBC maintains a completely unbiassed attitude – an attitude of austere balance, one might almost claim – which is the only guarantee of really good service to the public.

Christopher Stone[1]

Primarily, it is my job to put happiness and sunshine over the air.

Jack Payne[2]

The importance of music to sound broadcasting was never doubted from the outset. As early as 1916, when wireless development in both Britain and the United States was seen primarily in terms of military and commercial rather than social or domestic applications, the Marconi Company's commercial manager, David Sarnoff, was informing his employers by memo that 'I have in mind a plan of development which would make radio a household utility like the piano or electricity. The idea is to bring music into the home by wireless. The receiver can be designed in the form of a simple radio music box'.[3] Throughout broadcasting history the assumption has been frequently made that radio, as the prime aural medium of mass communication (or, to put it more correctly, of communication *to* the masses), is the 'natural' home for music of whatever kind, but we should note that in attempting to fill the vast, empty canvas that constituted the airwaves, the first practitioners of wireless had no broadcasting precedent to follow and no tradition of any kind to work within. To paraphrase Raymond Williams's account of the foundation of the BBC in *Television, Technology and Cultural Form* (1974), there was nothing in the technology of wireless to dictate either the form or content of radio programmes; neither did the forces in nominal control of radio's development – in Britain's case, the Post Office and the wireless manufacturers who combined to form the original British Broadcasting Company – give any specific direction as to what exactly would be transmitted.[4] The initial thrust in British radio, in the absence of either external guidance or a clear perception of the new medium's particular qualities or potential, was therefore to do no more than *reproduce* established features of culture and entertainment – the concert, the stage play, the variety turn, the public lecture – and present each individual programme as an event requiring the attendance (in both senses of the word) of the listener. Given this, the novelty of radio lay not so much in the nature of the entertainment it provided but, as Sarnoff foresaw, in its carrying of that entertainment *into the home.*

The tendency of the BBC's first programme-makers to appropriate existing forms of public entertainment (which Williams defines as 'parasitism') was, however, complicated by constraining factors like the prolonged refusal by the most powerful interests in the theatre, variety and press industries to co-operate with what they saw as a directly competitive medium. Plays and revues were broadcast prior to the BBC's establishment as a public corporation in January 1927, but it was some time before the Society of West End Theatres and organizations like the Moss Empires, whose network of variety theatres spanned the whole country, eased their pressure on performers not to appear on the BBC. Newspaper owners, too, feared declining public patronage as a result of the new medium's popularity and enforced a ban on radio news bulletins before 7 p.m. to protect sales of their morning and evening editions. The earliest BBC programming was therefore partly determined by what was available to broadcast, with the paucity of drama, variety and news accounting to a significant degree for a compensatory reliance on music programmes.

The BBC's early use of music – and music of all kinds, whether performed 'live' or heard on commercially produced recordings – was nevertheless not entirely a matter of convenience. The formulation of a policy on music became one of the BBC's first priorities, giving shape and expression to the notion of cultural responsibility enshrined in the BBC Charter and championed with particular ferocity and single-mindedness by John Reith, the BBC's first Director-General. Excellent accounts of the evolution of the BBC's constitution exist elsewhere, but it is enough here to underline that neither the BBC constitution nor the particular brand of paternalism that characterized the BBC's first ten years were wholly the product of one man's vision.[5] Rather, the direction that the BBC took in policy and administration was coloured by considerations about which both the BBC board (representing as it did a cross-section of Britain's cultural establishment) and the government itself were in broad agreement. These considerations included a commitment to the concept of a British national culture; an adherence to what can loosely be defined as upper-middle-class values, including the primacy of the family, notions of philan-thropic public service and belief in a classical education; and a strong vein of anti-Americanism, rooted in a distaste for the United States' supposedly vulgar and cultureless society and a suspicion of her growing challenge to British economic and political influence on the world stage. F.J. Brown, a civil servant reporting to the Postmaster-General, was one of several figures in government adminis-tration to observe at first hand the uncontrolled spread of local, commercially-run radio in the United States, and the widespread acceptance of the need for a centrally controlled, *national* broadcasting organization, with a fixed source of finance and therefore resistant to commercial interference, could in part be put down to a wish not to repeat the American experience.

Assured finance had the double importance of ensuring the BBC's indepen-dence from direct political or commercial intervention in its affairs (though political considerations could and did profoundly shape policy) and of enabling the Corporation to fashion itself as an institution at the very forefront of the nation's cultural life. With public funding via the licence fee guaranteed for an initial ten-year period, the BBC could afford to pursue a high-minded dedication to intellectual betterment, and to parallel its efforts in maintaining British artistic standards (of musical performance in particular) with the task of educating the masses. Implicit in all this was the assumption of clear and unquestioned dichotomies between 'high' and 'low' culture, between serious and inconsequential pursuits, one of Reith's aims being to educate the working-man out of his dependence on the fripperies of entertainment and towards an appreciation of the higher, finer things in life. This did not mean that the provision of entertainment was taken lightly by the BBC or deemed to be of no particular importance – broadcasting 'entertaining' programmes was a major part of its public service brief – nor that Reith's objective could be construed as simply force-feeding high culture to an ignorant proletariat. Rather, the education process took a particular form: Reith believed that 'the supply of good things creates the demand for more', so educating the listener meant encouraging him or her to discriminate, to develop the art of selective and attentive listening, to gradually wean him or herself off the more lightweight elements in programming (and particularly dance band music). This was paternalism in the literal sense – fatherly, guiding, encouraging self-discipline, the listenership likened to a child eager to learn.

## A 'democratization' of music

The principle of mixed programming – the scheduling of the more 'demanding' dramatic or musical fare alongside lighter, less intellectually taxing programmes of variety and light music – was central to the BBC's educative strategy. The aim was to discourage what was called 'tap' listening, the switching on and off of a radio set like a water tap, the use of radio as an ever-present (and therefore disposable) background sound, which was held to demean the content of programmes. Programmes in a series tended to be scheduled at different times from week to week, to keep listeners on their toes: it was believed that if, say, episodes of a drama serial were broadcast at a regular time, the wrong kind of selectivity would be encouraged and listeners would skip the more 'worthwhile' programmes in between.[6]

The presence of a captive audience gave the BBC's Music Department, formally established in 1927, a platform from which to pursue one of its prime policy aims – raising levels of musical appreciation among the public, what Controller of Programmes Basil Nicolls called 'the great missionary element of broadcasting'. Difficulties arose, however, over precisely at which level these 'missionary' programmes should be pitched – whether to assume some degree of musical awareness or assume none, whether to sugar the pill by concentrating on works by the better-known composers or even, as Nicolls himself favoured at one point, whether to foster wider public knowledge of classical works by allowing dance bands to dress such melodies in new arrangements with dance-floor appeal, this in the belief that listeners would then be moved to seek out the real thing. But the greatest conflicts arose over priorities in policy, particularly whether the pursuit of musical excellence and the raising of performing standards – the other great tenet of BBC music policy – should take precedence over the educational aim. According to BBC historian Paddy Scannell, the BBC's central administration was in general far more dedicated to this missionary aspect than was the Music Department itself, the staff of which were largely drawn from and in sympathy with the country's musical and academic cognoscenti. By the mid-1930s, the Music Department was using the vast resources it was allocated to cater for one particular section (in effect, a privileged minority, a cultural élite) of musically well-versed listeners.[7]

The BBC's attempts to bring about 'a true democratization of music' (as the 1928 *BBC Handbook* had it) foundered on conflicts like these, but the Corporation's concept of 'musical democracy' was a narrow one.[8] There can be little doubt that the works of Tchaikovsky, Mendelssohn, Brahms, and nineteenth-century composers in particular were popularized (or at least made familiar) by the BBC in an unprecedented manner, but the presentation of the classics was essentially conservative: works were generally explained or described in terms of the European tradition, and the emphasis lay firmly on encouraging *appreciation* of accepted masterpieces rather than on encouraging the listener to develop his or her musical interests in a creative or participative way. There were few programmes offering advice or instruction on either learning the basic rudiments of music or mastering an instrument, at a time when other pastimes such as gardening and (perversely) bridge-playing were given coverage. The failure of the BBC to acknowledge this participatory aspect and its reluctance to give time to amateur musicians (notably choral and orchestral societies and brass bands based in the regions) were partly consequences of the Music Department's concern for performing standards. 'It is always agreeable to consider choral and orchestral societies' performances with a view to relaying them by microphone', the 1928 *BBC Handbook* noted, 'on condition that *the performance given is of such a standard as to provide something of definite programme value*' (emphasis added).[9] It was taken for granted that the most able and committed musicians were not amateurs but those who studied at the required academic institutions and made music their profession, but there was also a strong element of cultural snobbery against the regions, which became manifest in the many conflicts between the BBC administration in London and its regional services.

These conflicts first arose in the early days of the Corporation, when the BBC's existing local stations became victims of the London-based administration's centralization policy. These stations had according to many accounts a commitment to, and an involvement in, the cultural lives of their communities and a marked informality of presentation that contrasted with the tightly scripted, dispassionate presentation heard on the national network. Their legacy was partly absorbed by the new regional system of radio introduced in the early 1930s, which saw the foundation of the Regional Programme in tandem with the National Programme, but the occasional insistence of the regions on broadcasting locally originated musical programmes as an *alternative* to those on the main network ruffled the administration and Reith in particular, who believed such acts of independence undermined his vision of the BBC as the voice of one homogenous culture. With the reorganization, the BBC channelled its involvement in locally-made music almost exclusively into the employment of professional musicians in regional orchestras. What musical programmes were made in the regions for local consumption were rarely thought appropriate for national exposure.

## Light music for all

The BBC's centrally imposed music policy sought to encourage a uniformity of musical knowledge and appreciation, if not of taste. Such ventures as the Henry Wood Promenade Concerts, the organization (effectively sponsorship) of which the BBC took over in 1927, epitomized the Corporation's commitment to the musical 'welfare' of the nation on a productive level – the concerts were showcases for the BBC's own fledgling orchestras. But the efforts of the Music Department did not represent the BBC's entire involvement in music: below classical music (the BBC's own preferred term) on the Reithian cultural scale, but each claiming a share of BBC resources, were three other categories – light music, popular music and dance-band music. Again, the 1928 *BBC Handbook* defined the categories: classical music meant opera, orchestral, symphonic and chamber music; light music was light opera, comic opera and light orchestral; popular music took in military band music, musical comedy, revue, the music of 'entertainers', and ballads.[10]

Light music represented the most familiar works of the classical repertoire, together with Victorian parlour music, songs from Gilbert and Sullivan operetta, Viennese waltzes and a range of light classical miniatures, and it was usually played or sung by small combinations and soloists rather than by full orchestras. Light music in the BBC sense was essentially a middle-class popular music of a slightly earlier period, and in content and presentation such programmes were analagous with the domestic musical evenings of Victorian and Edwardian times – conservative, traditional, *middlebrow* music for a listening public which, if not wholly middle class in profile, was 'offered direct access to the middle class community' (Simon Frith).[11] Light music in fact had a preponderance over classical music in BBC schedules, though the proportion of broadcasting time allocated to each during the BBC's first few years of existence did not in itself reflect the BBC's sense of priorities: full-scale classical works occupied the main evening hours, while light music, popular music and dance music, though heard more regularly, tended to be relegated to earlier or later hours of listening.

Although light music often crossed over into the other categories, the BBC's favouring of the former coloured its treatment of the latter, and especially dance-band music. Reading the early handbooks, it is difficult to escape the conclusion that the only dance music that the BBC took unreserved pride in featuring was that which incorporated elements (most obviously, string accompaniments) of the light music mode. The very term 'dance *band*' had American connotations, and when the BBC began involving itself in dance-music production, the term 'orchestra' was used in preference to it. But for some time during those early time during those early BBC years, dance-band music was effectively stateless, being one of the music forms – like operetta, musical comedy and cinema organ music – that the Music Department chose not to consider as one of its most serious responsibilities. It was the lack of any clear, central control over the BBC's dance-band output that led bandleader Jack Payne to suggest himself as Director of Dance Music in 1926. Because the BBC administration saw dance-band music as part of the show business world, and because its relationship with show business was strained at best, dance music remained on the fringes of departmental responsibility until after the establishment of the Revue and Vaudeville Section (which was itself later absorbed into the Variety Department) in 1930.

Popular music and dance music, as defined by the BBC, represented entertainment rather than culture. The BBC's attitude to entertainment was equivocal but by no means dismissive. Reith maintained that such programmes were 'not given grudgingly or under pressure from the public or press. To provide relaxation is no less positive an element of policy than any other'.[12] To Reith, the issue was one of moral principle: while entertainment for entertainment's sake, the single-minded pursuit of pleasure, was an indicator of moral failing, the true moral purpose of entertainment was to offer essential respite from the cares of the working-day. As Richard Dyer has pointed out, the word 'relaxation' – so commonly used by broadcasting professionals as a qualitative description of what they provide – carries 'an implication of prior tension [that] links entertainment directly with the stresses of work and life'.[13] In Reithian terms, then, entertainment was acceptable, within limits, as a source of refreshment and replenishment – a reward, in fact: 'mitigation of the strain of a high-pressure life, such as the last generation scarcely knew, is a primary social necessity, and that necessity must be satisfied'.[14] The prime criterion for broadcasting music outside the classical sphere was therefore its 'relaxing' quality – any music that disturbed or excited had no place on the BBC airwaves. Light music fulfilled this requirement admirably: dance-band music had to emulate it to justify broadcasting time. This involved a process of domestication in the double sense – 'Anglicizing' an American form and taking the music out of its original social context and rendering it suitable for the domestic environment. Essential to the success of this were the BBC's steady institutionalization of dance-band music – its move into the production as well as the dissemination of such music, through the formation of its own dance orchestras – and its exercise of strict control over the output of bands selected for broadcasting.

## A BBC dance music

Dance-band music was just that, music for social dancing, played by the leading bands of the day, but its development during the 1920s needs to be seen against the backcloth of increasing interest in American jazz in Britain, particularly following the 1919 visit of the Original Dixieland Jazz Band. The attempts by the Imperial Society of Teachers of Dancing to standardize dance steps were also part of a general establishment trend towards minimizing the American influence, while some of the larger dance halls banned such dances as the charleston.[15] These processes were already well under way by the time the BBC was a public corporation, and specific policy on dance music – which bands to hire, what standards to impose – was slow to evolve. In the pre-Charter years and for some time thereafter, the contracting of bands was not even a BBC responsibility but that of the hotels from which they broadcast. Within the London society scene, West End hotels were recognized as high-class providers of diversionary entertainment, and a quality band acted as both a status symbol and a means of attracting custom away from competitors. The hotel connection itself was originally just a matter of convenience – the first hotel with which the BBC had an arrangement, the Savoy, was barely yards away from the BBC's first studios at Savoy Hill and was used exclusively until November 1925. The ready availability of dance music in the hotels, the willingness of the BBC to associate itself with such prestigious London institutions as the Café de Paris (resident band Teddy Brown), the Carlton (Jay Whidden, Bert Firman), the Mayfair (Ambrose), Park Lane (Frank Ashworth) and the Hotel Cecil (Jack Payne), together with the BBC's aforementoned lack of access to other forms of entertainment, all combined to ensure that a strong dance-band presence was maintained at a crucial point in the BBC's development as a major entertainment institution (and employer) in its own right.

Announcers often prefaced dance-band programmes with invitations to listeners to 'roll up the carpet and dance', as if the objective was to recreate the ambience of a swish society dance floor in the humblest of abodes. But the new context that radio gave dance music implied a change in the music's original social function, and there was a growing tendency among bands from the mid-1920s onwards to elaborate and prettify their arrangements in order to keep the attention of the passive listener. Of major influence here was the example of Paul Whiteman and his Orchestra, established radio favourites in the United States who visited Britain in 1923 and 1925 and encouraged the adoption of what was called 'symphonic syncopation'. Whiteman's sweetly decorative arrangements (usually the work of resident arranger Ferde Grofé, whose aspirations to highbrow favour led to his orchestrating George Gershwin's *Rhapsody in Blue* and composing several extended works of his own including the *Grand Canyon Suite*) prompted British bandleaders to indulge in what Sid Colin, guitarist with Lew Stone's band, later ridiculed as 'opulent, over-orchestrated pomposities' geared to an armchair clientele.[16]

Of still greater impact on the development of British dance-band music as *radio* music were the Savoy Hotel's various house bands, notably the Savoy Havana Band and the Savoy Orpheans, whose radio success brought them a recording deal with His Master's Voice. Their music – which prior to their national exposure on the BBC had functioned as an unobtrusive, discreet musical backcloth to upper-class dining as well as dancing – developed into dance music of an easy-paced, unspectacular kind which, while suited to the sophisticated patrons of one of the most exclusive hotels in London, was also tasteful and decorous enough to be welcomed into people's homes. (The word 'welcome' is appropriate here, as Reith likened the broadcasters to invited guests.) The Orpheans in particular helped establish a mould of native British dance music to which even the more ambitious and musically adventurous bands were obliged to adapt, if only (and Sid Colin has elaborated, in *And the Bands Played On*, on the differences between live and broadcast dance music) for broadcasting and recording purposes. Although the BBC was not renowned for particularly high remuneration, radio appearances were much sought after because they brought prestige and the clout to command higher appearance fees from hotels and other venues. Establishing a radio reputation was also the only sure route to a recording contract, while for those bands who broadcast regularly there was always the chance to earn extra income from illicit song plugging, which was the arrangement by which bandleaders received payment from a music publishing company for playing its compositions on air. The practice was officially frowned upon as a form of clandestine advertising, but the BBC had few powers of investigation and the only serious counter-measure – a ban on the inclusion of vocal choruses in band arrangements and on the announcement of song titles, to make identification of particular songs difficult – was dropped by the Corporation in 1929, when the publishers' collection agency, the Performing Right Society, threatened to suspend its licensing agreement with the BBC.[17]

But if the practice of song plugging continued to cause problems during the 1930s, the BBC was able to exert a considerable degree of influence over the form, content and repertoire of dance-band music through its role as a major contractor of bands. While there were no set rules as to what constituted 'suitable' radio music, the bandleaders (who ran their bands as small businesses and usually employed their musicians on short-term contracts) competed for restricted air-time largely by anticipating and confirming the musical prejudices of BBC personnel like the anonymous writer of an article in the 1929 *BBC Handbook*, who suggested:

> It is probable that fashion more swiftly affects the playing of dance music than any other type of music. Everyone who has listened regularly for the last three years will have marked these differences in style. There exists a method in which all is sacrificed to rhythm and arrangement, otherwise 'hot' band-playing, but the present development tends, perhaps fortunately, to more melodious but highly rhythmic effects.[18]

The same writer noted 'the curious and interesting orchestrations' of Fred Elizalde, an arranger-pianist and bandleader from the Philippines who held the distinctly radical view that 'melody is an entirely secondary consideration as far as dance music is concerned'.[19] His experience with the BBC demonstrated how innovation and experiment were discouraged. Championed by the growing number of dance-band aficionados who formed a vocal part of the readership of the *Melody Maker*, he was taken off the air twice after broadcasts from the Savoy. The reaction of the dance-band establishment, personified by Bert Ambrose (who, interestingly, had come second to Elizalde in a *Melody Maker* readers' poll in 1928) was so unsympathetic as to suggest broad concurrence between the bandleaders and their BBC employers on questions of style. Criticizing Elizalde in a *Melody Maker* article, Ambrose wrote that 'there can be no doubt that Mr Elizalde is carrying out his "no melody" threat . . . if I tried it out at the Mayfair I feel certain that the floor would empty in a minute'.[20] In fact, Elizalde did make a number of concessions to the Savoy – adding a small string section, for example – but his removal from the BBC's list of acceptable bands reduced his recording options and his public visibility, leading to four years of relative obscurity and eventual emigration to Spain.

The Elizalde controversy highlighted the debate within dance music circles, which was mirrored in the pages (and particularly the letters and review columns) of *Melody Maker*, over 'hot' and 'sweet' music and the nature of jazz. It occurred not long after the BBC had taken the first step in formalizing its involvement in dance music by appointing Jack Payne as its first Director of Dance Music. According to Payne's autobiography, the appointment was his own idea, born of his close association with the BBC while leading the house band at the Hotel Cecil. While he had no direct concern with the hiring and firing of bands, his function was to give BBC dance music an identity and set an example to others, through his formation and leadership of a flagship BBC Dance Orchestra. There had been earlier versions of an in-house dance-band – the Dance Orchestra's precursor was the London Radio Dance Band, formed in 1925 and led by Sidney Firman – but Payne's band was the first that, in size and quality, rated on a par with the established, nationally-known dance-bands. Launched in 1928, the Dance Orchestra predated the formation of the BBC Symphony Orchestra by two years, but their terms of operation were very different. While the Symphony Orchestra comprised musicians in the BBC's direct employ, Payne's musicians were under contract to him alone; and while the former was created as part of an overall strategy to *improve* the technical and interpretative standards of British musicians (as Britain was considered to have fallen behind the rest of Europe in producing concert musicians of world stature), the Dance Orchestra was concerned primarily with *maintaining* professional standards.

Payne had a clear perception of his role, and he wrote proudly of being the only performer (the term was his) to have an office of his own at Savoy Hill. 'I look upon myself as being in much the same position as the editor of a widely circulating newspaper', he wrote in *This is Jack Payne*, 'I have to try to find out what the majority of people want and try to give it to them'.[21] In 1931, according to the BBC's own estimates, the Payne band enjoyed 650 hours of broadcasting time and played over 3,000 songs; of these, half were British in origin, 40 per cent American and the remaining 10 per cent European – a self-imposed balance Payne maintained with almost clinical precision.[22] He remained as musical director of the BBC Dance Orchestra until 1932, when he decided to trade on the name he had made at the BBC by taking a newly constituted orchestra – comprising mostly former-Dance Orchestra musicians – on a tour of Britain's variety theatres. That Payne's band should play to audiences in a theatre rather than a ballroom setting was indicative of the change in dance music's function that radio had brought about, from music for dancing – a social exchange, an expression of one-to-one communication, a physical activity – to music for listening, a passive and personal, even solitary, activity. The movement of dance-bands – or to use the increasingly preferred terminology, *show* bands – from the dance halls and night clubs into the theatres undoubtedly helped the latter venues to survive in the Depression-hit 1930s, though the bands' rapid elevation to top-of-the-bill status (purely on the strength of their radio reputations) was much resented by the established variety entertainers.[23]

Payne's replacement at the BBC was Henry Hall, a bandleader from Scotland who had broadcast regularly (nationally and regionally) during the 1920s from the Gleneagles Hotel, at which he and his band had a residency. Hall's background included a Salvation Army upbringing and Trinity College and Guildhall School of Music training, and he was a gifted administrator, having some years of management experience behind him as controller of dance music for a chain of railway hotels. His BBC position was resented within the mainly London-oriented dance-band world because he and the musicians he brought with him from Scotland were outsiders, but he had an astute understanding of the role of dance music in BBC schedules at a time when the BBC was tentatively expanding its entertainment output. The amount of dance music on the air increased under his careful direction, with new programmes appearing in the morning and afternoon as well as in the long-established late-night (10.30 p.m. to 12 midnight) time-slot, which had originally been timed to coincide with the evening supper dances mounted by the London hotels.

## Problematic musics

Hall helped weave dance music into the very fabric of BBC broadcasting, but his appointment also represented the culmination of a process of legitimization of dance-band music, to the exclusion of other forms of popular music. Two musical crazes of the 1920s and 1930s went almost unmentioned on the BBC, probably because of their amateur and working-class associations – that for accordion playing (its natural home being the cinema, where competitions for amateur and frequently very young accordionists were held prior to film showings) and for community singing, which was promoted by one of the BBC's most vocal press opponents, Beaverbrook's *Daily Express*.[24] Where popular movements in music-making were acknowledged by the BBC – for example, the revival of interest in regional folk music during the 1920s – there was a tendency to leave such programmes to the regions or, at best, to treat them in a documentary or magazine-type fashion and thereby accentuate their 'cultural' rather than entertainment value.

This distinction between cultural edification and 'relaxing' entertainment characterized BBC policy on many levels. Dance music could be tolerated and positively encouraged as long as it stayed within the bounds of entertainment-as-relaxation, and the bland, light, even soporific music of Henry Hall's Band – 'more BBC than Dance Orchestra', as Sid Colin complained – epitomized what was acceptable.[25] When dance-band music strayed beyond these bounds, in particular when dance-band enthusiasts (as in the Elizalde case) began voicing their opinions on the merits of certain bands and certain approaches above others, the administrators of BBC policy found themselves on much more difficult ground. One solution was simply to limit or ban outright offending styles or mannerisms: scat singing, for example, was officially banned in 1936, while American and American-influenced British jazz (an all-purpose and much misunderstood term, commonly equated by both its followers and detractors with 'hot dance music') was filtered through the thoroughly respectable record programmes of Christopher Stone, who had an informal yet slightly diffident, even non-committal style of presentation that had the effect of distancing him from the music he played. Stone's programmes, and those of Robert Tredennick on the Midland Region, were irregularly scheduled quarter-hour or thirty-minute 'recitals', and the only other jazz programmes of significance on the National Programme were those mounted by producer Leslie Perowne and Charles Chilton, his assistant. (It was left to the Regional Programme to broadcast performances by two of the most noted American jazz musicians of the period, Louis Armstrong and Duke Ellington, in July 1932 and June 1933 respectively.) Jim Godbolt, historian of British jazz, notes that Perowne's espousal of jazz was taken seriously by the BBC only in deference to his upper-class upbringing, he being the son of the Bishop of Winchester and the brother of the Political Officer of Aden; one of the conditions under which jazz programmes were allowed to continue was that Chilton, a former messenger boy from North London, be replaced as presenter of the *Swingtime* series (which began in 1937) by a duty announcer.[26]

The other solution to the hot music 'problem' was to accept the existence of internal distinctions within the general dance music mode yet confer intellectual validity only on those styles or approaches favoured by an expert élite. Stone's programmes took precisely this course, featuring a selection of 'worthy' jazz- and dance-band records in an instructive, recital-like (and therefore 'non-entertaining') setting. A 1937 programme, *Swing that Music* (featuring the Ramblers from Holland), was disdainfully defended by a senior BBC executive as being 'a jam session, whatever that means . . . primarily intended to inform and not to entertain'.[27] Another swing showcase, *Facets of Syncopation*, broadcast nationally at the rather daring time of 8.20 p.m., it was fiercely criticized within the BBC for being announced as a 'jam session'. Precisely because the 'entertaining' aspect of the programme had been stressed over its informative aspects, subsequent programmes in what was intended to be a series were reconstituted as 'recitals' and prefaced by some distancing explanatory remarks from the reassuring figure of Harmon Grisewood. The incident was a prime example of how, as Paddy Scannell writes, 'a non-cultural category (dance music) is transformed and renominated as a cultural category for the connoisseur'.[28] Compartmentalizing the more problematic extremes of popular music in this way – music which did not fit comfortably with notions of either entertainment or high culture – also meant that their impact could be softened and/or neutralized. Framed in the form of a music appreciation lesson, such music lost its ability to excite or disturb.

**Variety and stuffed shirts**

These rare intellectual excursions into the world of 'jazz' originated either from the Music Department or, more usually, from the regions. In the main, however, dance-band music was the concern of the Variety Department, the programme-making capacity of which expanded enormously as the 1930s wore on. This expansion suggested a change in policy towards entertainment for its own sake which was attributed, at the time and in subsequent accounts, to two developments: the spread of wireless to working class homes and the BBC's consequent 'awareness' of the need to cater for them, and the arrival of competition in the form of continental stations broadcasting a menu of variety shows and musical specials to Britain. To what degree the BBC was really troubled by all this is questionable, however. Audience research was practically non-existent until the establishment of the BBC's Listener Research Department in 1936 and only grew in influence within the Corporation after Reith's departure in 1938, so for some time the BBC itself had no concrete knowledge of the social profile of its listeners. The increase in the acquisition of radio licenses was in fact most marked among the lower middle classes between 1929 and 1935, and even though entertainers from northern working-class areas such as George Formby and Gracie Fields were heard on BBC radio for the first time, they were largely included as what Richard Middleton has called 'licensed eccentrics . . . [who] could be mostly contained by the stereotypes of working class humour, fatalism and exotic folk custom'.[29]

The expansion in programme-making by the Variety Department reflected more on the BBC's greater confidence in its handling of the variety industry, the agents' boycotts having largely petered out by the close of the 1920s, and on the BBC's growing income as a result of increased licence purchase; with more money available, the BBC could expand its programme-making capacities in all spheres. BBC Variety itself was a peculiar form, drawing more on the sophisticated (and West End-based) traditions of revue and musical comedy than on those of the music-hall, and it developed its own distinct musical language. Variety shows used music in a manner derived from both musical comedy conventions and the cinema, for which orchestrators and arrangers perfected the technique of scoring brief bursts of background music or slightly longer musical interludes to create a mood or delineate a geographical setting – a few bars of ac-cordion music, for example, to evoke a Parisian street scene. (This technique had its roots, paradoxically, in the silent cinema days, when orchestras and small instrumental combinations played from set scores in picture houses.) In variety radio, the function of musical accompaniment was to provide colour and accentuate the comic pace.

Alongside the expansion in programme-making came a simultaneous expansion in BBC bureaucracy that affected the former at the most basic levels and certainly helped explain the stilted tone of variety shows and dance music programmes during the first half of the 1930s. Particularly after the BBC's move from Savoy Hill to Broadcasting House in 1932, the BBC's administration grew relentlessly in size and influence: in the words of Maurice Gorham, a BBC employee since 1926 and later head of the Light Programme, 'from 1932 to 1939 was the great Stuffed Shirt era, marked internally by paternalism run riot, bureaucracy of the most hierarchical type, an administration that made productive work harder instead of easier, and a tendency to promote the most negative characters to be found amongst the staff'.[30] What Gorham called 'a sort of diarchy', with production staff in the subordinate role, was cemented by the appointment of Basil Nicolls as Director of Internal Administration:

> What it meant was that the head of every section, department and branch had as his right-hand man an executive responsible for money, accommodation, staff, salaries, and all the business and facilities side of the job . . . if everybody had followed the rules and accepted administrative Noes and delays, the BBC might easily have died of inanition before the war.[31]

These executive administrators enacted and interpreted the policies handed down by senior management, while the producers had the responsibility for turning administrative wisdom into programmes. There was some room for creative manoeuvre, but only by anticipating and accommodating executive decisions and making judicious compromises: the producer was, in effect, arbitrating between the needs of the listenership as he perceived them and the expectations of his superiors – whose major concern, at least during the 'stuffed shirt' period, was not whether BBC programmes were appreciated by the world outside but whether fellow management felt them worthy. (Gorham remembered being present at a Programme Board where Colonel Alan Dawnay, ex-War Office and newly appointed Controller of Programmes, tempered remarks that certain programmes had been well received by press and public with the comment, 'but of course that is not the final test. The real criterion is what we ourselves think of our work'.[32]) These attitudes infected entertainment programmes as much as the more serious output of concerts and talks, as production staff were continually making decisions on musical content – a dubiously ribald lyric here, an unsuitable subject for comedy there – based not so much on the sensibilities of the listeners as on those of the men upstairs.

A consequence of this indirect method of control was that all BBC programmes came to reflect a corporate BBC identity, a house style – safe, reliable, measured, and middlebrow in nature.[33] This was reinforced by a degree of self-sufficiency unparalleled by any other organization dealing in entertainment or the arts, which was consolidated rather than undermined during the late 1920s and 1930s by the important agreements forged between the BBC and what were in effect 'outside suppliers': musicians, represented by the Musicians Union (MU); the producers of commercial gramophone records, represented by Phonographic Performance Limited (PPL); and the music publishers, who received (via the Performing Right Society) revenue from the BBC for BBC usage of their copyright material on behalf of the songwriters contracted to them. Although the BBC restricted its use of records as a matter of policy – as early as 1925 the BBC's Control Board recommended that records be replaced by outside broadcasts, and it was 1927 before record programmes as such were re-introduced – the suspicion persisted within the MU and among the record companies that broadcasting institutions would (as was the case in the early days of American radio) use discs as a substitute for the programming of live music. That the BBC, at the request of PPL and the MU, agreed to limit the number of records it played and to pay for their use was a sign not of weakness but of the Corporation's confidence in its own programme-making strengths and cultural leadership. It also underlined the BBC's impact on the business of entertainment itself: just as dance-bands and their singers could become 'star' names on the basis of BBC appearances, so Britain's record industry developed a contracting policy heavily influenced by the BBC, with record companies signing artists and recording repertoire already familiar through broadcasting, rather than seeking out new talent of their own. (The promotional value of radio to the companies was understood, but they generally lacked the expertise to capitalize upon it; dance-bands recorded a catalogue of material for release over a period of time, which the company then issued in a manner analogous with book publishing, that is publicized by means of advertising in relevant newspapers and retail outlets, and with long-term sales in mind.) The emergence of the continental stations threatened this level of BBC influence, but not to the extent of fundamentally undermining it.

The coming of war necessitated far-reaching changes in policy and even more so in the attitude of the BBC programme administrators to their audience, but BBC bureaucracy was by no means a casualty of it. On the contrary, policy changes could only be effected if a tight administrative grip on programme-making was maintained. In the next chapter, I shall examine what those changes were, their apparent roots in pre-war continental broadcasting, and the bearing they had in the long-term on the BBC's attitude to and treatment of popular music.

# 2 Manning the defences: 1939–55

The Second World War was a watershed period in British broadcasting, the requirements of the war effort prompting a fundamental re-evaluation of the purposes, functions and applications of public service radio. It was a period in which the *ideological* uses of entertainment – its uses in binding people together in a common cause, its identification with and portrayal of national values, however contrived or self-regarding – were appreciated in very direct ways, and one that marked a distinct break with the principle of mixed programming and of catering for different interests and tastes within the context of one national network. As regards the broadcasting of popular music, the war years ushered in an era of greater reliance on gramophone records and considerably greater American domination of the music field as a whole. Typical of the post-war era, too, was an air of cosiness, conservatism and insularity in the broadcasting of music, born in part of protectionism and sustained by the mutually supportive relationship between the BBC and the British record industry, the copyright bodies and the Musicians Union. One long-term consequence of this was the failure to acknowledge and accommodate changes not just in musical taste but in the music marketplace, so that the BBC had neither the expertise nor the programme structures to successfully meet demand for various musics of identifiable 'youth' appeal – traditional jazz and skiffle, as well as rock 'n' roll.

But the story of radio between the late 1930s and the close of the 1950s is not wholly that of the BBC. A significant if often overstated role was played by the English-language stations operating from bases on the Continent, which acted as a catalyst for some modification of BBC policies even before the war and kept the issue of commercialization of broadcasting to the fore throughout the post-war period. While it is simplistic to suggest that the BBC responded to the stations – notably Radio Normandie and Radio Luxembourg – by attempting to beat the opposition at its own game, they did pose a real threat to the BBC in that they were used by commercial interests as a testing ground for and a stepping stone towards the establishment of sponsored radio in mainland Britain. Heading the commercial lobby both before and after the war were Britain's leading advertising agencies, backed in the main by American money and expertise, whose involvement in radio included not only the financing but also the *production* of variety programmes for sponsorship by British companies. Lobbying was particularly intense at times when the BBC was under political scrutiny, as during the Ullswater Committee's inquiry into broadcasting (1935–6) in the run-up to the renewal of the BBC's Charter.

The history of the stations can be briefly sketched. The pioneer of European-based, English-language, commercially funded radio was Captain Leonard F. Plugge, who by 1932 was running his own grandly titled International Broadcasting Company (IBC) from a single-room office behind the BBC's new Broadcasting House in Portland Place. Initially, he bought air-time on foreign stations within reach of Britain and sold it as advertising space to British firms, but he left programme content largely to the whim of the announcers he hired from diverse sources – Max Staniforth from management of Argentina's railway system, Roy Plomley from copywriting, Bob Danvers-Walker from Australian radio.[1] Much ingenuity went into making the IBC seem like an institution comparable with the BBC, to the point of building programmes around fictitious concerts featuring the 'IBC Dance Orchestra' (in reality an unnamed band on disc, sometimes even that of Jack Payne!) and improvising Test Match commentaries out of score flashes from the BBC.[2] Radio Normandie, based in Fécamp in northern France, became Plugge's main IBC outlet because its proximity to Britain made for particularly good reception; other stations from whom he bought time included Radio Côte d'Azur, Poste Parisien, Radio Eireann and some in Spain and Yugoslavia.

The days of makeshift programming and mock concerts came to an end with the entry of Radio Luxembourg into the commercial radio arena in 1933. The station was owned by the Compagnie de Luxembourgeoise de Radiodiffusion, which granted an English-language concession to the Parisian entrepreneur Jacques Gonat before passing responsibility for programming and advertising to its own London-based subsidiary, Wireless Publicity, in 1936. Everything about Radio Luxembourg was well organized and professional: it had the most powerful transmitter in Europe after that of Radio Moscow, and its financial position was such that it could afford to advertise its existence in the British press, though some newspapers refused to take insertions for fear of losing advertising revenue to radio. From the start, Luxembourg's *raison d'être* was purely commercial: it exercised little central control over content, and its air-time could be bought by any company or institution on the understanding that the advertiser would (as in the United States) provide the necessary programmes. In this way, the station could gain maximum revenue from the sale of air-time (far greater revenue than repeated 'spot' advertising could attract) without having to invest money or manpower in providing entertainment.[3]

Advertising agencies were best equipped to meet the needs of the commercial radio marketplace. Several of the bigger, American-owned agencies set up their own radio departments to assume virtually all those programming functions previously left to individual stations. In-house creative teams, working in liaison with the agencies' sales divisions, devised and developed programme ideas to the client's brief. They wrote the scripts, hired actors or musicians as required, and took full technical control of the programmes' production and recording. Two agencies in particular were renowned for their radio expertise, J. Walter Thompson and the London Press Exchange (whose radio department was headed by a former BBC freelancer, Howard Thomas). Their special skills lay in finding a programme format and a suitable personality (as singer, bandleader or comedian) to match the brand image of a client. The formats themselves followed a familiar variety pattern, with many programmes recorded before an audience. Because the Post Office, mindful of its relationship with the BBC, refused to rent its overseas lines to commercial radio concerns, all programmes had to be pre-recorded on discs and dispatched to Luxembourg for transmission.[4]

Music was vital to commercially sponsored programmes, but gramophone records played a generally minor role prior to the war. Record request shows were a feature of pre-Luxembourg days, before sponsorship and agency input made more ambitious programming possible, and the established presenters on the IBC stations – which quickly followed the sponsorship route to keep up with Luxembourg – complained of being demoted to the role of continuity announcer. High fees were offered to dance-bands to appear on commercial radio: Roy Fox appeared in association with Reckitt's Bath Cubes, Joe Loss by arrangement with Meltonian Shoe Polish, Geraldo on behalf of Cadbury's Chocolates. Many of the bandleaders and artists so contracted owed their 'stardom' to the BBC, while American companies provided shows spotlighting singers or musicians previously known to British audiences only via records or films – Morton Downey in the *Palmolive Hour*, Carson Robison and his Pioneers by arrangement with Oxydol. Luxembourg could also claim probably the most famous commercial radio programme ever, *The Ovaltineys*, which was made for Ovaltine by J. Walter Thompson and inspired a rival 'children's club of the air' in *The Cococubs*, created for Cadbury's by the London Press Exchange.

What impact, then, did the foreign stations really have? If the findings of the IBC's own research in 1938 were to be believed – and it was undertaken by Crossleys, an American research company with plans of its own for UK expansion – 82 per cent of the wireless sets in Britain were tuned to commercial stations on Sunday mornings, when the BBC was broadcasting talks, religious services and solemn music.[5] Audiences, it appeared, were not deserting the BBC wholesale but were turning to the foreign stations at times when the BBC chose either not to broadcast or to broadcast programmes with no discernibly entertaining features whatsoever. Luxembourg claimed its largest audience Sunday evenings and on weekday mornings between 8.30 a.m. and 10.30 a.m., at which point the BBC began its daytime programmes with the *Daily Service*. Reith's reaction was one of grumbling puzzlement: 'The Lord seems to have done nothing whatever', he wrote in his diary, 'in the matter of English advertising competition from Luxembourg all these years and soon we fear that this horrid place and others like it will hold English listeners even when we are operating. I am distressed but it is no case of my being weaker than I used to be.'[6]

The perceived 'success' of the foreign stations introduced a new element into policy arguments, as any apparent failure on the BBC's part to cater for the licence-fee paying mass audience undermined its political relationship with Parliament, which controlled the level of its funding. In a spirit of self-protection, the BBC had long had to accommodate itself, subtly and through various forms of self-censorship, to political pressures: particularly after the sudden and unexpected resignation of Reith in mid-1938, the Corporation found it politically imperative to begin shifting its ground, to modify its 'educative' stance and include more of the types of shows for which there was an apparent demand – quizzes, variety shows and of course more dance music. Some routinization of schedules was introduced, and the strictures of the infamous 'Reith Sunday' (hitherto devoid of dance music) were significantly relaxed. But the impact of Luxembourg and its rivals generally had little to do with any radical change in programming *conventions*: the agencies supplying the foreign stations tended to exploit programme forms like the variety show, the personality showcase and the dance-band half-hour that were already well established in BBC schedules. As already noted, many of the acts featured on commercial radio were well-known BBC 'names', and the BBC maintained clear advantages over its foreign competitors in key areas; it was able to present a far greater volume of dance-band music, for example, because of the availability of bands for live broadcasts, and because it had the resources and the administrative backing (unlikely to be matched by cautious clients) to launch new comedy shows and persevere with them until they caught the imagination of the public.

Certainly the presence of foreign rivals lessened the grip of the BBC on the careers of individual entertainers, scriptwriters and producers, but this did not necessarily mean greater scope for imagination: pressure from advertisers induced a conservatism in programming, an unwillingness to deviate from proven formulas, as marked as that of the BBC. Where the stations did have a strong influence was in the sophistication, professionalism and pace of their presentation, although on this point Eric Maschwitz (head of the Variety Department and the former editor of *Radio Times*) preferred to acknowledge the influence of networked variety radio in the United States, of which he had personal experience in the early 1930s.[7] One of his many innovations was *In Town Tonight*, which throughout its long run was an almost obligatory stopover for visiting American singers and comedians.

## Wartime radio

Ironically, the influence of the foreign stations was most felt within Broadcasting House in the period following the stations' war-enforced closedown, once the BBC's monopoly had been restored. Plans had been laid in 1938 for a reorganization of radio services in the event of war, and one of the priorities was to discourage non-BBC listening, as any station broadcasting from Europe could be prey to enemy propaganda. (Luxembourg closed down almost immediately after the declaration and was taken over by invading German forces in 1940, when it did indeed become the vehicle for William 'Lord Haw-Haw' Joyce's propaganda broadcasts.) In early 1940 the BBC split its services into a national programme (the Home Service) and a Forces Programme, the latter offering variety shows and dance-music programmes peppered with talks and the occasional classical concert. That the Forces Programme developed into something far more akin to pre-war commercial radio was almost wholly due to pressure from military circles, who recognized how useful radio could be in alleviating boredom among the troops, maintaining morale and keeping contact with home. The military emphasized the need to replace the recently closed (over Christmas 1939) Radio Internationale, which had been popular among the men of the British Expeditionary Force then landing in France. (Radio Internationale was operated from the studios of the now defunct Radio Normandie.) A report commissioned by the BBC from A.P. Ryan on the listening habits of BEF servicemen, *Listening by the BEF*, supported calls for a steady and uninterrupted flow of entertaining, undemanding programmes and a greater amount of dance music, pointing out that the men in the field simply turned a deaf ear to programmes of 'cultural' content and tended to listen communally rather than privately. Ryan ventured that the war situation gave the BBC an opportunity 'to get beyond its present position of public respect and to win also public affection. It can only do this if it establishes for itself a self-denying ordinance against the more austere kind of programmes'. The report suggested that the BBC could even learn from Internationale's mistakes – the troops regarded *excessive* familiarity on the part of announcers as patronizing, and the Corporation should instead adopt the persona of 'an officer addressing men informally ... simple, direct, sincere and, without self-consciousness, authoritative'.[8]

The outcome of this kind of internal policy discussion, founded on first-hand observation and questioning of the listening public at home and on active service, was that BBC programmes began to exhibit a restrained, quietly manipulative chumminess. Programmes on the Forces network (which fast attracted more civilian listeners than the Home Service) not only came to reflect the new-found understanding of public tastes and expectations in entertainment and music, they were presented in an adroitly tuned popular *manner* – the very tone of the programmes was bright, quietly optimistic, stoical, determined, never jingoistic. Some contained a pseudo-democratic element, involving audience participation or (far less often) that of members of the public at a production level, but this was inevitably limited: throughout the war, the BBC maintained tight control over its programmes and monitored reaction to them very closely. What seemed at the time like a relaxation of policy regarding popular music in particular – during 1942, dance music constituted 9.97 per cent of BBC output, an increase of 5.3 per cent on 1938 figures – disguised a wide range of 'gatekeeping' controls instituted to ensure that the music in question reflected positively on the war effort.[9] So 'Santa Claus is Bringing You Home for Christmas' was banned as tactless when forces' leave was cancelled; Noel Coward's sarcastic 'Don't Let's Be Beastly to the Germans' was deemed acceptable 'only if sung by a man' (female vocalists, the decision implied, were unable to handle irony convincingly); and 'My Prayer', 'Seagulls over Sorrento', 'Serenade in the Night' and a number of classical works by German and Italian composers were banned because of their origin in enemy countries. Even 'Lili Marlene', Austrian in origin but universally recognized as the song of the desert army in 1942, was initially featured only in news bulletins (where its popularity among the forces could be explained to those at home) and again only in a male vocal rendition.[10] Yet more intensive monitoring of musical output began following the establishment by Basil Nicolls of a Dance Music Policy Committee in 1942, which sought to eliminate 'crooning [defined as 'effeminate singing'], sentimental numbers, drivelling words, slush, innuendos, and so on'. (Nicolls' wish to introduce more 'waltzes, marches and cheerful music of every kind' was not followed up, however, and the administration's continuing lukewarm attitude to dance-band music was tempered by a thoughtful and informed report by Spike Hughes, a dance-band musician, composer and jazz critic of *The Gramophone*, in 1943. He advocated more programme time for dance-band singers and argued that the audience's use of radio dance music as essentially background music should be more openly acknowledged.)[11]

Particular music programmes were clinically conceived for morale-boosting purposes, though their impact could be a source of controversy. *Sincerely Yours*, started in November 1941 under the supervision of returning freelancer Howard Thomas, was ostensibly a showcase for singer Vera Lynn; consisting of sentimental, homespun songs, it prompted criticism within the BBC and Parliament as to whether this really was the stuff with which to send fighting men into battle. The counter-argument was that poignant reminders of loved ones were exactly what servicemen needed: songs such as 'We'll Meet Again', 'That Lovely Weekend' and 'The White Cliffs of Dover' reminded them of the values they were fighting to uphold. But the downbeat, almost melancholic ambience of the programme concealed an additional propaganda value that was not publicly appreciated at the time, as the shows were partly designed to counter the potentially damaging influence of the German broadcasts by a character called, suitably, Lili Marlene, who warned the Tommies in seductively decadent tones of unseemly behaviour on the part of their wives and girlfriends. Vera Lynn – sweet-voiced, demure, good-natured, the epitome of home counties England – was a homely antidote to the poisonous Lili, and her songs were carefully chosen by Thomas and Lynn's own musical director to strike just the right note of reassurance.[12]

The BBC discharged its wartime duty to mobilize and unite the nation to an almost constant background of music, whether broadcast live from concert halls or factory canteens, played on records, or featured in the large number of variety shows originating in Bristol or Bangor (to where the Variety Department was dispatched as part of a general dispersal of BBC departments beyond London). Most clinical of all in intention and execution were the daytime music programmes devised with the aim of steadying morale and improving production. *Workers' Playtime* toured the munitions factories, presenting variety acts and inviting sing-along participation from its audiences; Ernest Bevin,

Minister of Labour, was directly involved in the programme's evolution. Of most long-term relevance – if only because of its durability after the war – was *Music While You Work*, which the BBC introduced on 23 June 1940 for re-diffusion (relay by loudspeakers) in factories. This was a half-hour programme (broadcast twice a day) of non-stop instrumental music, played by dance bands, with the emphasis on the lively, cheerful popular tunes of the day. The factory applications of re-diffusion had been explored in Europe and the United States during the 1930s, but the idea was new to Britain and marked a departure from the BBC's conventional perception of the audience as passive and home-based. The principle was to keep the pace of mass production at a steady level through the broadcasting of even-tempo music, though it should be said that *Music While You Work* was hardly a re-diffusion experiment on the grand scale: a total of one hour per day was unlikely to make any great difference to the production lines. Nevertheless, the programme was taken very seriously within BBC and government circles, and reports from the factories were positive: 'the music exhilarates the workers without acting as a harmful distraction. When the set was shut down for a week there was a 20 per cent drop in production'.[13] To keep workers' minds from wandering and slowing down the production line, bands contracted for *Music While You Work* were instructed to play medleys rather than individually arranged tunes and to match the pace of their playing to the rhythms of the workbench. Some measure of the importance placed in the programme at the highest level can be gained from the famous banning, in 1942, of the song 'Deep in the Heart of Texas'. A participatory song, its inclusion disrupted production – too many workers downed tools to clap hands in the appropriate place. By 1944, over 8,000 British factories with a total workforce of over 4.5 million were taking the programme, and the age and gender profile of the audience was carefully noted in maintaining the right musical mix: a 1943 report quoted by Asa Briggs concluded that 'younger workers, and many thousands of women are in this group, prefer dance music'.[14] The success of *Music While You Work* helped establish the equation of radio music to background music – a pacifier and regulator both, for the workplace as much as the fireside – that came to pervade the BBC's treatment of popular music in the post-war period. The programme carried on in slightly altered form long after the war, when the title took on a new meaning: with demobilization and the replacement of women in the factories by returning servicemen, *Music While You Work* almost imperceptibly assumed a domestic character: 'work' now applied to housework as much as it did to paid employment.

### The post-war BBC

The war affected every facet of BBC operations, altering its programming, improving its image in the country and overseas, bringing in new personnel, and creating new expectations within its audience.[15] Plans for peacetime programmes were first discussed during 1943, with the BBC particularly concerned to anticipate what it expected would be renewed competition from the foreign commercial stations and extensive American involvement in European broadcasting. The best means of meeting that threat was to carry on with the network, the Forces Programme, that had to some extent drawn on Radio Luxembourg and Radio Normandie's pre-war example, and to retain the accent on variety and music. Renamed the Light Programme by its newly appointed Controller, Maurice Gorham, the readjusted service began on 29 July 1945. The established Home Service and (after September 1946) the Third Programme completed the BBC's new tripartite system of networks, the latter specializing in what were now acknowledged to be minority tastes in the arts and the concert repertoire in particular.

At first sight, the new system suggested a streaming of audiences, not only according to tastes and interests but to what Jean Seaton has called 'the new psychology of the listener': the Light Programme was to divert and entertain, while the Home Service would (as a 1944 memorandum had it) 'give talks which would inform the whole democracy rather than an already informed section, and be generally so designed that it will steadily, but imperceptibly, raise the standard of taste, entertainment, outlook and citizenship'.[16] By 1949 the Home Service was being described as reflecting 'the broad middle strand of the BBC's broadcasting', implicitly labelling the Light as a network for low-brows.[17] To Reith – cast adrift from the BBC since 1938 at his own behest, and resisting attempts by certain members of senior management to involve him in BBC affairs on a consultative level – the system spelt an end to mixed programming and the ideal of a homogenous service, catering for all yet informed by a strict sense of responsibility to the cultural welfare of the nation. It was, he wrote, 'an absolute abandonment of what I stood for'.[18]

In part, such streaming was simply the most convenient manner of coping with programme expansion: if there was enough potential programming to fill three radio channels, it was illogical that they should duplicate each other's output. Far from abandoning cultural objectives, as Reith supposed, the BBC was adopting a new kind of rationalized paternalism best defined by its post-war Director-General, Sir William Haley, in 1948:

> Before the war the system was to confront [the listener] with pendulum-like leaps. The devotees of [Irving] Berlin were suddenly confronted with Bach. ... Since the war we have been feeling our way along a more indirect approach. It rests on the conception of the community as a broadly based cultural pyramid, slowly aspiring upwards.[19]

Initially, the Light Programme and the Home Service differed more in tone of voice than in actual programmes. Both depended for their output on the various programme supply departments – Variety, Drama, the Gramophone Department and so on – and the two Controllers (Maurice Gorham heading the Light; Lindsay Wellington, the Home) were actively encouraged to compete for resources, with a co-ordinating committee set up by Basil Nicolls acting as arbitrators in any dispute. Variety shows appeared on both networks, and a particular oddity was the placing of a chamber music programme (albeit disguised under the innocuous title of *Music in Miniature*) on the Light against

Tommy Handley's ever-popular *ITMA* on the Home. 'I was to compete with Programme A [the Home Service's working title] as much as though it were run by an outside firm', Gorham wrote in his autobiography: 'I was expected to get a bigger audience: the target was set at 60 per cent for B [the Light] against 40 per cent for A . . . my brief was to entertain; the programme could interest people in the world around them but it must never cease to entertain'.[20]

The 60 : 40 target was based on the assumption that the wartime split between the Home and Forces networks in audience patronage would be maintained into peacetime, but it also implied a growing concern with listening figures as an end in themselves. This was evident in the growth of the Listener Research Department, building on the experience gained and expertise developed during its wartime monitoring of audience habits and views, after the Second World War. Internal rather than commercial competition prompted a clinical approach to the scheduling of programmes: 'to counter the familiarity of the Home Service we had to have novelty', wrote Gorham, 'All the time Tom [Chalmers] and I were studying the audience figures every week and discussing them with Silvey, trying new schedulings to take advantage of our strong points and to build up the weak ones'.[21] Gorham and Chalmers maintained a balance on the Light between those kinds of programmes non-existent in pre-war radio – daily serials, for example – and those that were extensions of shows first conceived for the Forces Programme. *Family Favourites* was a request show begat by *Forces Favourites*: in its new form, it set the pattern for similar request programmes whose large audiences proved Gorham's view that 'people will listen far more readily to a programme of records that other people have requested than to a pro-gramme of the same records without the requests'.[22]

Request shows of the *Family Favourites* and *Housewives' Choice* ilk tapped a new vein of radio populism.[23] They created an impression of democracy at work, listeners determining the programme content, although the crucial decisions as to which records to play were taken by producers working under the twin constraints of availability and 'suitability for broadcasting'. The return to peacetime conditions also dictated a change of tone in programmes such as this: as Cliff Michelmore, presenter of both *Forces Favourites* and its successor, wryly remarked in his autobiography,

> With the war in Europe over, *Forces Favourites* was demobbed to become a family concern and at once there was a problem. Having encouraged informality in wartime, how could the BBC get the cork back in the bottle and restore its former decorum to a programme as frivolous as *Family Favourites*?[24]

The main means of 'restoring decorum' was the Controller's edict: in the case of *Family Favourites*, an internal memo in 1945 listed a number of prohibitions such as 'noisy, advanced jazz' (Stan Kenton was cited as an example), songs containing references to public schools or pubs (as that would constitute advertising), requests on behalf of fiancées or girlfriends (the title of the programme was to be taken literally), and requests carrying specific messages – even wishing a happy birthday was forbidden, as giving out the age of a listener might offend.[25] Then there were the songs banned by that relic of wartime censorship, the Dance Music Policy Committee. These included songs with allusions to religion or commercial products, and some (but not all – the decision was at the Committee's discretion) based on classical themes. So 'The Wedding Cake Waltz' was denied airplay because of references in the lyric to 'pasty choirs and tasty churches/prudish old preachers on their perches', and 'Oodles of Noodles' was ignored because it was held to give publicity to a well-known brand of soup. Ribaldry and sexual innuendo were as frowned upon as ever: Asa Briggs cites 'Get up Those Stairs, Mademoiselle', 'Two Old Maids in a Folding Bed', and 'A Huggin' and a Chalkin' ' as examples of offending lyrics.[26] And while certain songs, subjects and styles were automatically excluded, the inclusion of at least one item of classical music per request programme was mandatory. In the cases of *Family Favourites*, *Children's Favourites* and *Housewives' Choice*, the classical piece was always placed at the end of the programme, because to insert it between 'popular' items was thought to demean it.

## Protectionism and the record industry

External agreements also affected what was played, notably that between the BBC and the Songwriters Guild of Great Britain (formed only in 1947) to ensure the broadcasting of more songs by British composers. The foundation of the Guild was in fact directly related to the failure – or unwillingness – of the Music Publishers Association (MPA) to bring pressure to bear on the BBC on the matter of coverage of British-made music.[27] (The catalogues of MPA members contained a growing amount of repertoire licensed from the United States, and a number of American publishers were actively buying into their UK counterparts.) The most significant restriction placed on music output as a whole, however, was that regarding 'needle-time' – the number of hours agreed between the BBC and Phonographic Performance Limited (acting on behalf of the record companies and in league with the Musicians Union) for the playing of commercially produced records.

The background to this agreement is worth tracing. If the 1920s was a time of uncertainty and competition within the British record industry (exemplified by the numerous outlets in which companies placed their products – electrical shops, general stores, newspaper stands – and by the absence of a standard price for records), the early 1930s brought a bullish change of mood. A bout of frenzied share-dealing activity on the Stock Exchange and a sharp decline in record sales precipitated wholesale mergers of record companies – notably the Gramophone Company with His Master's Voice to form Electrical and Musical Industries (EMI) – and a series of important protectionist moves.[28] Falling sales of records were blamed on their increasing use by restaurants and hotels, and also by the BBC; the MU objected to such usage because it provided broadcasters with a cheap alternative to hiring musicians. A test case was brought by the Gramophone Company against a Bristol restaurant, Cawardine and Company, under the 1911 Copyright Act, to establish the principle of permission and recompense for public use of products sold for private enjoyment. The Gramophone Company won, and in 1934 the PPL was founded by the British Phonographic Industry (representing all the major record manufacturers) for the distribution of licences and the collection of revenue. Total revenue received during PPL's first full year of operation, 1935, was £23,781, and in 1938 its annual receipts topped £67,676.[29] Under the original agreement, revenue received for public performance of records went direct to the participating companies, but this was modified in 1935 under pressure from the MU, whose members could in law claim no royalties for the public performance of their re-corded work (the copyright resting with the companies themselves). Under the 1935 agreement, 20 per cent of PPL's net distributable revenue was to be set aside for allocation to the musicians named on record labels and contracted to member companies.[30]

The initial sum negotiated between the BBC and PPL was £20,000 per year for a period of three years, beginning in 1935. For the future development of the BBC's relationship with the record industry, this first agreement with PPL was vital. Forged at a time when records were not of any great importance to British broadcasting, it set a precedent that ensured that any wider use of records in later years would be both expensive and subject to a degree of outside control, and it effectively restricted that use for a long period (and with it the BBC's ability to accommodate the changing musical tastes of its audience) by strengthening the hand of the MU within the BBC.

The BBC's use of records did increase, briefly, during the war. Gerald Abraham, head of the Gramophone Department, tellingly referred to the gramophone record (in an article for the 1945 *BBC Yearbook*) as an 'understudy':

> While it is the policy of the Gramophone Department to promote the gramophone as far as possible from the position of a useful stop-gap to the position of a definite factor in radio entertainment, it is on the other hand, as an understudy probably the most efficient understudy in the world. When war was declared the gramophone was fully prepared to act as a sub-stitute. All through the bombing of Britain gramophone records were collected and prepared to 'shadow' certain actual performances, so that if they were interrupted by enemy action the programme was immediately resumed on records.[31]

Conscription limited the number of bands and individual musicians available to keep up the BBC's in-house supply of music, and in 1940 the MU agreed to relax its restraints on needle-time for the duration of the war: 4.22 per cent of air-time had accounted for record programmes on the one national network in 1939, but a year later that figure increased to 18.34 per cent of air-time on the Forces Pro-gramme and 5.08 per cent on the Home Service.[32] In 1946 the MU rescinded the agreement and insisted on new restrictions on the pre-recording of music programmes and repeat broadcasts, to protect the livelihoods of musicians who were returning from overseas service to find former workplaces destroyed by bombing and their old jobs gone. New negotiations between PPL and the MU, meanwhile, resulted in PPL (now representing just two companies, EMI and

Decca) increasing its revenue allocation to working musicians; in recognition of the army of session musicians or dance-band or orchestra members who contributed to the recording process but received only session fees, PPL granted a further 12.5 per cent of its annual revenue to the MU to distribute among this relatively 'anonymous' section of its membership.[33]

One unforeseen side-effect of the BBC's greater wartime use of records was growing public exposure to American popular music; few records were issued in Britain during the war because of the shortage in raw materials, so the BBC came to rely extensively on imported American discs. But American musical influence was most profoundly felt through the presence of US troops in the country; also the BBC's regular transmission of US-made variety programmes (minus the sponsor's message), which featured the likes of Bing Crosby, Bob Hope, the Andrews Sisters and Frank Sinatra; and the programmes of the American Forces Network (AFN).

## Americanization at bay

Maurice Gorham recalled that when AFN began in 1943, 'it was the preordained programme for the bobby-soxers, with its American comedy, American swing and entire freedom from restrictions. AFN could use the *Oklahoma!* music two years before the BBC could. If anybody complained of breach of copyright they just said "Sue Uncle Sam".'[34] Although Gorham, for one, thought that the popularity and influence of AFN were exaggerated, British popular culture as a whole did undergo an insidious 'Americanization' as the war progressed. American influence was probably at its height as the Allied invasion of Europe loomed and the numbers of US army and air force personnel stationed in Britain increased. A few months prior to the D-day landings in June 1944, plans were laid for an integrated radio service for the British, American and Canadian troops forming the invasion force; launched on D-day itself, the new Allied Expeditionary Forces Programme (AEFP) was administered by the Overseas Service of the BBC in close co-operation with AFN and the Canadian Broadcasting Company, under the directorship of Maurice Gorham. Its programmes reflected, deliberately, the proportion of national forces serving in the field – 50 per cent were of American origin, 35 per cent British and 15 per cent Canadian – and heavily featured the official dance-bands of each, namely the American Band of the Supreme Allied Command (effectively Glenn Miller's civilian band, now in uniform), the Army Radio Orchestra under the direction of RSM George Melachrino, and the Royal Canadian Artillery Band. These bands, and smaller combinations of musicians assigned to them, contributed a huge amount of broadcasts (most of them live) to the AEFP, and the Miller band in particular made a major and lasting impact. Virtually unknown to British audiences prior to 1944, Miller's reputation was built on AEFP programmes which, theoretically, the civilian audience in Britain was not meant to hear: relatively few of the shows were broadcast on the Home Service or the Forces Programme in what was interpreted by *Melody Maker* writers and by many British dance-band musicians as a deliberate attempt to keep American swing music at arm's length.[35]

How to protect the nation, and the nation's youth in particular, from the effects of supposed American economic and cultural imperialism was a preoccupation of both right- and left-wing opinion-formers throughout the late 1940s and 1950s. The BBC was in the front line of the defence against Americanization. US-originated shows were quickly dropped from the schedules after the end of the war, on Haley's instructions, and Alistair Cooke began sending his *Letter from America* in March 1946, a programme which in part sought to redress the United States' culturally vulgar image (a task that could not apparently be trusted to American-born broadcasters). In the debate surrounding the future of the BBC that was initiated by the Beveridge Committee in 1950, the American system of broadcasting and the role that commercial operators played in it were continually cited in arguments against the introduction of advertising or sponsorship on radio or television.[36] Behind all this lay a sense of national economic inferiority, exacerbated by Britain's dependence on American finance for post-war reconstruction, and a feeling that Britain's cultural 'superiority' over the United States (and the values reflected in its history and traditions) was under threat. Americanization had political implications, too, in that it could be held to create unrealistic expectations of material improvements at a time when the government was preaching austerity. American popular music in particular was seen by BBC personnel as having what Dick Hebdige has called a 'potentially subversive' impact on public morale.[37]

This point requires qualification, however, as it was not American popular music *per se* that BBC programme-makers sought to control but the *presentation* of it in undiluted, unmodified form. The BBC acted as a filter, recognizing the qualities and the popularity of American music but re-presenting it to the British public in a form devoid of much of its spark and charm. BBC radio had long wrapped American music in a British packaging, and it continued to feature home-grown dance-bands playing their own arrangements of the latest American hits right through to the 1960s in programmes such as *Music While You Work* and *The Billy Cotton Band Show*. One of the marked changes in American music during the mid to late 1940s – generally seen as a consequence of a wartime recording boycott by the American Federation of Musicians, which prompted dance-band singers to break with their bands and begin solo careers – was the sharp decline in popularity of the dance-bands and the parallel rise to stardom of singers like Frank Sinatra, Perry Como, Dick Haymes and Ella Fitzgerald. In Britain, however, the absence of industrial unrest and the BBC's continuing (and by now unequivocal) patronage of the dance-bands ensured that a similar development in Britain was delayed. When solo singers did begin to make their mark on British popular music during the early 1950s, most were established BBC 'names' – Donald Peers, Lee Lawrence, Jimmy Young, Dickie Valentine, Dennis Lotis – who had previously sung with the orchestras of Ray Martin, Ted Heath, Cyril Stapleton and others. When recording success came, it was invariably with 'cover' versions of American songs which were favoured over the American originals by BBC producers: Jimmy Young, for example, remembers how his version of Nat 'King' Cole's 'Too Young' began picking up sales after Jack Jackson chose to include it in preference to the Cole version on his Saturday show, *Record Rendezvous*.[38] The favouring of British discs over American was by no means systematic – records by such US stars as Jo Stafford, Frankie Laine and Guy Mitchell were regularly featured on *Housewives' Choice* and *Family Favourites*, despite the existence of British 'covers' – but the regularity with which British singers appeared on the radio and a general sense of loyalty to British-made product made it more likely that the British version would be given the more frequent airplay. The success of British acts in the Top Selling Artists survey published by *New Musical Express* in 1955 reflected precisely this form of protectionism: the list was headed by Britain's Ruby Murray and Jimmy Young, while two of the most established US singers, Johnnie Ray and Frank Sinatra, were placed at seventeenth and eighteenth respectively (with Tony Bennett and Dean Martin just above them).[39]

The treatment of jazz, that most quintessentially 'American' of idioms, was as problematic as it had been before the war; in fact more so, because of its association with and apparently increasing appeal among college-educated, middle-class youth. The jazz community of musicians and critics, as represented by the perennially influential *Melody Maker*, was a very vocal one that could not be ignored altogether, however much certain senior BBC personnel may have wished to impose a blanket ban. Seen at best by these same personnel as a minority music worthy of a 'specialist' spot, jazz was thought by some to warrant inclusion on (or, looking at it negatively, exclusion to) the Third Programme. A number of jazz programmes were indeed mounted by the Third, thus confirming jazz as the property of a cultured élite and exemplifying another familiar BBC tactic: to appear to accommodate the tastes of a minority community (in effect, to grant 'rights' to it) while at the same time deliberately distancing those tastes from the mainstream. Even when broadcast on the Light Programme, jazz was featured in low-key fashion, introduced by 'experts' who clearly assumed some foreknowledge of the jazz field among their listeners. Unlike Latin American music, which enjoyed a post-war vogue in Britain, jazz could not be easily incorporated into the daily musical output of the Light: the nature of jazz was that it entailed a spontaneous interplay of instruments rather than detailed pre-arrangement, and strict adherence to the melody line of a song was never a priority.

The issue was complicated further by the various post-war conflicts within the jazz community over the direction, style and approach of jazz, notably that between the revivalists (who worked diligently at recreating Dixieland jazz) and the progressives, who followed the example of Charlie Parker and others. Programme producers like Jon Foreman, responsible for *Jazz Club* from 1950 onwards, acted as arbitrators, though he for one came out firmly on the side of the revivalists. Foreman told *Melody Maker* that he would not feature 'bop' or 'progressive music' on the programme (which was an offshoot of the wartime *Radio Rhythm Club*), citing practical considerations: genuine be-bop could only be heard on disc, not 'recreated' (a reactionary notion, anyway, in the progressive view) by British jazz musicians in BBC studios, so why should precious needle-time be used up on something of such limited appeal and so obviously 'unsuited' to domestic dissemination? But revivalist jazz was favoured over modern jazz because it came closest to matching conventional BBC notions of musical culture – it had tradition, history, an air of permanence, along with what George Melly called a 'potential respectability', because of the strength of its following among an educated middle-class audience.[40]

However, the BBC could only do so much to keep the tide of Americanization in check. Other media – juke boxes, the cinema, commercial television (after 1955), Radio Luxembourg and, though to a lesser degree, AFN – offered the listener far greater opportunity to hear American popular music in its original form. They also provided the foundation upon which post-war youth culture was to build its ascendancy, although it is important to view the story of post-war 'youth music' in Britain in terms of *both* the importation of mainstream musical idioms *and* a growing bohemianism (initially centred on jazz) modestly but significantly encouraged by the BBC's treatment of jazz as a music of a minority élite.

# 3 Pop and piracy: 1956–67

For radio listeners, the prime source of music *on record* in the post-war years was not the BBC Light Programme but Radio Luxembourg, which was permitted to resume broadcasting to Britain in 1946 after its use by the BBC in the period immediately following the Grand Duchy's liberation. The station did not immediately re-establish itself: prevailing economic conditions and the consequent paucity of advertising revenue, the lack of experienced creative personnel in the advertising agencies (many copywriters having joined either the BBC or the Ministry of Information during the war), and changes in listening habits left it in an uncertain financial state for some time. To the surprise of some within the BBC, there was not the expected demand in the country, or even from commerce, for sponsored radio; even the Institute of Practitioners in Advertising, while favouring a commercial system, advocated a restricted use of advertising by the existing BBC networks rather than the creation of any new, competing service.[1]

By the beginning of the 1950s, Luxembourg's programming was taking two distinct directions. On the one hand there were sponsored shows, no longer the variety showcases of pre-war years but generally quiz shows or talent contests on the American model, like *Double Your Money* and *Opportunity Knocks*, which were relatively inexpensive to produce and offered the kind of big-money prizes which the BBC was prohibited from offering under the terms of its Charter. On the other hand, record shows – the early mainstay of commercial radio in the United States and Europe – assumed a far greater importance for economic reasons, as they incurred very little expense (Luxembourg was outside PPL territory) and attracted audiences comparable in size with those of the audience-participation shows. The station had two types of record programme at this time, the request show and the hit parade programme, both of which had antecedents in BBC wartime programmes. The request shows followed the BBC formula of familiar music and dedications but dispensed with a script – right up until the reorganization of the Light Programme's service departments in 1963, all BBC record shows had to carry an approved script – while the inspiration for the hit parade programme (which started in late 1948) was apparently an earlier dance-band show which Maurice Gorham had initiated for the Forces Programme and which had featured the currently most popular songs as evaluated by sheet music sales. (That said, the idea of a programme based entirely on sales *rankings* originated in the United States during the war with *The Lucky Strike Hit Parade*. The 'hit parade' concept itself grew out of the pre-war monitoring exercises mounted in the United States by market-research companies and financed by music publishers, who ranked songs according to the number of times a song was performed live on air.[2]) Luxembourg's 'chart' of best-selling songs was compiled by the Music Publishers Association and was again based on sheet music sales.

The growth in television set ownership during the early 1950s and the incursion of the BBC's television service into the evening leisure hours began tilting the balance in favour of the disc shows, particularly as television entertainment programmes tended to replicate many of the features of radio variety. The arrival of Independent Television in 1955, its programme-making capacity entirely dependent on advertising revenue, spelt the end of variety programmes on Luxembourg for good; advertisers withdrew their sponsorship of such shows and switched their resources to the making of 'spot' commercials for television. As a result, Luxembourg lost not only revenue but also a number of key programmes: several of ITV's most-watched programmes were straight adaptations of Luxembourg successes (*Double Your Money, Opportunity Knocks* and *Take Your Pick* included). Many of the personnel in ITV production and administration were ex-agency figures like Howard Thomas, who had served an apprenticeship in commercial radio production prior to the war. By 1957 Luxembourg was itself supplementing its remaining sponsorship by selling 30-second slices of air-time to advertisers, à la ITV. One of the advantages of this form of spot advertising was that the advertiser could use the soundtrack of a made-for-television commercial rather than incur the extra expense of creating advertisements specially for Luxembourg use.

## Sponsorship and the record companies

The loss of Luxembourg's hard-core *family* audience to television necessitated its cultivation of a narrower listenership, but the solution to the station's declining patronage – programmes aimed specifically at the younger listener – took time to emerge. The catalysts for the solution were the record companies, which first be-gan sponsoring record shows in piecemeal fashion after the war. The first company to build a true marketing strategy around them was Capitol Records in 1951, whose half-hour showcase of latest releases was produced in Hollywood; Decca and EMI subsequently began their own, the latter under the supervision of Promotions Manager Harry Walters, who booked a regular time-slot for his company after noticing that EMI's products were selling exceptionally well in

Scotland and the north of England, where Luxembourg's signal was particularly strong. At first, these 15- and 30-minute shows were conceived as public relations exercises, designed to heighten awareness of that company's presence in the marketplace rather than maximize sales of particular releases, and choice of content was often left to the Luxembourg staff presenter (who, as Pete Murray admitted in his autobiography, would frequently play records released by a rival label).[3] In time, however, the companies assumed complete control of their programmes by recording them in London and hiring their own 'name' presenters, some of whom were Luxembourg regulars like Murray and Teddy Johnson and some BBC freelancers such as Jack Jackson and Sam Costa. By 1957 EMI, for one, was sponsoring shows at the rate of one per day, at a total annual cost of £35,000.[4]

The shows were effectively extended advertisements, the novelty being that the product advertised was *itself* the entertainment provided. They offered British radio listeners the opportunity to hear a range of commercial releases generally wider than that featured by the BBC, though it did not necessarily follow that Luxembourg's attitude (or that of the sponsoring companies) was any more sympathetic towards young tastes or fashions. Far from offering a haven for music of 'young appeal', Luxembourg's record shows were at first extremely selective, one of their functions being to reflect the broad *span* of a company's entire weekly output. The shift to a more pop-based policy (defining pop music, in this case, as music targeted at teenagers) was gradual and coincided with a more general realization on the part of advertisers regarding the youth market's potential profitability. Luxembourg only became fully committed to a 'pop' service in 1957, when Barry Alldis took over the English Service and the last vestiges of the station's variety programming were dropped. This paralleled, and was to a great extent inspired by, a concerted attempt by the major British record companies to woo the teenage record-buyer with discs by carefully groomed British counterparts to the American rock 'n' roll idols: Decca, after initial success with Tommy Steele, achieved still more with Marty Wilde and Billy Fury, while the cluster of labels affiliated to EMI (and particularly Columbia) produced Cliff Richard, Adam Faith and Helen Shapiro and many less durable names. All were promoted and in many cases launched by made-for-Luxembourg programmes, which were also used as vehicles for star showcases or portraits and for recruitment of members to fan clubs. As a general rule, what constituted 'pop' on Radio Luxembourg was, because of the record companies' direct control over programme content, a calculatedly pallid version of American rock 'n' roll.[5]

Luxembourg's post-1957 strategy had the effect of strengthening the hold of the major companies on the record market and stifling the expansion of smaller, independent companies such as Top Rank and Oriole. It meant, finally, that the record manufacturers were able to exert a considerable degree of control, unmatched at any other time, before or since, in British record industry history, over the ultimate destiny of their product, be it a Top Twenty placing due to repeated exposure on Luxembourg or the *failure* of a record to achieve a chart placing due to deliberately *limited* exposure. The Beatles' first British release,

'Love Me Do', fell into the latter category during late 1962 because their company, the EMI subsidiary Parlophone, was not accorded the same pre-Christmas promotional backing given to the senior EMI label, Columbia: only covert action by Brian Epstein, who ordered 10,000 copies of the record (few of which were eventually sold) for his Liverpool record store and thereby ensured its appearance in the lower reaches of the Top 20, forced EMI to give it greater exposure on Luxembourg and, subsequently, to promote the group's *second* release ('Please Please Me') as an *expected* bestseller.

One further point should be made about Radio Luxembourg at this time, if only to correct a distortion of music radio history that accounts such as BBC Radio 1's *The Story of Pop Radio* have compounded. Despite certain parallels with American radio in the 1950s, what Luxembourg offered its listeners was hardly rock 'n' roll radio in the romanticized, almost mythical sense. Certainly radio in the United States at the start of the 1950s faced similar problems to those of Luxembourg, with television attracting away sponsorship and advertising, but the main factor in the growth of all-music (i.e. gramophone record based) radio in America was the switching of investment by the big radio networks into television and the consequent requirement of network-affiliated local stations to originate much more of their own programming. Music programming was cheap programming, and it was not uncommon to find a radio station run by a staff of five or six catering for a potential audience of around 100,000. Lowered costs of entry into US radio in turn brought increased competition and, with it, specialization, as the stations identified particular audiences or sections of audiences (usually defined by age, ethnic background or musical taste) and geared their programmes, music selection and advertising to them.[6] One such was the adolescent audience for rock 'n' roll music, the emergence of which was directly related to the patronage of black neighbourhood music stations by young white listeners. As rock 'n' roll (stylistically an offshoot of black rhythm and blues) grew in popularity and record companies began to exploit a hitherto untapped market, so the rock 'n' roll radio format of rhythm and blues records and frantic presentation (imitative of the black stations) took hold nationally. The parallel development and mass marketing of portable transistor sets and in-car receivers placed radio and rock music at the very centre of the teenage life-style. The image of a young, mobile, noise-loving, slightly delinquent young listener entered the iconography of rock music.

In Britain, the earliest 'pop radio' – in the sense of disc shows on Luxembourg, aimed at a young record-buying audience – had none of these qualities. Transistor development lagged behind that in the United States; British teenagers were less affluent than their American counterparts and few drove cars: listening to the radio was a *domestic* rather than out-of-house activity and usually restricted to bedrooms, commonly as a background to homework. When reminiscing about the Radio Luxembourg of the late 1950s, former listeners invariably dwell on the pleasures of listening to the station's fading signal under the blankets. There was a clear qualitative difference between the British and American experiences of rock 'n' roll, which the respective means of dissemination underlined.

## Youth appeal

Luxembourg continued to be seen, nevertheless, either as an agent of American cultural imperialism or as a harbinger of cultural debasement, and often as both. Eric Maschwitz complained that Luxembourg was out 'to catch the cinema-queue, dance-hall audience in order to bamboozle them into combating night starvation' and that the BBC was following the station's line in pandering to 'the semi-Americanized "teen-age" listener who in these times of high wages and full employment, has an excess of pocket money to spend upon foolish, often vulgar, musical fads'.[7] It was clearly with Luxembourg in mind (the description did not fit the Light Programme at this time) that Richard Hoggart, in *The Uses of Literacy* (1958), criticized 'the lowbrow gang-spirit of some gramophone-record features in which young men, accompanying their items with a stream of pally patter, offer programmes whose whole composition assumes that whatever the greatest number like most is best and the rest are the aberrations of "eggheads" '.[8]

But a change could be detected across the whole of British broadcasting in the 1950s, and especially after the advent of ITV, a service operated by commercial consortia made up of the same kind of investors (including equipment manufacturing and entertainment concerns) that had been barred from investing in broadcasting when the BBC monopoly was created. Obliged to compete for audiences in order to justify the continued provision of public funding, BBC television became more populist in approach, not so much in the scheduling of 'mass appeal' programmes as in programme presentation. *Tonight*, which began in 1957, was the perfect example, offering a magazine-type mixture of serious features and comical items and presided over by a master of chummy informality, Cliff Michelmore, who had initially learnt his trade with the British Forces Broadcasting System (BFBS) in Germany, co-hosting *Family Favourites*. Within BBC radio, the impact of ITV was more subtle but still considerable, its main effect being to encourage the expansion of television set ownership and thereby accelerate the process by which radio was already being turned from a primary source of entertainment and news into a secondary source. One of the purposes of the reorganization of BBC sound output in 1957 was to dovetail the Corporation's radio programmes with its television output: more resources were pumped into daytime programmes on the Light, and the network's transmission time was brought forward from 9 a.m. to 6.30 a.m. The daytime Light Programme became a mixture of music and magazine programmes, while the evening and weekend programmes (less patronized because of increased television watching) were gradually given over to more 'specialized' streams of programming.[9]

Specialization (i.e. the making of programmes for different communities of tastes and interests) provided the context in which BBC radio made its first tentative steps towards recognizing a 'youth' audience. A seminal programme in this respect was *Jazz Club*, which began in 1947 as a replacement for *Radio Rhythm Club*. By the mid-1950s it was faithfully mirroring yet another split in the jazz camp – that between the revivalists and a new breed of young, diehard traditionalists led by Ken Colyer, who had travelled to New Orleans and had returned to spread the gospel of pure, unsullied Crescent City jazz. The traditionalists scorned any deviation from the early New Orleans model, but it was an offshoot of traditional jazz – skiffle, a re-creation of the washboard and kazoo jug-band music played at jazz parties in low-rent neighbourhoods – that most unexpectedly captured the public imagination. A former member of Colyer's band, Lonnie Donegan, joined the Chris Barber Jazz Band in 1953 and introduced a skiffle session into the band's gigs, playing American folk songs with Barber and Beryl Bryden while the rest of the band took a beer break. Donegan's career took off when one of the tracks he had recorded with Barber, 'Rock Island Line', became a Top Twenty hit in Britain; within months, record companies had signed a string of promising skiffle outfits and new groups were forming all over the country.

Skiffle's importance to the development of British popular music, the manner in which its play-it-yourself qualities introduced the nation's teenagers to music-*making*, has been described many times, but of more relevance here is the role it played in the image of youth that the media constructed.[10] Skiffle was welcomed by an odd alliance of churchmen, politicians, schoolteachers and media professionals: emerging just as American rock 'n' roll was gaining a foothold in Britain (and finding a particularly ready audience among young working-class 'Teddy Boys'), skiffle presented youth in a much more positive light. Skiffle was closely identified with the school, the church and the youth club (where many of the groups first formed) and with a music, jazz, that already had a history and a tradition of indifference to commercialism behind it – a music that in a sense belonged to the older generation. Rock 'n' roll carried connotations of rebellion and violence – the screening of the films *The Blackboard Jungle* and *Rock Around the Clock*, both featuring Bill Haley soundtracks, had supposedly prompted 'teenage riots' – but skiffle was a supposedly healthier and more durable alternative:

> Skiffle will continue. One can say this despite the fact that from time to time voices are heard proclaiming that Skiffle is dying. ... Such individuals are probably confusing Skiffle with other forms of music today, which are neither Skiffle nor Jazz, and which therefore do not possess a very high survival value, being very largely commercialised products ... the terms 'Skiffle' and 'Rock-and-Roll' are not synonymous. Their histories and origins are so very different, and one only has to study these, and to listen to examples of their music, to be convinced of the fundamental difference between them.
>
> Rev. Brian Bird, *Skiffle*[11]

Rock 'n' roll was held at arm's length by the BBC: Stuart Coleman of BBC Radio London remembers being astonished at the number of records of the 1956–8 period carrying green 'restricted' stickers (a practice that dated from the war years) he found on his first visit to the BBC's record library. Restriction did not necessarily mean blanket censorship, but it did signify unsuitability for regular or repeated broadcasting in specified programmes. Elvis Presley's 'Heartbreak Hotel', for example, was never banned outright by the BBC but was rarely heard on BBC record shows at the time of its release in 1956, in spite of its sales success; one of the seminal moments in the history of rock 'n' roll in Britain, referred to by numerous rock stars-to-be in discussing their first exposure to the music, was the single play that the record received on *Family Favourites* during that year. By contrast, skiffle was accommodated to a startling degree. The seal of approval was the launch of *Saturday Skiffle Club* in 1956, which was conceived as a youth club of the air and a radio counterpart to BBC-TV's *Six-Five Special*. Like that programme, it featured a professional front-man (Brian Matthew), whose function was to act as a go-between, a chaperone, between youngsters and adults like a tolerant but responsible teacher.

There was another distinct difference between rock 'n' roll and skiffle: while the former was a music heard mainly on record, the latter was an idiom best heard in the live setting of a club or even a BBC theatre. Donegan's discs apart, skiffle did not translate at all well to record, it sounded too tinny, too unsophisticated, too amateurish against standard record company product, and few other artists in the field even enjoyed hit records. It was too basic and too easily imitated to endure, and those young musicians whom the skiffle fad had initially encouraged moved on to playing rock 'n' roll itself. (This point was well appreciated by television producer Jack Good, who moved from BBC's *Six-Five Special* to ITV's *Oh Boy!* in 1957, in which he not only gave rock wider coverage but helped establish a visual – and faintly parodic – house style for British rock 'n' roll.[12]) That the BBC was not really on top of the newly crystallizing 'teen scene' was obvious to any teenager who followed the record sales charts printed in *Melody Maker* or *New Musical Express* or read the music press with any diligence. The 1957 *BBC Handbook* could quaintly claim that 'millions of young listeners followed the BBC's programmes devoted to the contemporary cult of the gramophone record',[13] but these programmes were thin on the ground and were usually made up not just of carefully screened discs but of in-house re-creations of current hits, either by BBC bands or by those contracted by the BBC under its MU agreement.

## Beat across Britain

Nevertheless, the amount of air-time given by the BBC to 'pop' music – the record industry's own favoured term, 'rock 'n' roll' having too many negative associations – did increase between 1957 and 1962. *Skiffle Club* evolved into *Saturday Club*, the first edition of which was broadcast on 4 October 1958; under Brian Matthew's direction, it featured a skilful mix of newly released records, Top Twenty items and studio sessions by BBC regulars like Bob Miller and the Miller Men, and became something of a radio equivalent to the music papers. Simultaneously a consumer's guide and a forum for modest debate, it did at least give the appearance (which the Luxembourg programmes could not of course do) of acting independently of record company influence. In November 1961, for example, Matthew blew the gaffe on a phoney request-card racket, the cards apparently originating from record company press offices. However, *Saturday Club* began as a special-interest programme and continued to be regarded as such, despite its large audience (inherited in part from *Children's Favourites*, which ran for the previous hour). Far from illustrating the potential of pop programming on BBC radio, the programme's success confirmed the status of youth-oriented music in BBC thinking – as something to be acknowledged and accommodated, even modestly encouraged (the success of *Saturday Club* prompted a Sunday morning equivalent, *Easy Beat*, again with Brian Matthew as host), but to be kept apart and treated differently from mainstream programming.

How and why, then, did BBC radio's attitude towards, and treatment of, pop music change as the 1960s went on – and did it in fact change at all? Initially, there were few real changes beyond the introduction of regular lunchtime pop shows from the regions (*Pop Inn*, from Manchester, was one example), most of which were live programmes acting as showcases for the various regional dance orchestras, who played big-band arrangements of current hits. The most significant long-term innovation was the launch of *Pick of the Pops* in 1962, an hour-long Sunday afternoon chart show hosted first by David Jacobs and later, far more memorably, by a presenter with experience in Australian radio, Alan Freeman. But it was after 1963 that the most marked changes occurred, partly as an indirect result of internal organizational changes brought about to streamline the efficiency of BBC radio within the new television age, partly because of the advent of pirate broadcasting. That the new pirate stations acted as a catalyst for changes in the shape and (though to a lesser extent) character of the networks themselves is indisputable; what needs to be properly assessed, however, is the degree to which change was already under way within BBC radio itself.

What has to be borne in mind, too, is that the commercial pop world was itself far from static at this time. The early years of the 1960s marked the start of what Iain Chambers has called 'an internal remaking of British pop music',[14] when the amateur and semi-professional groups populating the underbelly of provincial music-making finally broke through to achieve mainstream recognition. Made up mostly of ex-skifflers, rock 'n' roll fans and/or enthusiasts for black American rhythm and blues, these groups played a generally harder, more-intense, less-polished music than that offered by the Top Twenty, being most interested in American musical sources (including rockabilly and Tamla Motown) that the British record companies either had little access to or simply ignored. Physically isolated from the main hub of record industry activity in London, such groups became the sudden focus of record company attention following the success that EMI enjoyed (much to its own surprise) with the Beatles.[15]

This beat group 'boom' was the catalyst for an unprecedented global expansion of British influence, with British artists and UK-produced records making a particularly huge and enduring impact in the hitherto unyielding US market. After years of American domination of British popular music, the tide appeared to turn, although such groups as the Beatles and the Rolling Stones initially drew heavily on American styles which had found only fleeting commercial favour in their country of origin. In Britain itself, home-made pop of the Beatle ilk formed a musical backcloth to the start of a spending boom among young consumers comparable with that in the United States in the mid-1950s; it coincided, too, with a burst of creativity in fashion, film-making and other areas of Britain's popular arts, including television, where would-be proletarian dramas like *Z Cars* and *Coronation Street* depicted the north as the spiritual heartland of 1960s England. In the face of continuing political and economic difficulties that were rooted in Britain's post-war industrial decline, the various branches of the nation's popular culture helped modify Britain's own downbeat image of itself.

But one of the most remarkable aspects of this flowering of British pop was the very minor role which radio played in it. *Saturday Club* and the various 'Beatle specials' mounted by the Light Programme (the Christmas show, *From Us to You*, for instance) during their first flush of national popularity certainly sustained the commercial impetus of the early beat boom, but BBC radio's role here was reactive rather than creative. Radio Luxembourg, as we have seen, consistently reflected a mild, diluted record-industry interpretation of American pop. Dependent as it was on the record companies (for programmes as well as the records themselves), the station could only respond to changes in fashion and taste as the companies recognized and responded to them. Although Luxembourg, supplied by EMI's Promotions Department, did run a number of Beatles specials of its own during 1963–5, the sponsored shows continued to showcase an across-the-board selection of company releases, including those by established solo artists to whom the labels had a long-term commitment. Just as in the mid-1950s it was television – particularly *Six-Five Special* and *Oh Boy!* – that did more than any other medium to disseminate skiffle and rock 'n' roll respectively, so in the early to mid-1960s television shows like BBC-TV's *Top of the Pops* and ITV's *Thank Your Lucky Stars* were the vital programmes for 'breaking' new artists and making hits. The Beatles' first media appearance was on regional television, on a Granada TV magazine programme broadcast from Manchester in late 1962, and press interest in the group only began in earnest after their spots on ITV's *Sunday Night at the London Palladium* in October 1963.

A turning-point in British radio's relationship with pop music came in 1964 with the appearance of the first of several pirate radio stations, each broadcasting day-long sequences of programmes featuring currently best-selling records and disc-jockey chat. The pirates' existence was brief – little more than three years – and certainly of crucial importance to the pattern of radio which followed, but their influence has been exaggerated (not to say mythologized) to such an extent that the real nature of their contribution to British music radio can be overlooked. The degree to which the stations supposedly shaped the course and character of British pop has been frequently overstated, as has the 'boost' they gave to record sales and to the growth of the record industry's independent sector (which historians of pop music have consistently portrayed as the pioneer of the new and experimental, in contrast to the major companies whose role is supposedly to exploit or dilute such innovations). In considering the pirate era, it is easy to be beguiled into locating the stations within the mythology of the Swinging Sixties, to be honoured alongside Carnaby Street fashions, mods and rockers, flower-power and *Ready Steady Go!* as manifestations of young affluence and high-spirited youthful rebellion and enterprise. But the consequences of this for radio have been almost entirely negative: contemporary romanticization turned into a cult of nostalgia almost as soon as the pirates were outlawed, and so much of what followed in British radio – the establishment of Radio 1, the setting up of legal commercial radio stations on land, even the metropolitan pirates of the late 1970s and early 1980s – came to be judged according to how well it recreated pirate radio's narrow mid-1960s ambience.

## Top Forty radio: the US model

Pirate radio was Top Forty-based format radio, imported to Britain from the United States and crudely adapted for domestic consumption, but the history and mechanics of the format should perhaps be sketched out before we consider its British application. The US variety of Top Forty radio involved the round-the-clock playing of a carefully selected and programmed mixture of the highest-placed hits on *Billboard* magazine's Hot Hundred chart, newly released discs that were *expected* to reach the chart, and a sprinkling of past hits ('golden oldies'). When first introduced in 1949, by stations affiliated to the Todd Storz-owned Mid-Continent Broadcasting Company, it was a radical departure from the established US radio convention – known in radio circles as the 'bandstand' concept – of playing 15-minute segments of records by a single artist or band. Storz had noticed that juke-box patrons, in choosing what records to hear from a list of between fifty and sixty discs that the juke-box suppliers changed weekly, tended to select the same discs again and again; applying this to radio, he developed the principle that the most popular current records (i.e. the best-selling and fastest-rising discs on the Top Forty chart) should be given the most plays, and often. Supposing that more listeners would tune in if they could be sure of hearing their favourite records, a rotation system was introduced to ensure that the biggest current sellers were played at set intervals. As American radio became fiercely competitive and the format was widely adopted, so the mechanical details that Storz had outlined were intensely refined and a whole range of audience-catching elements – time checks, weather reports, station call-signs, trailers and typewriter sound effects (to give an impression of urgency during newscasts) – added to the mix. As one of Top Forty radio's best chroniclers, Philip Eberly, describes:

> At the interior of Top 40 was a basic management understanding of nuances – nuances of timing, of sound reproduction, of listener empathy. Nothing was left to chance. Top 40 radio was quality-controlled all the way. . . . Reverberation units were installed to give the station a 'big' sound; records were transferred to tape cartridges to eliminate scratches from constant use . . . filter mikes and other sound devices were built by engineers to give select disc jockeys 'character voices' and alter egos.[16]

Top Forty radio in the United States predated rock 'n' roll but became a main-stream format as the music itself grew in popularity. The pace, excitement and gimmickry of Top Forty radio made it an ideal setting for rock 'n' roll and teen-age music in general, and many of the newer disc jockeys based their styles of presentation and took much of their hip vocabulary from their counterparts on black rhythm-and-blues stations. The appeal of Top Forty radio to advertisers lay in its teen orientation, as it could deliver a ready market for such leisure commodities as hair grease, skin cleanser, sportswear, jeans, chewing-gum, make-up and fan magazines. The spread of such stations also suited the electronics industry, which began marketing the portable transistor radio set in the early 1950s but saw sales soar between January 1956 and July 1957 (the period spanning Elvis Presley's first eleven Top Forty hits) when 2 million sets were sold.[17]

Most of all, the spread of Top Forty radio in the United States aided the record industry's own exploitation of the teenage market, with companies concentrating their promotional efforts on getting their new releases on to the playlists of the highest-rated stations. For a time, 'payola' (payment for airplay) was rife, with the smaller labels fighting for their share of a congested market by trading cash and gifts for radio play from the most powerful disc jockeys. A long-running war of words between the music publishers' licensing and collection agency, the American Society of Composers, Authors and Publishers (ASCAP) and the radio networks (who in 1941 had set up their own rival licensing agency, Broadcast Music Incorporated (BMI), to which many publishers of country music and rhythm-and-blues material affiliated) culminated in the former lobbying for, and finally winning, a congressional inquiry into payola within radio.[18] But although the inquiry generated much ugly publicity and individual careers were ruined (notably that of Alan Freed, self-styled rock 'n' roll entrepreneur, whose career encompassed not only syndicated radio but song publishing, concert promotion and film appearances playing himself), Top Forty radio emerged considerably strengthened: station managers assumed responsibility for selecting the playlists, and the format became further refined to prevent abuses, to the extent that disc jockeys on some stations became almost anonymous figures, 'making the disc jockey a mechanical figure, an automaton from which all humanness was drained' (Eberly).[19] This trend reached its nadir in 1965, when disc jockey and radio consultant Bill Drake introduced a new version of the Top Forty format in the form of 'Boss Radio' (its name derived from English slang, then enjoying currency in the United States through the Beatles), which featured a much-reduced playlist (the top thirty in the *Billboard* chart only) and a 20-second limit on talk between discs.

Britain's pirate radio stations had little of this sophistication of approach, but virtually all of them took the Top Forty concept and adapted it to their own uses. The idea of round-the-clock music broadcasting was of course totally new to Britain, even though facile analogies were made (and continue to be made even now) between the 1960s pirates and the continental stations of the 1930s. The differences were that the pirates lacked the backing or even the benign tolerance of foreign governments, had none of the resources required to mount anything other than record programmes, and aimed to cater for a much narrower audience in age terms. The only real similarities lay in their dependence on advertising and an affirmed populism in their programmes. There were a few precedents for broadcasting from outside territorial waters – the *Daily Mail* had planned to fund such an enterprise in the late 1920s and gambling ships anchored off the coast of California in the 1930s had broadcast commercially sponsored programmes – but it was in Europe in the late 1950s that the idea took hold, with Radio Mercur operating from three miles beyond the Danish coast, Radio Veronica off the Dutch coast and Radio Nord from an anchorage just outside Swedish waters. Veronica began an English service on 16 February 1961, while one of the figures behind Nord's launch just under a month later was Gordon McLendon, an associate of Todd Storz and one of the architects of the Top Forty format in the United States. Known in American radio circles as 'the P.T. Barnum of Broadcasting', he brought promotional pizzazz to Europe's fledgling version of pop radio with station-identification jingles, competitions and merchandising.

All these developments were noted by Ronan O'Rahilly, a one-time method actor who in 1963 became the agent of singer Georgie Fame, then without a recording contract. In trying to interest the Light Programme's various programme producers and Radio Luxembourg's programme planners in a Fame demonstration record, he discovered at first hand how near impossible it was for artists who did not have the backing of a major record company to secure airplay. His initial plan was to simultaneously launch a record label of his own and a Veronica-like radio ship to promote its products, but the latter project eventually superseded the former. Raising £250,000 from various business and family sources, he bought and refurbished a former Danish passenger ferry called the Frederika and installed on board two 10-kilowatt transmitters and a 168-foot-high radio mast. The station, named Radio Caroline, after the late President Kennedy's daughter, came on air on Easter Sunday, 29 March 1964, with a record show presented by Simon Dee. Positioned some four miles off Harwich, the station was soon joined by a potential rival, Radio Atlanta, whose ship the Mi Amigo dropped anchor off Frinton-on-Sea in Essex. In July, the two stations merged: the Frederika sailed for the Isle of Man to take up a new identity as Radio Caroline North, while the former Radio Atlanta became Radio Caroline South.

Attempts to silence the stations began almost immediately. The GPO cut Radio Caroline's ship-to-shore link within days and lodged an official complaint with broadcasting's international ruling body, the International Telecommunications Union, over Panama's registration of the two Caroline vessels. The PPL, stating that 'indiscriminate broadcasting of records is detrimental to the interests of the industry, the musicians and artists', unsuccessfully brought an injunction against Caroline over unlicensed use of PPL-registered material.[20] Political action, however, was delayed because of the Conservative government's insistence that the European countries should be seen to act together in banning radio piracy: a bill was promised once concerted action had been taken through the Council of Europe's Convention on Broadcasting, due to meet later that year. Meanwhile, other pirate operators appeared. Radio Sutch, the brainchild of an eccentric (and markedly unsuccessful) pop personality named Screaming Lord Sutch, began broadcasting in late May from an abandoned wartime fort in the

Thames estuary; Sutch eventually sold his interest in the station to his manager, Reg Calvert, who renamed it Radio City. In June 1964, Radio Invicta was launched from another fort and lasted under that name until January 1965, when it was relaunched as King Radio. Radio London – the most professionally run and most 'American' of all the stations in terms of both financial backing and style of presentation – commenced broadcasts on 19 December 1964. And as the new Labour government (elected in October 1964) inherited its predecessor's apparent reluctance to take unilateral action against the pirates, because of the precariousness of its parliamentary majority, so the pirate ranks swelled to take in Radio 390, Radio Essex and (in January 1966) Radio Scotland.

## Sinking the pirates

Radio piracy in the mid-1960s was a haphazard, amateurish affair, heavily dependent for its popularity (and its advertising revenue) on its novelty value. Pirate radio protagonists were divided between those who wanted to make a quick killing and those who saw the stations as a means to the establishment of commercial radio in Britain, in national or local form. Ownership of the stations rested mainly with obscure American trust funds: Radio England, for instance, was registered in the name of a British company (Pier Vick Ltd) but was almost wholly financed by a syndicate of US investors, while Radio London was owned by the Marine Investment Company Inc. of Freeport in the Bahamas, which spent £500,000 on launching the station and registering the ship in land-locked Liechtenstein.[21] The pirates gave American broadcasting interests long-denied opportunities to invest in British radio: as Erik Barnouw described them in his *History of Broadcasting in the United States*, 'almost all [were] financed by American capital. Along Madison Avenue in New York, girls in pirate costume drummed up business for this novel form of international freebooting, which for a time earned small fortunes'.[22] With such backing came expertise: Radio London's managerial staff included Philip Birch, who had worked in the United States for J. Walter Thompson and had an insider's knowledge of how commercial radio could work. Birch's press release announcing the launch of Radio London gives some measure of how seriously the station took itself:

> The responsibility for programming and presenting Big L [*sic*] lies with the programme director. He works on the principle that people like packaging and uses the system of 'Formula Radio' and Top 40 format. Formula broadcasting has been tried and proved all over the world, in fact wherever there is commercial radio. The programme controller's job is to present it to the average British listener, and to adapt it to the public's taste. The conclusion so far is that people want – and are getting – the top forty records in Britain. . . . Selected records from the hit parade are played together with revived records, a new release and an overseas hit or track from an LP. On the half hour there is a newscast and weather forecast with time-checks at various intervals. This method ensures that no record is played more than

once in the three-hour programme presented by each disc jockey, and the top forty are only heard five times in any one day, and the thirty American or LP tracks are not repeated that day. There are six minutes of advertising each hour, and each three hour programme takes its name from the disc jockey.[23]

This was high-powered stuff, calculated to win over advertisers who had hitherto shied away from pirate radio, fearful of its illegality or unimpressed by its hyped-up listening figures (Radio Caroline claimed an audience of 8 million after one month of operation). In practice, Radio London's choice of music was more wayward than the press release suggested, based not on the national sales chart but on its own, curiously compiled listing – the 'Big L Fun 40' – which was mostly the work of head disc jockey Tony Windsor. He favoured a fast-changing turnover of records and a policy of plugging American hits immediately prior to their British release; discs could be suddenly and mysteriously dropped from the forty after 'reaching' Number 3 or 4.[24] All this added to London's reputation as a pace-setter, while in hiring staff the station literally pirated disc jockeys from other stations and brought in a number of presenters with experience in commercial radio in the United States, Canada and Australia.

The stations' income came from spot advertising, with Caroline charging £90 for 30 seconds of air-time, London charging £56 and Radio Essex (which had the weakest signal of all the pirates) asking a modest £8 10s for the same amount. Findus, Shell, Weetabix, VP Wines, the *News of the World*, Alberto Shampoos, the National Coal Board and Egg Marketing Board (both government-funded bodies) all used the advertising facility, booking their commercials through leading London agencies.[25] Some stations also had dealings with wealthy American religious organizations such as the Radio Church of God and the Seventh Day Adventist School, who paid handsomely for the privilege of broadcasting 15-minute sermons. It was an open secret, too, that Radio Caroline had financial arrangements with certain record companies, not only charging £8 per play but promoting discs that had Caroline-owned songs (published by a sister company) as flipsides. The station's main dealer was Major Minor, a small independent company whose roster of artists included Irish folk group the Dubliners, French orchestra leader Raymond Lefevre and a Bob Dylan-type folk singer, David McWilliams, none of whom slotted in easily alongside Caroline's otherwise mainstream pop fare. Emperor Rosko, an American disc jockey who worked for Caroline for a year prior to joining Radio 1, has recalled intercepting boxes of pay-for-play records as they arrived on ship and throwing them overboard: 'that they could make more records than I could throw away there is no doubt . . . if someone had sat down and said this is the only way the station can stay on the air maybe I would have seen it differently, but the way I saw it, it was just someone profiting from my integrity'.[26]

A bill to make offshore broadcasting virtually impossible to fund and promote from mainland Britain was finally announced by the government in July 1966. Based on Swedish legislation that had forced Radio Nord off the air in 1962, the Marine, Etc., Broadcasting (Offences) Bill had clauses prohibiting the supply of advertising, programme material, goods or services to offshore broadcasters and outlawed the publication of programme schedules in British newspapers or magazines. With a comfortable working majority, the government pushed the bill through Parliament with relative ease, though they were aided immeasurably by the distinct change in public mood towards the pirates that followed the death of Radio City owner Reg Calvert at the home of Radio Atlanta founder Major Oliver Smedley and Smedley's subsequent trial on a manslaughter charge. The trial brought many unsavoury facts to light about the exact nature of the stations' financial backing, the behind-the-scenes double-dealing and the occasional acts of real piracy that belied the pirates' buccaneering 'Jolly Roger' image. Initially regarded as harmless and even admirable upholders of the spirit of free enterprise – especially in backbench Conservative circles – the pirates lost prestige and support. Despite a concerted anti-government campaign mounted throughout the autumn of 1966 and the winter of 1967, the bill duly reached the statute book on 14 August 1967. All the stations bar Radio Caroline – which opened offices in Holland – closed down.

## The pirate legacy

Outlawing the pirates was not, in the end, a party political issue. Anyone who doubted that a Conservative government would have brought in similar legislation was fooling themselves, particularly in the light of the pirates' continued appropriation of internationally allocated frequencies and the very real prospect of acute congestion of the airwaves if the spread of stations went unchecked. Rather, political arguments centred on the direction that radio broadcasting should take in the pirate aftermath. Recognizing the political advisability of setting up a service of some kind to replace the pirates, yet unwilling to embark on a wholesale reorganization of radio, the government proposed a dual response in its White Paper on broadcasting:[27] the BBC was to allocate its 247 metres medium-wave frequency (at that time used by the Light Programme) to a new daytime service offering 'a continuous popular music programme', and was to operate nine experimental local radio stations from funds provided by local authorities and organizations. Commercial investment in the latter was to be barred, partly for ideological reasons and partly because of the effect that the introduction of radio advertising might have on the advertising revenues of local newspapers. The BBC's pop music service, Radio 1, was finally unveiled six weeks after the closure of the pirates, and the first of the BBC's local stations, Radio Leicester, opened on 8 November 1967.

The enforced closure of the pirates precipitated the *timing* of these changes, but it is appropriate to see them in a wider BBC context. The possible development of local radio was one of the issues discussed by the Pilkington Committee of Inquiry into broadcasting in the new post-ITV era, which reported in 1962. Independently of any events in the North Sea, BBC network radio was already undergoing some changes: most significantly, in 1963, the supply departments servicing the Light Programme had been reorganized, with the new Popular Music Department assuming responsibility for programmes featuring in-house, pre-recorded or live music and the Gramophone Department taking charge of all the disc shows, among them *Pick of the Pops* and the hour-long weekday *Midday Spin*, which from 1965 onwards became a showcase for ex-pirate disc jockeys (beginning with Caroline's Simon Dee) seeking to prove their worth to the BBC. Another development was the interpolation of pre-recorded musical items into the Light Programme's daytime record programmes (notably the early evening *Roundabout*) to create the *impression* of a continuous disc format; this was a clear break with the BBC convention of highlighting the performances of individual bands or orchestras in separate showcase programmes. In 1964 the Music Programme was started as a distinct segment of the old Third Programme: in concentrating so much of the BBC's serious music output into one block of programming, it marked another stage in the BBC's shift – which began with the formal launch of a three-tier system of networks in 1945-6 – towards generic broadcasting. The pirate radio issue simply offered the BBC an opportunity to take the generic principle still further, albeit a great deal further than anyone would have envisaged at the start of the decade. Under the supervision of Frank Gillard, Director of Sound Broadcasting, BBC radio was to be reshaped into four networks, each with a separate identity: Radio 1 as a pseudo-pirate, pop-based station; Radio 2 as a slightly modified, revamped Light Programme, specializing in variety, light music and sport; Radio 3 as a successor to the Third Programme; and Radio 4 as a modified Home Service.

Whatever their impact on Radio 1 in terms of presentation and content, it is therefore doubtful whether the radio pirates were really responsible, as was claimed, for the physical restructuring of BBC radio; the wheels had already been set in motion. As for their supposed impact on Britain's pop music industry, here again one must be cautious, particularly when claims like the following are made on their behalf:

> In the short period that the offshore stations existed, the entire record market changed. Many new independent record companies were formed, and because of the tremendous amount of airplay given to new discs, hundreds of pop groups and singers were 'discovered'.
>
> Mike Baron[28]

The use of the word 'independent' to describe the small-scale operators who competed with larger, well-established companies like EMI and Decca does imply a kind of philosophical alliance between the former and the pirate stations, as if both had a recognized common interest in fighting the music business establishment and providing the consumer with 'alternatives'. The reality, however, was different, and there is no evidence that disc jockeys or playlist managers necessarily gave preferential treatment to independent releases (unless, of course, there was payola involved). The obvious exceptions were releases on the Motown and Stax labels, but both were *American* independents distributed by British majors. During 1966, UK-based independent companies accounted for 3.8 per cent of Top Ten single releases, a significant number of them on the Immediate, Reaction and Page One labels, the principal acts of which were groups (the Small Faces, the Who and the Troggs respectively) which had already established their chart pedigree while with major companies. The independents' share of Top Ten singles increased to 12.5 per cent in 1967, but that year's most significant newcomers – Island (actually established in 1962, but by this time moving into the pop field), Track and Blue Horizon – were launched too late to take much advantage of any special relationship with the pirates.[29] The British independents began making their greatest impact on record sales *after* 1967, and then by capitalizing on the new demand for albums. The best that can be said is that the pirates, through what might kindly be described as a reasonably egalitarian playlist policy, enabled the first flush of British independents to gain a toehold on the domestic market.

Assessing the effect of pirate radio stations on record sales as a whole is more difficult. First, pirate radio reception was by no means countrywide: thousands of regular or potential record-buyers in many areas of Britain simply never heard the stations. In a survey quoted by Richard Mabey in his book *The Pop Process*, one record company found that sales of singles were up to 20 per cent higher in Cardiff, where no pirate stations could be heard, than in the home counties, where the signals of Caroline and London were at their strongest.[30] PPL therefore appeared to have a point when it complained that the greater availability of broadcast music made consumers less inclined to pay for it on record, especially at a time of increasing competition for teenage expenditure from the fashion and cosmetics industries. (This did not, of course, stop the majority of record companies affiliated to PPL from keeping the stations regularly supplied with promotional copies of their releases; this schizophrenic attitude to radio play on the part of the industry is discussed in Ch. 6.) Patterns of sale and manufacture of single records between 1964 and 1967 did suggest a somewhat depressed market: production of singles declined from 72,841k in 1964 to 51,196k in 1966, picking up slightly during 1967 to reach 51,576k,[31] while the total value of UK-manufactured records (albums as well as singles) remained steady at around the £25 million mark between 1964 and 1966, rising to £27.93 million in 1967.[32] Total consumer expenditure on recorded music – including those discs manufactured in the United States and Europe for UK sale – showed a similar pattern, declining from £55.8 million in 1964 to £51.8 million in 1966, and improving to £53.7 million in 1967.[33]

Summarizing the qualitative impact of the pirates on British pop music presents yet more problems. Pirate supporters claimed that the stations offered a far wider variety of music than either the BBC or Luxembourg: the 'freedom' of the disc jockeys to pick and choose what they played according to their own personal tastes, the argument went, meant greater exposure for unknowns and music that would otherwise have found little place on the airwaves – American soul and west coast rock, for example. John Peel's late-night *Perfumed Garden* programme on Radio London is commonly cited as an example, but since 1967 he has been one of the most persistent defusers of pro-pirate romanticism. Comparing Radio London to Radio 1:

> there were more disciplines on London, they banned more records. Radio 1 always gets slagged off for banning records, they don't ban that many, the

pirate ships used to ban a lot more and for the most peculiar reasons. You always assume at some stage you are going to go through periods when you are restricted by the requirements of the people that you work for, but you just get in there and try and work at it all until you have got what you want. I did that on the pirate ships, just taking advantage of the fact that nobody was listening.[34]

Individual disc jockeys championed particular artists and particular discs, and it would not be difficult to compile a list of records whose chart fortunes depended entirely on initial exposure via pirate radio. In selecting records of interest from the weekly piles that the record companies sent and 'rescuing' a number of them from otherwise certain obscurity, the disc jockeys and playlist compilers did provide a service which, within the narrow terms of pop consumerism, had some value. But Peel's point has consistently been that the relentless cheerfulness of the presenters, the superficiality of so much of their patter, and the pirates' exclusion of all programming elements other than music, patter, news and self-aggrandizing announcements militated *against* an appreciation of pop music as anything other than a background sound. On the fringes of pop activity and contributing nothing to the music-making process on either a commercial or creative level, the pirates used pop uncritically and arbitrarily, and their success encouraged Radio 1 programme-makers to do the same. The effect was to make 'pop radio' more disposable, less special and, ironically in the light of the pirates' origins in and association with the youth-obsessed 1960s, ultimately far less youth-centred.

# 4 BBC radio – restructuring and beyond: 1967–87

... there were signs of change in the public's listening habits. The success of the music programme and Radio 1 suggested that the public wanted specialized rather than all-purpose channels. The old 'brow level' concept of Home, Light and Third was outmoded. The public wanted to know where they could easily find the kind of programme which fitted its mood or its age, pop, sweet or light music, serious music or speech.

Lord Hill of Luton, BBC Chairman, 1967–72[1]

The BBC have copied the best ideas from the illegal stations. They've turned out to be the biggest pirates of them all.

Screaming Lord Sutch[2]

Radio 1, the most publicized product of the BBC's restructuring of its radio services in 1967, was in practice less a fully fledged network than a junior partner to Radio 2, sharing not only the bulk of its programmes but the same production and management team. But the repercussions of this and other, seemingly purely cosmetic changes – a retitling of the old Light Programme, Third Programme and Home Service – only began to be fully appreciated in the summer of 1969, when a Policy Study Group comprising senior BBC executives and outside management consultants published their report on the future of radio, *Broadcasting in the Seventies*. Acknowledging the growth of a daytime audience for radio and the need to reshape regional broadcasting in the light of local radio expansion, the report looked ahead to the ultimate separation of Radios 1 and 2 and advocated reductions in the BBC's music budget to help fund future developments.

The report was the catalyst for fierce internal debate within the BBC and some political controversy, particularly over the threat posed to at least four orchestras – the BBC Scottish Symphony, the Northern Dance Orchestra, the London Studio Players and the Training Orchestra. In Lord Hill's words, the BBC was accused of 'cutting serious music while manufacturing an extra output of pop',[3] though the plans were more accurately read as an attempt to make the four existing services yet more output-specific and to a great extent self-reliant, eliminating the similarities in programme content between Radios 3 and 4, shifting serious music almost entirely to the latter, and granting Radio 1 a measure of independence. With a general election looming in 1970, the government's response (aside from agreeing an increased licence fee and a BBC plan for up to forty new local radio stations, and asking the BBC to maintain its current levels of employment of musicians) was the classic delaying tactic of appointing a Committee of Inquiry into broadcasting, to be chaired by Lord Annan, the Provost of London's University College. Appointed in May 1970, the Committee was an early casualty of the Conservatives' unexpected election victory one month later, after which the political focus switched abruptly from internal BBC planning to the threat of externally imposed changes, with the future of Radio 1 and BBC local radio in particular thrown into immediate question. Paradoxically, it was the new government's decision to press ahead with commercial radio on a local rather than national basis (see Ch. 5) – and freeze rather than force the abandonment of the BBC's own local radio plans – that finally removed Radio 1 from the political arena and secured its continued existence.

Quite why Radio 1 was left untouched had much to do with its proven popularity (according to the BBC's own figures) and its cost-effectiveness. Prior to the unveiling of the government plans, Hill reminded Christopher Chataway, Minister of Posts and Telecommunications, that 'if the wavelengths of Radio 1 were taken away we should have to introduce pop material into the other services in order to remain comprehensive. We had to make an appeal to the young, however little the stuff appeals to us personally. Anyway, the savings would be only three-quarters of a million pounds a year'.[4] In political terms, closing Radio 1 would have been unpopular and pointless – and that, in turn, was a measure of the success of BBC management in nursing the whole enterprise through a very fragile and uncertain infancy. In particular, it was a vindication of the Radio 1 team's pragmatic approach in adopting (in an effort to build a large audience) a musical thrust to its programmes that was decidedly middle-of-the-road. The paradox behind Hill's remarks to Chataway was that Radio 1's audience by 1970 was neither particularly young, nor was it offered a surfeit of what any listener to the pirate stations would have defined as 'pop material'. Upon that paradox, Radio 1 built a programming strategy that remained intact until well into the 1980s.

## The infant service

Radio 1's brief was vague from the outset. According to Robin Scott, joint controller of Radios 1 and 2, the BBC was originally asked 'to provide a service of popular music during the hours which lie outside the period of peak viewing of television'. As for what 'popular music' itself constituted, 'rightly it was left to the broadcasting authority to decide', and he qualified his belief that 'if the new service was to be dynamic and attractive, it must go for pop' by suggesting that 'pop' had a broad appeal beyond teenagers:

> We should not forget that the young housewife of 27 – perhaps with two children or more – was a 17 year old when rock 'n' roll music first hit this

country and that it is nearly five years since four brilliant Liverpudlians first began their imprint on the world of entertainment.[5]

A daytime service aimed primarily at 'housewives', which looked back rather than forward to seek a musical identity, was therefore how the BBC saw Radio 1 establishing itself. This was in contrast to the conventional media view that Radio 1 was a carbon copy of pirate radio – a view given apparent credence by the BBC's hiring of fourteen former pirate disc jockeys on short-term (eight or thirteen-week) freelance contracts, with the promise of longer contracts once they had proved themselves on air. It was true that the cosmetics of the new network suggested a strong leaning on the sequential, highly formated programming of Radio London in particular: the trailers, dedications, jokes and jingles (commissioned from the same company in Austin, Texas, that had made the jingle package for London) were all new to BBC radio, as was the concept of self-operation – the presenter taking charge of the physical operation of putting records on turntables and needles on records. An instant review of the station by George Melly in *The Observer* on the day after Radio 1's launch on 30 September 1967, described the extent of its apparent emulation of the pirates:

> It was all go at Auntie's first freak-out. The solemnity with which the conventions evolved by the pirate radio stations have been plagiarised is almost Germanic in its thoroughness: the little burst of identifying plug music, the comperes gabbling over the opening bars of the records, the fake excitement ('Beautiful song, beautiful words, must make it'), even the deliberate amateurism and fake fear of the sack, are all there. And yet somehow the effect is of a waxwork, absolutely lifelike but clearly lifeless.[6]

But Radio 1 began life on a weekend. Melly had not at that time heard the weekday programmes, which revealed where Radio 1's true heart lay. However many ex-pirate presenters the BBC took on (and many were dropped within six months), the larger proportion of disc jockeys on the new network were established Light Programme regulars – Keith Fordyce, Barry Alldis, Bob Holness, Jack Jackson, Pete Murray, Alan Freeman and others. The key daytime show was the mid-morning programme compered by singer Jimmy Young, who had been presenting record shows (produced by the BBC's Gramophone Department) and a vocal showcase (produced by the Popular Music Department) on the Light since 1964. His Radio 1 show mixed records with BBC-made recordings, many featuring Young himself backed by one of the BBC's own orchestras, and was the flagship programme in the latter Department's interpretation of the Radio 1 brief. Department head Donald MacLean told Young that 'the sort of presentation you are going to do will be the salvation of this radio network',[7] while Young's personal perception of the programme was entirely in keeping with the Light Programme ethos of a family audience of which 'the kids' were only a small part:

> The kids, as the business fondly knows young record and transistor fans, were not the only audience in Britain. There were the people who liked it sweet, the people who went to the film *The Sound of Music* by the million

and made it into one of the world's greatest money-spinners, the people who just had to see the Black and White Minstrels, another money-spinning phenomenon. What we really wanted to get on the air was the middle-of-the-road stuff, which is the music that gets good figures. But we had to be sharp as well, playing some of the sharp hairy music without appearing to be too sharp. It was a pretty narrow tightrope we were going to walk.[8]

The objective behind such programmes – and the afternoon shows presented by Terry Wogan, Pete Brady, Dave Cash and David Hamilton into the late 1970s – was to deliver an audience that would justify the expense and upheaval of creating a new network. It was not necessarily, as some of the more imaginative writers in the pop press of the time claimed, part of a BBC plot to keep pop music at arm's length even within the concept of a 'pop service': MacLean and others simply assumed that Radio 1 could not even begin to prove itself to either its paymasters or to the public at large (in theory, of course, one and the same) without taking on board much that had been learnt during twenty years of the Light Programme. The BBC's version of pop radio became, in essence, a selective assimilation of aspects of American-style Top Forty radio – the emphasis on chart hits, time-checks and jingles (used by the pirates to aid station identification, but by Radio 1 for pure aural decoration), and the ridiculous promotional plugs for cross-network programmes (Tony Blackburn trailing Max Jaffa, for example) – into traditional light entertainment radio programming. The hiring policy of the Popular Music Department, which stuck by tried and trusted Light Programme bands like Bob Miller and the Miller Men and Ray Davis and his Button Down Brass, underpinned this conservatism, so much so that the morning and afternoon weekday programmes on Radios 1 and 2 became virtually indistinguishable and certainly interchangeable.

Programme-sharing with Radio 2 was argued to be necessary because of the scarcity of resources, and the responsibility for the output of both Radios 1 and 2 remained with Gramophone Department and Popular Music Department producers rather than producers assigned to each network. Despite its identification with chart music, Radio 1 had no playlisting system until 1973, the choice of records being left entirely to the producers, most of whom worked in isolation from one another. With little perception of pop music as anything other than ephemeral – a perception rooted in the pre-Beatle years, in notions of pop as a kind of junior version of show business – programme producers restricted themselves to 'safe' record choices, favouring conventional balladeers of the Tom Jones/Engelbert Humperdinck ilk to the point that, as Derek Chinnery (Radio 1's first network head) later admitted, some chart records hardly ever got played.[9] This problem was compounded by the continuing limitations on needle-time, by which Radios 1 and 2 were restricted to an allowance of seven hours a day of records between them. To make up the shortfall, Radio 1 programmes featured in-house, studio-made recordings of currently popular hit songs, recordings that were either wholly imitative of the originals or showcased the song in a big-band arrangement of the type commonly heard on the still-running (now on Radio 2) *Music While You Work.*

Radio 1's Light Programme inheritance was also apparent in its marginalization of (and simultaneous reverence towards) pop musics of a supposedly more intellectually appealing character. Just as jazz had always figured on the periphery of the Light Programme schedules, beloved of radio producers yet kept separate from the mainstream almost as an act of deliberate intellectual apartheid, so 'progressive rock' assumed a similar mantle after 1967. Progressive rock was not so much a specific, identifiable musical idiom as a general term encompassing any pop or rock music with an obviously intellectual bent: 'progression' was equated with musical maturity and a discarding of the commercial trappings of mainstream, singles-oriented chart pop music in favour of expansive, experimental suites of music following particular concepts or themes. Precursors of progressive rock included the Beach Boys, the Byrds, a stream of bands associated with the drug culture of the US west coast, and the Beatles, whose *Sgt Pepper's Lonely Hearts Club Band* album took pop albums into the arts review columns of 'quality' newspapers and gave credence and respectability to the idea that pop music could constitute an art form. Progressive rock encompassed 'art-rock', which took in grand musical statements (often with classical overtones), meaningful lyrics and all the decorative ingredients – artistic album covers, gatefold sleeves, sound effects – that the Beatles had pioneered on *Sgt Pepper*; it also included the quirky, psychedelia-laced music played by bands associated with London's 'underground' culture, which had its own select events and clubs and even its own newspaper in the shape of *International Times*. A third and most widely adopted strain of progressive rock grew directly out of the largely London-based rhythm-and-blues club scene, frequented by bands who by 1967 were adopting a new range of influences, particularly the jazz-laced playing of blues guitarists B.B. King and Freddie King, and developing their improvisational skills on the jazz pattern.[10]

Progressive rock, in all its many forms, had bohemian appeal: protagonists and opponents alike equated it with the counter-cultural values propounded in the pages of *International Times*. Its popularity with a young, educated, streetwise élite, together with its existence on the fringes of commercial pop music – as an *oppositional*, alternative music – was recognized in Radio 1's pre-launch planning, but the manner in which the network framed such programmes was instructive. First, progressive rock's claims for itself – or, rather, the claims made for progressive rock by both its musicians and the writers (particularly those on the *Melody Maker* staff) who proselytized it – were accepted almost unquestioningly by Radio 1's management. Coverage of progressive rock was initially limited to a three-hour programme of records and studio sessions on Sunday afternoons, but more time was allocated as the extent of the programme's popularity became clear and especially that of John Peel, who was voted top disc jockey of 1968 in a *Melody Maker* poll. However, instead of seeking to incorporate progressive rock within the daytime schedules – 'I don't believe there is anything at all to be gained from playing it on mainstream radio' (Derek Chinnery)[11] – Radio 1 emphasized its distinction from Top Forty pop by giving it air-time at weekends, in the early evening and (from 1970 onwards) late at night. Progressive rock followers complained of discrimination against them, but the very separation of 'progressive' programmes from the conventional daytime disc shows – and the former's transmission on Radio 2's FM frequency, so that the music could be heard in full stereo – suggested compliance with the notion of a distinct split between the serious and the trivial, the intellectually valid and the inconsequential and disposable, the élitist and the mass appeal, the 'difficult' and the easy. In other words, it implicitly legitimized the notion that progressive rock was culturally *superior* to Top Forty pop: the former 'demanded' more of listeners. As *Top Gear* producer Bernie Andrews described his programme,

> We use groups that aren't acceptable or sufficiently familiar to be that easy to listen to generally. By and large, our material is not suitable for other programmes because it needs more listening to. We're not exactly trying to set trends, but are offering these sounds as an alternative to the more conventional type of programme.[12]

Radio 1's late-night programmes, collectively titled *Sounds of the Seventies*, had a premise of featuring 'adventurous contemporary sounds' within what appeared to be a fairly free format and a style of low-key, almost conspiratorial presentation modelled in part on American FM radio. In reality, however, the musical policy of these shows was extraordinarily narrow, each offering a predictable mix of latest American and British album releases and sessions by bands who mostly already had recording contracts – in contrast to Peel's original policy, in his *Top Gear* series, of searching out unknown acts and using the programme to create record company interest in them. Although Peel himself remained pleasingly perverse and defiantly idiosyncratic in some of the music he chose to play, those presenting and producing shows in the other progressive slots settled for the safer option of simply presenting the latest industry product, wrapped in the trappings of exclusive interviews, pre-release scoops and affirmative critical comment that were so criticized as elements in Top Forty radio.

Radio 1's policy on 'alternative' musics gave credibility to the artistic claims that progressive musicians made for their work and, to paraphrase the argument of Andrew Weiner in an excellent *Story of Pop* article on progressive rock and Pete Fowler's seminal essay (in *Rock File*) on class differences in late 1960s British rock tastes, legitimized the musical snobbery of its mainly middle-class, collegiate following. Andrew Weiner:

> Who listened to progressive music? Not primarily, as one might suppose, the people who formed the original audience for psychedelia – the freaks and drop-outs and hippies – but, rather, the affluent sections of the rock audience who identified to some degree with those elements. In particular, students who demanded ever more intellectual and challenging rock music. It was students who largely bankrolled the new movement, through the lucrative college circuit. It was students who were excited by the idea that rock was art. Predominantly middle-class, middlebrow students . . . progressive rock [was] middle-class rock, enshrining and propagating

middle-class values and aspirations: creativity, individuality, intellectuality. The music of a minority culture. And yet, through the enormous buying power of that minority and through the middle-class orientation of the mass media in this country, it was able to wreak a disproportionate influence upon the shape of British rock.[13]

One of the paradoxes of the supposed progressive alternative was that it very quickly became part of the commercial music mainstream. Briefly, the emergence of progressive rock suited the strategies of the record industry: the massive sales success and influence of *Sgt Pepper* not only inspired many groups to shed their teenybopper image and restyle themselves (musically and fashionwise) in progressive garb; it also precipitated wholesale exploitation of the album market, which was potentially more lucrative than that for singles not only because profit margins were higher but because it was made up mainly of older record buyers with a higher level of disposable income. (This was an international trend. In the United States the introduction of stereophonic sound and the marketing of cheap hi-fi equipment gave an added boost to album sales, while FM radio developed into the major promotional outlet for companies like Columbia and Warner Brothers, prime movers in the signing of student-appeal acts with aspirations to artistic respectability.) All the talk of alternativism and breaking with commercialism belied the extensive investment of British record companies both in the signing of suitably non-Top-Forty-minded acts and in the creation of subsidiary labels as quasi-independents with fashionable hippie-like names (Harvest by EMI, Dawn by Pye, Deram by Decca) as outlets for the same.[14]

Along with the opening up of colleges and universities as venues for rock concerts and the embracing by *Melody Maker* of the progressive ethos, the creation of Radio 1 was perhaps the most significant factor in shaping the British pop landscape after 1967, particularly with regard to the marked polarization in taste and attitude within what had previously seemed to be a fairly unified youth market for pop. After 1967, described by Pete Fowler as 'the year of the great divide',[15] pop tastes in Britain appeared to split almost on class lines, with skinheads (working-class teenagers) and teenyboppers favouring Top Forty pop, soul music and reggae, and the predominantly middle-class grammar school children and students looking to the progressive field. A 1973 study by Graham Murdock and Guy Phelps, *Culture, Class and Schooling: The Impact of Pop*, confirmed this division and noted the mutual antipathy between the two sets of record buyers.

## Competition and after

By the early 1970s, then, Radio 1 appeared to be a station with two distinct (and opposing) identities: a pop-cum-middle-of-the-road network by day and a pseudo-FM station, broadcasting on VHF, by night. But behind the apparent schizophrenia Radio 1 was simply following the familiar BBC convention of drawing a distinction between programmes that *entertained* and programmes that *stimulated*, between programmes of background music and those of 'music that perhaps requires *more actual listening* rather than being a background to other activities' (Derek Chinnery).[16] This carried connotations of cultural prioritization, the most 'fulfilling' programmes being tucked away in the evening, for the discerning, non-television-viewing listener, in the way that the old Light Programme had featured concerts of light classical music (and sometimes much heavier fare) only in the evening, leaving the daytime hours to the likes of Edmundo Ros, Frank Chacksfield and Stanley Black.

As suggested earlier, there were solid pragmatic reasons for Radio 1's reassertion of Light Programme values through its cultivation of a daytime audience of 'housewives' (a dubious categorization challenged elsewhere in this book) with ballads and novelty singles, and the devotion of non-prime airtime to supposedly more demanding fare. Once the network's future appeared stable, new priorities informed its approach to programming – principally the challenge to ratings and prestige presented by the commercial radio stations, the first two of which (LBC and Capital Radio) opened in London in October 1973. As Johnny Beerling, then a staff producer, remembers:

> The thinking at the time of ILR was that this brash new baby would come on the air and that they would be giving away Ford Cortinas every day and hundreds of dollars in cash prizes, and they would have so much money to spend that they would probably cream off all our major DJs, so it did make a number of us sharpen up and think, well, how are we going to respond to this. The immediate response was to put most of the DJs who we thought were worthwhile in those days under long-term, two-year contracts.[17]

The changes made to programming and presentation in anticipation of commercial competition were not particularly dramatic; the daytime/evening dichotomy remained. But they were accompanied by key changes in the administration of the network. Having previously been overseen by a controller (Robin Scott) whose responsibilities also covered Radio 2, Radio 1 gained its own head in former Gramophone Department producer Derek Chinnery. A departmental reorganization, originally envisaged in *Broadcasting in the Seventies*, transferred programme-making responsibilities from the Gramophone and Popular Music Departments to the networks themselves, making for a greater sense of continuity between programmes and the emergence of something like a clear station identity. The amount of programme-sharing was reduced, Jimmy Young departed to Radio 2 and was replaced on the Radio 1 mid-morning slot by Tony Blackburn, who had presented one of the network's few all-disc programmes, the 7 a.m. to 9 a.m. breakfast show.

Most significantly of all, Radio 1 introduced a playlist system to eliminate the notorious inconsistencies in its producers' selection of records. Derek Chinnery again:

> You could listen for a whole morning or a whole day and never hear the top three records played at all because of the way they were compiling their programmes – perhaps they'd played them all on the Monday! If you're working through the week you tend to plan your programmes horizontally, as it were, whereas listeners listen vertically during the day. So we

decided that it would make a better service if we actually got those guys together and had a common music policy during sections of the week, during the daytime, so that people who switch on at random would know exactly what style of music they were going to hear, some of the top ten hits of the day at some time within the coming hour or so, so we started a playlist for that purpose. . . . It was connected with ILR starting, there was to be an alternative popular radio, so we thought we ought to smarten ourselves up if you like and make ourselves more obviously a certain style of service.[18]

The playlist consisted of fifty records to be 'regularly featured' during the weekday daytime output; on average, this represented two chart records in any one half-hour, together with three or four that the producer would pick either as oldies or as up-and-coming hits. The strategy was loosely based on that of the pirate Radio London, though Tony Blackburn and his producer Tim Blackmore had run the breakfast show on a 'mini-playlist' principle since early in Radio 1's life; in his autobiography, Blackburn credits himself with being one of the architects of the station's new-found post-1973 sophistication.[19]

All these changes were made on the assumption that, because of the number of ex-pirate personnel employed by the new commercial stations in presenter or management capacities, Radio 1's would-be competitors would set out to re-create the pirate formula of rapid-fire patter and Top Forty pop. This was a mis-judgement, as the newcomers generally pitched their programmes somewhere between those of Radios 1 and 2; Capital Radio, for example, was dubbed 'Radio 1 and a Quarter' by the *Daily Mail*'s radio critic the day after the station came on air. ILR stations adopted music policies aimed at attracting the kind of audience profile of most interest to advertisers – listeners whose musical tastes, research showed, were hitherto more closely matched by Radio 2 than Radio 1, and to whom a preponderance of Top Forty pop was of no special relevance. One of the most curious side-effects of the coming of ILR was therefore that Radio 1 modified itself into something resembling a Top Forty station without really needing to, with the result that its position of dominance within British music radio was not only left unchallenged but was very much cemented. Certainly the adoption of the playlist increased the station's importance to record company strategies – getting a record on to the playlist was nine-tenths of the promotion process – and Radio 1 also benefited from an increase in needle-time, granted by PPL to the BBC to balance out its allocation of nine hours per day of needle-time to the ILR stations.

The most telling aspect of all these changes (which were effected with a deliberate lack of fanfare) was that they were undertaken primarily for marketing reasons. Radio 1 was ostensibly created by public demand, or at least to replace a service with a proven popular following, and its only reason for existence *was* its popularity. No matter how much Radio 1 presenters or producers made 'cultural' claims for it (citing its evening coverage of progressive rock, the status of pop music as a form of popular art, its 1973 launch of a twice-daily news programme called *Newsbeat* and of the first of many documentary series), Radio 1 was fundamentally a music-based entertainment network working in a commercial sphere. After 1973, Radio 1 became a commercial in the sense that nearly every aspect of its daily operation – the pursuit of audiences and satisfaction of same, the maintenance of a particular image and sound for the station, the attempts to involve listeners in the life of the station through competitions and meet-the-people roadshows – drew much from commercial radio precedents. Radio 1 continued to carry an indelible BBC stamp because of its close adherence to the established listener stereotypes, but the very presence of competition brought the populist tendencies that had informed Light Programme output since 1945 into play as never before. The station even flirted briefly with outright commercialism in the promotion of its first major documentary series, *The Story of Pop*, each episode of which carried what could only be called an advertisement for an independently produced partwork of the same name, published by Phoebus. Complaints were made in Parliament that the BBC was breaking the terms of its Charter by associating itself with a private publishing venture, echoing earlier protestations over the Corporation's involvement with Time-Life Inc. in the funding of *The British Empire* television series and accompanying partwork.

**Towards independence**

Radio 1 adapted easily to the threat of ILR thanks mainly to the relatively free hand that Chinnery's management team were given, an early sign of the quasi-autonomy to be enjoyed by the network as the 1970s went on. The team was made up of three executive producers, to whom a total of eighteen producers reported: Teddy Warrick acted as Chinnery's deputy and controlled the network's internal financing; Doreen Davies supervised the live music sessions, the weekly compilation of the playlist and Radio 1's productions for the BBC World Service; and Johnny Beerling took charge of competitions, trailer production, outside broadcasts and station promotion in general, together with the auditioning and recruitment of new disc jockeys. On programming matters, the most influential of the trio in the long term was Beerling, one-time producer of two of the most inventive Gramophone Department shows of the pre-Radio 1 years, *Pick of the Pops* and *Roundabout*, as well as those shows featuring the more individualistic ex-pirate jockeys on the network's roster – Tony Blackburn, Simon Dee, Kenny Everett, Chris Denning and Emperor Rosko included. A keen student of commercial radio techniques (and one of the very few BBC employees to visit a pirate ship (Radio London) in the run-up to their abolition and replacement by Radio 1) he gradually introduced to Radio 1 a whole range of promotional gimmicks that were extensively copied, ironically, by ILR stations. These included the creation of a Radio 1 logo, its depiction on a specially purchased fleet of vans and roadshow equipment, mass-production of car stickers and T-shirts bearing the logo, and involvement in publicity stunts and motor sport events.

Beerling wrote in 1977 of

a constant need for advertising and promotion to keep one step ahead of potential rivals . . . fun ideas and stunts to keep the station alive and full of friendly fun. The more successful promotions produce an added bonus when they are reported by other media, either press or television, so that we reach an even wider audience.[20]

This concern for maintaining Radio 1's status as a market leader extended to open association with the promotional activities of record companies – typified by the almost saturation coverage of visits by American teenybopper stars (and rivals) the Osmonds and David Cassidy in 1973 and 1974 – and to combing of the newly competitive airwaves for new voices. Whereas early in Radio 1's life recruitment of disc jockeys had been undertaken in piecemeal, haphazard fashion, the process had become much more systematic and professional by the mid-1970s, with possible new presenters monitored in action at their various stations (often without their knowledge) and approached only after considerable internal discussion. Radio 1's image of itself as a personality station made presenter requirements quite specific – good looks, perversely, were among those requirements, as the presenter would be expected to front *Top of the Pops* on occasion – and the station became less inclined to hang on to big-name disc jockeys once their appeal and their sympathy for changing fashions in pop music began to falter. From 1973 onwards, Chinnery and Beerling took to reviewing the programme schedules on a three-yearly basis (three years being the length of the longest freelance contract under which disc jockeys were hired), though the major changes of 1976–7 – the arrival of ex-Luxembourg and Radio Trent jockey Kid Jensen and Radio 2 early morning show presenter Simon Bates, both eager to enhance their credibility by joining John Peel in espousing (albeit in a much more limited way) punk-rock – came about because of the decisions of Rosko and Johnnie Walker, two of the network's most respected ex-pirates, to depart of their own accord.

Although the possibility of temporary reamalgamation with Radio 2 reared its head in 1975–6, at a time when all BBC departments were called upon to make severe economies, Radio 1 was by the end of the decade an almost fully independent network and could boast a majority of externally recruited disc jockeys. The fact that most came either from ILR stations (Jensen, Andy Peebles, Mike Read) or Luxembourg (Peter Powell, Noel Edmonds) illustrated the position of Radio 1 at the top of the music radio career pyramid, but probably the clearest evidence of the changes at Radio 1 over a thirteen-year period was the removal of former Radio 1 regulars like David Hamilton, Terry Wogan and Ed Stewart to Radio 2 and the moving aside of Tony Blackburn to just three weekly spots, the Top Forty chart show and the two editions of the children's request programme, *Junior Choice*. (*Junior Choice* was the network's final link with the old Light Programme, where it had existed for many years as *Children's Favourites*, and was itself dropped from the schedules in 1984.)

With the 1980s came recognition by BBC management of Radio 1's claims to equal status alongside the other three networks, in the form of the creation of the new post of Controller of Radio One, which Derek Chinnery filled until his retirement in 1985. Meanwhile, the station's physical separation from the main body of the BBC organization at Broadcasting House, in offices in neighbouring

Egton House, and the plans (first announced in 1983) for the construction of new, completely self-contained offices and studios for the network, tended to accentuate the view – frequently voiced by non-Radio 1 BBC staff – that Radio 1 was tantamount to an autonomous body, free to formulate its own policies and reliant not on BBC-trained personnel but specialist freelance staff. Radio 1's 'independence' may have been purely notional, but again its ratings success and comparatively low running costs appeared to justify continuing disinterest (in the literal sense) in the network's administration and programmes on the part of senior BBC management: Radio 1's operating expenditure for the year ending 31 March 1984, stood at £13 million, as opposed to £28 million incurred by Radio 2, £28 million by Radio 3 and £39 million by Radio 4, while its share of radio listening stood at 28 per cent of the total radio audience, Radio 2's at 22 per cent, Radio 3's at 2 per cent and Radio 4 at 13 per cent.[21] It was even possible to believe that, in cultivating a separateness and making audience maximization the major tenet of policy, Radio 1 was itself preparing to accommodate a politically imposed switch from public to commercial funding, and it was widely assumed in the run-up to publication of the Peacock Committee's report in 1986 that Radio 1 would be the first network to be so 'privatized' if any hiving off of BBC services was contemplated.

Within Radio 1, the most obvious sign of self-confidence and independence during the early 1980s was the dropping of the playlist – on the grounds that it had outlived its usefulness, that producers automatically chose hit material anyway, that a little more adventurousness in programming was needed, and that playlisting had been discredited by ILR's over-reliance upon it. A further sign of independence at that time was the extension of broadcasting hours to allow for 18 hours of programming per day from 6 a.m. to 12 midnight. This was made possible by a 1982 agreement which gave BBC radio as a whole an extra 30 hours of needle-time per week at a cost of £15.1 million payable over three and a half years.[22] Half of the extra time went to Radio 1, enabling it to introduce showcase programmes for three new disc jockeys (Janice Long from BBC Radio Merseyside, Pat Sharp from Radio Tees, Gary Davies from Piccadilly Radio in Manchester) and fill the mid-evening gap, previously abandoned to Radio 2, between the end of the daytime shows and John Peel's late-night slot. The new weekday evening schedule comprised a one-hour speech programme, usually related to 'youth issues' like unemployment and drug abuse to give the network what Nick Higham of *Broadcast* called 'a bolt-on social conscience',[23] plus two hours of session and album music on the Peel principle. The speech experiment was dropped during 1983, however, on the discovery that listeners were switching off at 7 p.m. and not tuning back once the programme was over.

This continuing concern for maximizing audience patronage was given added edge by the acknowledged popularity at this time of Laser 558, an offshore pirate station with American disc jockeys that had a policy of minimum chat and maximum music – 'where music is never more than a minute away', as its slogan promised. Laser's powerful signal and its slick, professional, all-American presentation ate into ILR figures far more than those of Radio 1, but its appeal and professionalism were noted by Johnny Beerling, who became Derek

Chinnery's successor as Radio 1 Controller. While Chinnery had made no secret of his dislike of Laser – 'Laser is rock musak, it doesn't tell you the time, it doesn't tell you what the weather is or give you any news, it doesn't react to the day's events . . . our people talk to their audience as real people, that's what real live personality radio is about, not an anonymous voice telling you here's another fine piece of music'[24] – Beerling was much more enthusiastic, and the string of changes he made in 1985–6 reflected the Laser influence. His attempts to curb the semi-legendary verbosity and egotism of the established Radio 1 disc jockeys were front-page news in the tabloid newspapers during the summer of 1986, but of much more significance was his decision to reintroduce the playlist – paradoxically to ensure that a mandatory amount of *non*-Top-Forty music was featured, Laser-style, in daytime shows.[25]

As of early 1988, Beerling's chief impact has been in making Radio 1 appear and sound a far more streetwise and contemporary station than its ILR and pirate competitors. There have been many cosmetic changes but few of a fundamental nature, and he remains acutely aware of the difficulties inherent in attempting to update Radio 1 – particularly the risk of alienating the station's older listeners, who have stayed with it over the years, despite changes in musical fashion, and who form a larger part of the audience in numerical terms than the under-18 audience at which contemporary pop music (and certainly Top Forty music) is supposedly aimed:

> The difficulty is that rock music's heritage is getting longer. If we had started Radio 1 in 1967 and played music that was 25 years old we'd have been playing Glenn Miller records. There's a constant battle going on between the people who think you should be playing more of the Beatles and early Elvis Presley, which means nothing to a kid of 15 years old.[26]

Meanwhile, population projections for the future indicate a decline in the number of 16 to 24 year olds by 11 per cent between 1987 and 1992, again questioning the wisdom of retaining a teen-oriented pop policy.[27]

The problem really lies in Radio 1's original brief as a pop music station rather than as a young people's service: pop may be youth music, but its ever-lengthening history precludes it from an exclusivity of appeal based on age. Increasingly, Radio 1 finds itself in a similar position to that of the Light Programme in the early 1960s, obliged to cater for all ages and a broadening range of specialist tastes within a single network.

## Radio 2: the multi-headed monster

Compared to Radio 2, however, the obligations placed upon Radio 1 have been and remain very light. Radio 1 is a music station, no more and no less; Radio 2, by contrast, has had to inherit many of the Light Programme's original commitments not only to music-making – providing an outlet for BBC dance orchestras, and for the majority of those bands contracted by the BBC for in-house recording under its agreement with the Musicians Union – but to such specific (and expensive) programme areas as sport, light entertainment (situation comedies and variety shows) and religion. In addition, Radio 2 serves traditional specialist tastes with weekly programmes of vintage jazz, organ, brass-band and big-band music, alongside a number of specialist programmes originally associated with Radio 1 – *Folk on 2*, *Country Club* and *Rhythm and Blues*. Together with the presence on the network of several ex-Radio 1 voices, all this has tended to strengthen Radio 2's image as a repository for the unfashionable and the unwanted.

As Bryant Marriott, Controller of Radio 2 from 1984 onwards, describes it, the station is 'a multi-headed monster with too many responsibilities'.[28] During 1985 an internal BBC committee chaired by the Director of Finance, Geoff Buck, suggested the virtual extermination of the monster by recommending the transfer of Radio 2's FM frequency to Radio 1 and the effective amalgamation of Radio 2 with BBC local radio, thereby making the resources of the network's Music Department available to the needle-time starved local stations. According to a report in *Broadcast*, 'only vigorous advocacy by radio's managing director, Dick Francis' persuaded the BBC's Board of Governors to reject the proposals: he pointed out that, while the switch of Radio 1 to FM might save several millions of pounds on the building of an extra series of transmitters, turning Radio 2 from a fully fledged network into a supply service for local radio would hand over 17 to 20 per cent of the radio audience to the independent stations. It would also have meant moving particular streams of programming, notably sport and light entertainment, across to Radios 1, 3 or 4, thus disrupting the tone and character of those services and causing untold administrative upset.[29]

These proposals were made as part of a cost-cutting exercise, but Radio 2's long-term problems lay in muddled perceptions over programming objectives and target audiences. Administratively, Radio 2 was originally geared to the making and broadcasting of *individually conceived* programmes, as the Light Programme had been. One of the lessons of Radio 1's success, however, was that 'stripped' programming – literally, a sequence of music-based programmes stripped across the daytime hours – was more practical and less expensive to mount and gave the network a greater cohesion and identity. The departmental reorganization of 1972–3, which gave Radio 2 its first team of network-specific producers, had the effect of turning the network into a kind of somnolent Radio 1: with increased needle-time, more records were brought into the daytime shows and producers balanced records from the Top Forty with album tracks by artists like the Carpenters, John Denver, Simon and Garfunkel and (a little later) Barry Manilow – all big-selling acts whose records were never heard on Radio 1 unless they happened to have a current chart hit. At a time when the market for so-called 'easy-listening' music (a catch-all record industry term, synonymous with 'middle-of-the-road', for music of appeal to the over-25s) was growing apace, Radio 2 began to excite record company interest, and there were a few instances in the mid-1970s of singles becoming hits on the strength of Radio 2 airplay alone.

A deliberate attempt at updating Radio 2, this change of policy created more difficulties than it solved. In going for a younger sound, the network risked losing faith with a large part of its old Light Programme constituency, those older listeners (45 and over) who favoured the light classical milieu of *Friday Night is Music Night* and *These You Have Loved*. Updating the network also brought Radio 2 dangerously close to Radio 1 territory – an ironic outcome in view of the latter's deliberately middle-of-the-road nature in its early years. The success of Radio 1 in holding on to its audience as it grew older meant that Radio 2 failed to pick up new listeners, with the result that its listenership remained static in number and grew progressively older. By 1984, four out of five Radio 2 listeners were estimated to be over 35 and three out of five over 45.[30] These tendencies were obscured during the latter half of the 1970s and well into the next decade by the high figures and high public profile achieved by two shows in particular, Terry Wogan's breakfast time programme and Jimmy Young's deft mixture of music, consumerism and political chat which followed it. Although Wogan's show was adversely affected by the advent of breakfast television in early 1984, it was his departure for a three-nights-a-week television chat show later that year that precipitated the intense internal debate about Radio 2's future: patronage of the breakfast show dropped by 19.5 per cent within a month of Wogan's replacement by Ken Bruce from BBC Radio Scotland. BBC Audience Research also noted a decline of 13 per cent in the station's daily patronage during the first quarter of 1985, and there were persistent rumours as the year went on of disenchantment among presenters and producers.[31]

A rethink of the whole purpose and status of Radio 2 was clearly necessary, and the result was the unveiling in April 1986 of a new programme schedule and a substantially revised music policy. Ken Bruce was moved to a mid-morning slot and the breakfast show given to Derek Jameson, former editor of the *Daily Express*, *Daily Star* and *News of the World* and presenter of BBC-TV's *Do They Mean Us?* He had very little radio experience but had the Wogan-like traits of a quirky personality, a catchphrase or two, and Clapham Omnibus-type street wisdom. He also made some instructive analogies regarding the new direction being plotted for the network:

> Television and radio are getting more populist because of the ratings war and fierce competition, the same reason that caused Fleet Street to go hell for leather and Press Council be damned. . . . The job I have enjoyed most was being editor of the *Daily Express*, I see [that] as the level I will aim for on Radio 2. I hope to inform, delight and stimulate everyone, as I did then.[32]

Radio 2's head of music, Frances Line, described the revamped music policy as not so much new as 'a reversion to what we used to do, which was to play middle-of-the-road music and sit happily between Radio 1's very clear pop policy and Radio 3's classical music policy'.[33] The change was immediately noticeable in both the records played and the greater incorporation of BBC-re-corded orchestral music into the daytime shows – a reversal of 1970s policy, which relegated much in-house material to the hours of 12 midnight to 6 a.m. on the assumption that Radio 2 listeners had an innate preference for music on record.

As Line explained to *Music Week*,

> We may have lost listeners by playing material better suited to Radio 1. But

we are now concentrating on MOR in all its forms over a broad spectrum, with the emphasis on melody and excellence. There are over 22 million people over the age of 45, and perhaps the youth market has been over-indulged.[34]

In the long run, however, could such a profoundly retrospective music policy – one that essentially harks back to the pre-rock era – attract any *new* patronage? In all the discussion about music policy it was easy to miss one of the paradoxes of Radio 2, that its best-rated shows (Jimmy Young, Derek Jameson, Gloria Hunniford) are those with a high speech content, which use music primarily for strategic reasons, to break up or conclude interviews, to isolate particular programme items, to enhance the pace of the show or provide a light contrast to 'weighty' topics. This is in complete contrast to the manner in which music is used on Radio 1, where speech simply constitutes the inconsequential patter between the records, and the music itself (in theory at least) becomes the focus of the programme. The *tone* of Radio 2 over twenty years has been consistently cosy, familiar and safe – even the news bulletins are prefaced by a soothing jingle – but it is its speech content that saves the network from what would otherwise be an all-enveloping blandness. As the successes of Young, Wogan and Jameson show, getting the *voices* right is really the major part of Radio 2's battle for survival.

## BBC local radio

Radios 1 and 2 at least had traditions of a kind to draw from and build upon. BBC local radio, that other product of the class of '67,[35] was a completely new departure in which few Corporation personnel had any expertise or experience and which was rationalized internally as 'not merely an addition to radio ... [but] an element in a new structure in which we destroyed the old regions and re-placed them by local stations appealing to the local community'.[36] The primary benefits that would accrue to the BBC from having a local network of stations were in the news-gathering area, though there remained an expectation that the stations would provide .the four major networks with a steady flow of programmes suitable for national dissemination, just as the regional system had done. Politically, however, the BBC's venture into local radio was unloved from the outset and regarded simply as an expedient measure on the Labour government's part to deflect criticism from its apparently unpopular outlawing of the pirates without playing into the hands of the commercial radio lobby. Although the Corporation could fairly claim that its plans for local radio predated the arrival of both the pirates and ILR by some years (their plans were broadly endorsed by the Pilkington Committee's report in 1960), claims of empire-building and expansionism were still being levelled at the BBC as late as 1977, when the Annan Committee delivered its recommendations for the future of local radio as a whole, and again in 1985–6, when the Peacock Committee considered the issue of whether the BBC should be in local radio at all.[37]

The BBC local radio story has to date covered two main phases, pre-ILR and post-ILR. Between 1967 and 1973 the local stations suffered from a chronically low profile, exacerbated by the high priority the BBC invested in promoting Radios 1 and 2 and by the restriction of the new services to between 6 and 12 hours a day and on VHF only. Programme content was generally an uncertain mixture of BBC-owned library music (needle-time being limited to two hours), local news and chat, and individually produced programmes on local themes such as farming, the activities of the Women's Institute, or student life in the district. Music programmes and speech programmes were generally kept separate, and the impression was of a worthy, local answer to Radios 2 and 4. The chief effect of the introduction of commercial radio was a new concentration on building a solid local image and on *promoting* that image within the locality:

> ILR taught us how to sell radio stations, basically. ILR marketed itself, certainly in its early years, very well indeed, with its car stickers and its promotional activities, its buses, its T-shirts, its mugs. Up to then, most of the promotion of the BBC local stations was low key . . . I think it's only since ILR that the BBC has seriously marketed its radio stations. Now it's very much down to individual stations how they do it, we take marketing the station very seriously here. Through the summer our bus will be out doing as many shows as we can get to . . . and the on-air trailing is quite strong. For many years the BBC stations didn't have anything like the kind of glitter that the ILR had. Some of our stations could have been criticized in the early days for being very worthy but rather dull, now I think we would say we're exciting and worthwhile.
>
> Tony Fish, BBC Radio York[38]

Programming, too, began to follow the ILR formula of records interspersed with information and dedications, especially at stations now facing direct local competition from a commercial service – for example in Nottingham, Sheffield, Manchester, Newcastle and London itself. Existing BBC stations switched to medium wave with the arrival of ILR, meaning they could at least begin to compete on equal terms for audiences, and there was a freeflow of personnel between the two systems, initially from BBC into ILR (especially at engineering level) but later in the reverse direction, as BBC stations were seen to offer greater job security. 'The BBC wants you to get on. In ILR you have to move on to get on. I'm fed up with that', Tony Gillham, late of Mercia Sound and Chiltern Radio, told *Media Week* after being recruited by BBC Radio Bedfordshire in 1985 as presenter of its daily music-and-news show.[39] The most obvious signs of growing competitiveness on BBC local radio's part were the decisions to launch new stations in established ILR areas, notably in Bedfordshire in 1985 and in Essex in 1986. Despite its name, Radio Bedfordshire adopted a catchment area almost exactly the same as that of ILR's Chiltern Radio, taking in much of neighbouring Buckinghamshire and Hertfordshire; BBC Essex, meanwhile, upset the existing ILR contractor, Essex Radio, by all but stealing its name and – so the latter complained – capitalizing on the confusion caused. Both stations were symptomatic of another general trend in BBC local radio, away from small-town stations (though BBC Radio Manchester did run a 'community radio' experiment in the form of local opt-outs for the Trafford and Bury areas in the early 1980s) and towards large county or semi-regional stations, both for cost-saving reasons and to meet the increasing regionalization of ILR. In 1985 came a fundamental reappraisal of BBC local radio's central services[40] and in June 1987 a radical reorganization of local radio management was effected, with stations now falling under the control of regional centres – threatening, as dissenting voices within the stations had it, local autonomy and squeezing station budgets still further.

Perhaps the greatest oddity of BBC local radio is that the stations, although dependent entirely on licence-fee funding,[41] are considerably less publicly accountable than their ILR counterparts: although every area has its machinery of local consultation (in the form of a sixteen-member Local Advisory Council supposedly representative of the community at large), there is no requirement on them to submit programme plans to a higher authority – programming is entirely an internal BBC matter. Nor is there any direct obligation to supply the locality (as is nominally the case in ILR) with cross-community, cross-generation appeal programmes. Bizarre differences in programming therefore occur between stations, some directly competing for ILR audiences, others deliberately aiming their programmes at an older age group in an attempt to sweep up those left behind by ILR's pursuit of demographically defined audiences of interest to advertisers. Because the stations still suffer from lack of needle-time, many tend to continue in Radio 2 fashion, mixing a few current hits with orchestral music from non-PPL labels; others – notably Tony Fish's Radio York, which during its first year attracted bigger audiences than any of the national networks or the peripheral ILR stations in its area[42] – adopt a tight playlisting policy, making astute use of bought-in, non-PPL vocal music and particularly oldies, all wrapped in a pleasantly professional style of presentation involving all the paraphernalia of jingles, trailers and phone-in requests. As in ILR, BBC station management ostensibly tailor their music policies to local research, though in an area as huge, as cosmopolitan and as demographically varied as London, that can be meaningless: BBC Radio London has one of the lowest audience reaches of all the BBC's stations and has suffered more than most from internal BBC threats of either closure or radical reorganization. Among the options considered during a major review of the station in 1985 were that it could be reshaped as a quasi-community station, feeding material to local opt-out stations serving ethnic minorities; or as a woman's station, run and fronted by women:

> [Alan] Rodgers envisaged a station run mostly by women and fronted by women – not a feminist station (though that would form part of the output) – appealing to a mix of ages, incomes and ethnic groups. Audience research on the proposal got a warm response: half of the London women sampled were very or fairly interested in the idea. But Rodgers and the study group lost their nerve: they ended up clearly recommending another option, which would build on the known strengths of radio, rather than try something new.
>
> Anne Karpf, *New Statesman*[43]

In fact, Radio London did begin to develop a new identity for itself between 1985 and 1986, thanks largely to the mixture of sexism and soul music offered by its mid-morning presenter, Tony Blackburn. (The BBC's own figures, published in 1987, showed that the station's audience was virtually non-existent at weekday breakfast time yet the highest of the London stations while Blackburn's show was on the air.[44]) The station already had a good reputation among soul followers through Robbie Vincent's long-running Saturday lunchtime show, but it was the ratings success of Blackburn's programme – in which he had a free hand in selecting the music – which prompted London's management to explore soul programming on a wider scale. The results were mixed: Blackburn's posturing contrasting with the raucous chumminess of Gary Crowley introducing a late-night, all-stereo soul show. Again the changes were aimed at increasing London's competitiveness (Crowley was recruited from Capital), at making the station appear to have a value and fill a need. Radio London again came under close internal scrutiny during 1987, when a wholesale change of the station's management team was effected, and its future remains as uncertain as ever at the time of writing: even its late-night soul shows, usually broadcast live from London clubs, survive more for the fact that they pay for themselves (admission charges covering all production costs) than their high profile within soul music circles. In 1988, as the BBC announced plans to reshape the station's programming and relaunch it as Greater London Radio, Blackburn departed to Capital and Vincent to LBC.

However precarious its affairs, Radio London has been the leading British example of the 'find a niche and stick to it' school of radio, but whether such a policy would have any application outside the big metropolitan areas is doubtful. If BBC local radio as a whole does have a strength, it lies in its ability to provide programming for audiences otherwise disfranchised by radio: ethnic minorities and minorities of taste and interest alike, those audiences in which commercial stations take an interest only out of what Tony Fish identifies as 'the brownie points syndrome', as a means of convincing the IBA that they are honouring the terms of their franchises to serve all sections of the community. Radio London, in particular, can claim at least two 'minority' programmes not only of real merit but of solid contribution to the capital's musical welfare – Charlie Gillett's *Honky Tonk* show, which began (in 1972) as a rock 'n' roll-oriented programme using minimum needle-time, and evolved into a major showcase for new London rock bands during the punk and new-wave era of the late 1970s; and Alex Pascall's *Black Londoners*, a programme which deftly mixed commentary on the various strands of black music-making in London with discussion of black issues. That the BBC stations follow the same policy of effectively ghettoizing such programmes, by confining them to the fringe evening or weekend hours, is indicative of their main failing – the tendency to replicate not only ILR but Radios 1 and 2 as well, in an attempt to capture an ill-defined middle ground.

# 5 ILR – The road from regulation: 1973–87

An Independent Local Radio station cannot afford the luxury of directing its output at just one section of the population. ILR stations are obliged to provide programming which meets the full range of radio needs from their local communities . . . they must attempt to appeal to all sections of the population – men and women, the young and the old, people at work and those at home.

*Television and Radio 1981* (IBA official yearbook)[1]

The young professional market is a very affluent sector, very influential with a high disposable income. In the selling of Capital's commercial airtime that sector must be of considerable importance to 85 per cent of our advertisers. They are simply a sector of our existing audience, and one that could be more precisely targeted.

David Lees, Sales Controller, Capital Radio[2]

Officially sanctioned commercial radio arrived very late in Britain, over fifty years after the creation of the BBC and nearly twenty years after the introduction of commercial television. It was, in part, a child of political opportunism, a response to the sustained lobbying of business organizations like the Local Radio Association (which in 1966 had published proposals for 276 commercially funded stations[3]) and an accession to the youth vote that was widely believed to have helped the Conservatives to power in the 1970 general election, the first in which 18 to 21 year olds had voting rights. But although the acceptability of commercial radio to a young public had been amply demonstrated by the success of the pirate stations, this was never going to be enough on its own to ensure the new medium's viability. More importantly, as a latecomer to the British media scene, commercial radio had to establish itself within an advertising market long dominated by television and to operate within an administrative structure (commercial companies supplying local broadcasting services under franchise) originally devised purely with television in mind. In addition, the infant medium was obliged to compete with a range of well-established, popular, *national* BBC services from a position of reliance on local resources, and to look to BBC radio as a prime source of managerial, engineering and presentation staff.

All this had ramifications for the kind of programming offered by the new stations and for the scale of their operations. In many ways the subsequent history of commercial radio in Britain is that of a medium seeking to free itself from its subordinate relationship to television – institutionalized by its placing, in 1972, under the umbrella of a revamped Independent Television Authority, renamed the Independent Broadcasting Authority – and from the BBC-like 'public service' requirements imposed upon it. As to why such requirements were initially perceived to be necessary, we must first examine the political background to the setting up of the Independent Local Radio (ILR) system.

## ILR: Conservatism in action?

A week after the 1970 election, BBC Chairman Lord Hill recorded in his diary that the new Conservative administration 'may say that we can have our local radio but that there must be a competitor'.[4] The Corporation quickly began what was in effect a period of negotiation with the government, promising co-operation on the transfer of little-used wavelengths to commercial radio but insisting that its own plans for local radio development were essential to both the maintenance of its news services and the decentralization process to which the BBC had been committed since the early 1960s.

The issue soon crystallized into one of whether the government, in paving the way for commercial radio, would be prepared to make it economically viable at the expense of the two services likely to provide the greatest competition, BBC local radio and Radio 1. But, given Edward Heath's exhortation to business to 'stand on its own two feet', independent of any legislative or financial assistance from the government, such a blatant act of favouritism towards the commercial sector would have been politically unacceptable. For all the supposed radicalism of its intentions on radio, the White Paper published in March 1971, *An Alternative Source of Broadcasting*, was remarkable for the modesty of its proposals and the traditionalism of its outlook. Most surprisingly, it was clear that the BBC had not only won the argument for its own retention but would, even allowing for competition, maintain a large part of its supremacy in radio. Not only was there to be no national element in commercial radio, but the terms under which the new stations were to run were very much 'public service' dictated. Competition was to be on the BBC's own terms: the Sound Broadcasting Act of 1972, which was largely based on proposals in the White Paper, was essentially a restatement of the paternalistic ideology that had underpinned the development of both BBC and ITV broadcasting.

The Conservative plans simply applied to a radio context many of the features of Independent Television, launched by an earlier Tory government in 1955. The Act allowed for the establishment of stations on a franchise basis under the aegis of the IBA, whose responsibilities with regard to radio would be precisely as they were for television: to select suitable contractors to run radio services in designated areas, to supervise programme planning across the new network, and to undertake the actual transmission of the output of each station. The only major differences between the ITV and ILR systems related to the number of franchises to be advertised – a total of sixty ILR stations were envisaged, in contrast to the sixteen companies serving ITV – and to their local rather than regional base. Provision was even made for the creation of a network news service in the manner of Independent Television News, which would be funded by an annual subsidy from all the ILR stations.

The approach to broadcasting embodied by ILR was paternalistic in the senses most affirmatively outlined by Sir Brian Young, Director-General of the IBA from 1970 to 1978, in the 1983 Watt Club Lecture.[5] Britain's 'paternal tradition of broadcasting', he maintained, rested on the assumption that 'broadcasting belongs in some way to all the people and all their needs . . . not just something to be bought and sold'. Paternalism as operated by the IBA was essentially protective and preservative; television and radio should be available everywhere, not just in the obviously profitable metropolitan areas, so that the individual's 'equal right to the signal' was upheld. Paternalism ensured high technical and artistic standards and a commitment to quality – 'output must not consist only of programmes that pay their way' – which overrode the commercial imperative. It guaranteed impartiality and balance on matters of controversy and protected the programme-makers (and, by implication, the public they represented) from editorial interference by political parties or advertisers.

All these points were reflected in the structure of the ILR system, its most significant aspect being the retention of nominal parliamentary control (via Parliament's 'representatives', the IBA) of the means of transmission. Because the airwaves were deemed to be national property, ownership of the transmitters was vested in the IBA, from whom the contracting companies effectively 'rented' air-time. On the principle of 'universal right to the signal', ILR was planned to eventually cover the whole country. That stations in economically disadvantaged areas would fail to attract the same level of advertising revenue as those in more affluent areas was expected and allowed for: it was assumed that ILR *as a whole* would generate sufficient revenue to allow for redistribution to the less profitable stations. (This was to be effected via the imposition of a secondary transmitter rental on the more profitable stations.)

The Act also attempted to safeguard community interests by setting requirements which had to be met before an applicant contractor could be considered for a franchise. Investors, whether companies or individuals, were to be denied a major role in the operation of more than one station: the maximum shareholding allowed in other stations was fixed at 20 per cent. Investment by other (possibly competing) media interests was restricted: television companies were allowed a maximum stake of 12.5 per cent in ILR companies, while newspaper shareholdings were to be subject to IBA approval when 'it appears to the Authority that the existence of these shareholdings has led or is leading to results which are contrary to the public interest'. Foreign investment in ILR contractors was effectively barred under section 12, subsection 5(a), as were individuals employed by (or in management of) advertising agencies.

The Act set down in general terms what the IBA's criteria would be in the selection of contractors, the final responsibility for which lay not with the IBA's professional staff (around 150 staff were appointed to the newly created radio division) but with the twelve members of the Authority. Equivalent in status to the governors of the BBC, these were all part-timers on a nominal salary, nominated by the Postmaster-General (after 1974, by the Home Secretary) and chosen to represent a contrived cross-section of the nation, including one member each from Scotland, Wales and Northern Ireland. Their prime function was to ensure that companies applying for franchises in particular localities were actually capable of running a radio service: this included assessing the economic viability of companies which had not yet begun to trade (and which could only appoint professional staff once a franchise had been awarded!) and judging, purely on the basis of programme submissions and the track records of individuals with a personal stake in the company, both the desirability of the projected programming and the ability of the said individuals to provide it.

The IBA stated in its own guidelines for applicants that it wanted to promote a wide range of 'ownership, control and influence among independent radio companies'.[6] In the case of the London, Birmingham, Glasgow and Manchester franchises – potentially the most lucrative contracts – the Authority was met by broadly similar applications from consortia boasting finance from relevant regional ITV companies, local newspapers and local businesses; market-research findings to back up their programme submissions, showing there would be a demand for the kind of service offered; and a board of directors packed with local dignitaries and media personalities. The IBA played an active role in encouraging competing consortia to amalgamate – London Broadcasting Company (LBC) won the very first franchise advertised, for a London-wide 'news and information' service, after the Authority had advised the company to offer a shareholding to two rival applicants, Associated Newspapers and City Sounds – and initially took a far from predictable course in allocating contracts. The appointment to London's 'general and entertainment' franchise of Capital Radio, who were markedly non-specific in their programme submissions and lacked even a programme controller, in preference to the heavily backed, public relations-primed Network Broadcasting was a surprise decision that signified an important shift in IBA policy in the wake of its wayward handling of the reallocation of television franchises in 1968. Pilloried at that time for appointing a number of new contractors on the basis of extraordinarily far-fetched and naively conceived programme plans, the Authority had the opportunity to re-establish its credibility through ILR, and it seized it.

In conception and execution, therefore, ILR hardly had the look of a great new commercial enterprise. Not only was it subject to paternalistic constraints on programming, it was not even intended to be an internally competitive system; the only ILR stations to directly compete for listeners were LBC and Capital in London, but their services were planned as complementary rather than competing and they shared the same transmitters. One of the first to recognize that the money-making possibilities of commercial radio, ILR-style, would be severely limited was TV-show host and one-time Radio Luxembourg child star Hughie Green, who pulled his company Commercial Broadcasting Consultants out of the franchise hunt soon after the IBA guidelines for contractors were published. Anticipating the financial burdens to come better than anyone on the administrative or operational side of ILR, Green complained that the Act's disallowance of sponsored programming would deter major, national advertisers and that the cost of starting up a station – £1 million in the case of the London entertainment station – were simply too high:

Only the people with fantastic incomes can afford it. You're paying 30 per cent of your money in copyright charges and rent to the IBA even before you've got four walls, before you've even paid the tea girl ... we could have borrowed the money and built our own transmitter. Allowing for depreciation it would cost £700,000 and that's doing it rich. If you're kicked out after three years then at least you'd have an asset. Now you're being asked to pay for something which isn't yours and never will be.[7]

Green's complaints were echoed on many occasions in subsequent years, particularly when arguments for outright deregulation of ILR began to surface early in the 1980s, encouraged by a political climate in which the principles of cross-subsidy, community-led programming and tightly monitored investment were no longer fashionable. But it is within the political context of the early 1970s that ILR requires locating, almost as a paradigm of a style and philosophy of Toryism on the verge of becoming outmoded, a vein of traditional Macmillanite Conservatism, presided over by a former Macmillan lieutenant in Edward Heath and temperamentally suspicious of radical change. The moulding of ILR in ITV's image appears, in this light, an act of perfect political logic: introduced by a Conservative administration, ITV had played a significant part in fuelling the consumer spending boom that neatly straddled the beginning of the Macmillan years and the fall of the Tory government in 1964. If the electoral success of the Tories between 1951 and 1963 was a consequence of the Macmillan administration's skill in delivering its promise of 'capitalism for the people', as Stuart Hall has it in *Policing the Crisis*, of forming a 'high-wage, mass-production, domestic-consumer-orientated modern economy' and tying 'the working class, through the mass market, hire purchase and the well-timed budget, to the Conservative Party's success at the polls',[8] then ITV's establishment had the twin effect of legitimizing the materialistic aspirations of the populace and suggesting, as much through 'popular' programming as through the advertisements it transmitted, the existence of a political and economic consensus based on notions of material well-being, consumer choice and class harmony.

Conservative enthusiasm for launching commercial radio was partly based on the belief that history could repeat itself, that consumer spending would be boosted and new marketing opportunities created; Christopher Chataway also suggested that ILR would have the same 'beneficial' effect on BBC radio that ITV had had on BBC-TV in the 1950s, when the BBC service had been forced into widening the scope of its programmes and developing more of a 'common touch'.[9] If ITV was a product of its period, in conception and organization a compromise between traditional Tory paternalism and pressure for business expansion from the party's entrepreneurial wing, ILR was an exercise in similarly regulated capitalism entirely in keeping with the Macmillan inheritance – the business world being seen to work in the people's interest, as a servant of the nation. Convincing the electorate of the business world's commitment to the 'public interest' was an essential part of the Conservative strategy in the early 1970s, hence Heath's public condemnation of the Lonrho affair during 1972 as 'the unacceptable face of capitalism'. The ILR system was therefore subject to a range of controls that simultaneously protected the tradition of public service broadcasting in Britain and attempted to forge – particularly through guidelines as to the make-up of consortia applying for franchises, requiring a balanced representation on consortium boards of trade union and business figures, and a balance between local and national investment – a new economic and political alliance of interests, or what Heath in another context called a 'trade union for the nation'. Paradoxically, huge profits for ILR companies could have undermined that strategy, just as ITV profits had reached such a scale by the early 1960s that a levy was imposed to cream off the excess. To keep a check on ILR profits, a similar levy was placed on its companies, to come into effect once the profits of a contracting company exceeded 5 per cent of total income. ILR, one must conclude, was never intended to become a huge money-spinner, but simply to become comfortably self-financing.

## ILR programming

Nowhere was ILR's place in the traditional mainstream of broadcasting paternalism better illustrated than in its programme content, which was required to meet specifications laid down in the Sound Broadcasting Act (which was consolidated with the 1964 Television Act to form the Independent Broadcasting Authority Act in 1973). As the episode of the Capital franchise award showed, grandiose programme plans were far less likely to impress the IBA into dispensing a franchise than a general commitment to the principles that the Act embodied – namely, the provision of programmes with cross-community appeal, including special programmes for ethnic minorities; public access to the airwaves, either by means of community involvement in programme-making or, more usually, the mounting of programmes (phone-ins) based on a 'dialogue' between broadcaster and listener; and a more nebulous promise to produce programmes of inherent intellectual merit, whether arts programmes, drama or documentaries. Capital's franchise application not only promised plays, current-affairs slots and discussions but cleverly presented the station's proposed music policy in 'quality' terms, insisting that 'the top forty will be played, not to distraction, but with an awareness that much of it is unoriginal and manufactured on a conveyor belt process that leaves little time for real talent and professionalism'.[10] In what read like a calculated dig at the populist tendencies of Radio 1, Capital simultaneously offered the promise of an intelligent and discerning listenership and portrayed itself as a broadcasting institution both aware of its 'cultural' responsibilities and dedicated to the highest programme standards.

Capital was, of course, a special case: music was a major part of its 'general and entertainment' brief, and the sheer size of its potential population coverage (taking in the whole of London and a large slice of the home counties as well) made it more of a regional, even quasi-national station from the outset. Much broader, and more local, programming was required of the other ILR stations, who had to 'provide a proper balance of information, education and entertainment' and combine the usual elements of entertaining radio programming with programmes of a strong local flavour, in order to provide a service which can develop into a true alternative to the BBC services, particularly in news, news commentary and information.[11]

In effect, each of the ILR stations outside London had to provide the full range of BBC services within a smaller, localized framework, and entirely from commercial resources. (The IBA Act of 1973 does in fact contain a far clearer formal statement of public service requirements, particularly regarding 'balance, neutrality and impartiality' within programmes, than the BBC's own Charter, while BBC local stations are not and never have been subject to the same theoretical level of public scrutiny as ILR stations; their programming policies and financial affairs remain internal BBC matters.) The contractual obligations on ILR companies included an undertaking to ensure that 'programmes broadcast ... contain a suitable proportion of matter calculated to appeal specially to the tastes and outlook of persons served by the station' and that 'programmes broadcast from different stations for reception in different localities do not consist of identical or similar material to an extent inconsistent with the character of the services as local sound broadcasting services'.[12] Precisely which local 'tastes and outlook' should be catered for within a franchise area was defined by the IBA itself on the basis of preliminary consultative work carried out by its staff in the run-up to the advertising of a franchise, with due regard to various sectional interests within those communities. Swansea Sound, for example, was required to allocate a fixed number of hours per week to Welsh-language programmes.

Implementing these requirements cost money, and most of the early financial difficulties experienced by ILR stations stemmed directly from a miscalculation of overheads and operating costs as a proportion of income. ILR was a newcomer to a broadcasting market where labour and equipment costs were to a great extent conditioned by the BBC, and in which unavoidable day-to-day costs such as copyright and performance fees, payments to freelancers and use of news agencies had to be negotiated in relation to what the BBC already paid for similar services. A particular burden was the cost of news, adequate coverage of which was one of the most important tenets of ILR; one of the first actions of newly appointed franchise-holders was to hire a full complement of news staff, features editors and researchers on the local newspaper model (and from which many were recruited). When both Capital and LBC were launched to a run of poor audience figures and a shortfall in advertising (compounded by the effects of the three-day week and the looming oil crisis), news staff were the first to be cut. In Capital's case, the newsroom was disbanded completely at a saving of around £100,000 and news bulletins taken from LBC. Similar cost-trimming exercises in the provinces put a strain on the fledgling Independent Radio News service (IRN, operated by LBC), the efficient operation of which depended on a flow of news from other stations, and the industrial action it prompted in defence of jobs not only disrupted programmes but brought compensation claims for untransmitted commercials from disgruntled advertisers. In response to such an inauspicious start, the IBA was forced to be pragmatic, waiving transmitter rental for one year in the case of LBC, agreeing to labour savings while attempting to negotiate adequate compensation on the unions' behalf, and – with the reluctant approval of the new Labour government, elected in February 1974 – breaking one of the cardinal points of principle of the original legislation in allowing foreign broadcasting interests to take stakes in both London stations. By February 1975, Selkirk Communications of Canada held a 49 per cent holding in LBC, and the UK division of its chief Canadian rival, Standard Broadcasting Corporation, acquired 24.9 per cent of shares in Capital. Both rescue packages precipitated important changes in programme policy, including the curtailing of LBC's through-the-night magazine programmes and their replacement by short, on-the-hour bulletins and a test signal.[13]

All this indicated failings in the basic structure and financing of ILR and lent some justification to the government's decision to freeze further expansion of the system until after the reconvened Annan Committee made its report. The launches of Radio Clyde in Glasgow, BRMB in Birmingham, Piccadilly Radio in Manchester and the stations that followed in Newcastle, Swansea, Sheffield, Liverpool and Nottingham – all franchises allocated prior to the freeze – were considerably less traumatic. Such stations, born of generally more modest commercial expectations than their London predecessors and serving less diffuse localities, gave a better taste of how ILR was to develop. This is not to say that their programming approaches necessarily evolved in a uniform way, as clear distinctions emerged between that developed by a station like Swansea Sound – small-scale, covering a rural as well as urban populace, with a large number of potential listeners in the 35 to 45 age group – and that of a station such as Piccadilly, with its comparatively young listening profile, its base in the entertainment capital of the north, and under the management of a team (headed by ex-Radio London chief Philip Birch) with strong connections with 1960s pirate radio. Central to the long-term success of both – Swansea's weekly reach in 1984 was almost 50 per cent of its total potential audience, while Piccadilly's financial position was strong enough by that year for its operating company, Greater Manchester Radio, to seek flotation on the stock market[14] – was the application of a shrewdly devised, professionally executed music policy tailored (with advertisers in mind) to the economic profile of the respective localities.

**Music in the mix**

ILR was never intended to develop as a network of music stations, but it was perhaps inevitable that it would come to be regarded as such. Competition from Radios 1 and 2 dictated that music had to be at least a prominent ingredient in ILR programmes, and it was in anticipation of this that the IBA negotiated an agreement with PPL, on behalf of the stations, that set each station's daily needle-time quota at nine hours. (This agreement was formalized in 1976, with each ILR contractor being obliged to pay PPL a fee of 3 to 7 per cent of its net advertising revenue. Additionally, the contractors guaranteed to spend 3.5 per cent of annual advertising revenue on the employment of musicians.[15]) The task of winning over listeners from Radios 1 and 2 fell largely to ex-BBC personnel – for example, Keith Skues at Radio Hallam (Sheffield), Colin Burrows at Radio City (Liverpool) and Aidan Day at Capital – who, as programme controllers or heads of music, introduced daytime programme schedules on the 'strip show' model favoured by Radios 1 and 2. And, again like Radios 1 and 2, the ILR stations concentrated their needle-time allocation almost entirely into the daytime hours and limited their choice of records to currently best-selling singles, some oldies and album tracks.

ILR's BBC inheritance extended to the sectioning-off of the less patronized evening programmes to the student audience and 'minority interest' shows (typically, of country, folk, classical and brass-band music) to the weekends; and to the purloining of some of the standard features of BBC local radio – 'what's on' spots, sports bulletins, listeners' swaps, phone-ins with celebrity interviewees, outside broadcasts from shopping centres and local hospitals. Superficially, ILR combined two seemingly disparate conventions of sound broadcasting: radio journalism, and what IBA literature called 'the companionable style of music radio'.[16] But the principle of mixing news, information and entertainment *within* programmes, as opposed to isolating these elements to separate programmes was hardly new. Distinctions between news and entertainment had become increasingly blurred in broadcasting as a whole since the advent of ITV, and one of the key influences on local radio content (BBC and ILR) was the folksy magazine style of topical journalism fashioned by BBC-TV's *Tonight* programme in the late 1950s and exemplified during the early and mid-1970s by *Nationwide*, a programme with 'local' input in the form of stories gathered from the BBC regions. Such programmes featured a mixture of 'hard' news stories, consumer items and light relief – tales of eccentric characters, unexplained happenings (hauntings, flying saucers) and the occasional singing dog. This kind of approach came late to national radio (though distinct changes in the style of news presentation were evident in Radio 4's *The World at One* and *PM*, both started in the late 1960s), and it was significant that the first successful venture in this direction, Radio 2's *Jimmy Young Programme*, began life in July 1973, just months before the start of ILR.

The IBA itself defined ILR programming as 'flow programming ... a constant stream of varied items, mixing popular music, national and local news, local information, features, competitions and interviews, linked together in a lively style'.[17] Bill Macdonald, Managing Director of Radio Hallam, described his station's programming as 'like a tapestry which weaves in non-antagonistic but not bland music, news and information'.[18] Where ILR differed from BBC radio was not so much in the elements in this flow as in its execution, the efficacy of which helped determine the scale of its commercial funding. 'Flow programming' was a pragmatic way to provide entertainment while maintaining (and being *seen* to maintain) public service commitments, and one of the ways in which ILR attempted to stay ahead of its BBC competitors was by adopting a harder, slicker approach. Obviating the inherent parochialism of local radio required considerable concentration on the nuances of programming, on getting right what Bob Snyder (Programme Controller of Radio Trent between 1975 and 1978) called the 'typography' of a station – working out a programming formula in which all the necessary elements could be smoothly and strategically interpolated and setting out the points at which a presenter should talk. This helped to create a sense of aural style and an environment in which commercials sounded neither obtrusive nor completely ignorable:

> The key thing is that we're a radio station, not a collection of programmes
> . . . our programming is clinical and disciplined, and the way you do things
> in radio is actually more important than what you do, it's a 'how' medium.
> Style is paramount, it's more crucial to sound professional. Style must come
> before content if you're starting a radio station, because otherwise it will
> lack a recognisable identity. Style is what matters, the typography of a
> station comes before everything else, and I don't believe people in my job
> in other stations are clinical enough or technical enough about what
> they're doing.[19]

Particular programme elements – records, news items, weather checks – were collectively important but individually subservient to the *sound* of the station, to its aural identity, its 'signature'. What mattered was the manner in which those elements were framed and presented, and whether the placing and scheduling of these individual items persuaded the public to listen and keep listening. Although an indispensable part of a station's output, even news could be subject to manipulative scheduling in the interests of programme continuity: Piccadilly Radio set a house rule that news and information items were to be limited to a maximum of two minutes to discourage listeners from turning their dial in search of music, while in 1976 Radio Trent refashioned their audience-losing lunchtime news programme – a straight half-hour bulletin sandwiched between two music shows – to include records, which were played without announcement between the main news items. The revamped show not only checked what research showed was a wholesale retuning to Radio 1 but, more importantly, held Trent's audience into the post-1 p.m. rating period, when advertising was charged at a slightly higher rate.

## Music as a marketing tool

Instances such as these confirmed the importance of music as the ILR stations' primary marketing tool, as the main means of attracting listeners who collectively form the 'product' (and, in the absence of sponsorship, the only product) which the stations can then 'sell' to advertisers. According to the customary equation, the higher the audience figures, the more advertisers would be attracted and competition for advertising time would force up the station's rates; conversely, a poor-quality product (i.e. low figures) would deter advertisers, keep rates and revenue low and necessitate changes in output – the more dramatic the better, to inspire the confidence of advertising agencies and their clients. Faced with disappointing results, a station's first priority was invariably to reassess all aspects of its music policy: whether its musical ambience suited the listenership, whether a Top Forty bias should or should not be retained, whether the problem lay in the choice of music made on the listeners' behalf or in its presentation.

These points are well illustrated by the experience of Capital, which set the precedent for abrupt changes in music policy as early as Christmas 1973, when it stopped aiming its programmes at the middle ground between Radios 1 and 2 (the research on which Capital based its original policy identified a collective 89 per cent listenership for these two networks in London[20]) and switched to a more Top Forty-based strategy, projected unequivocally at the 15 to 35 age range. For Music Director Aidan Day it was a blow to his stated belief that London audiences were more 'progressive' in outlook than Radio 1 assumed: in practical terms, the policy change meant fewer album tracks and more hits, but with the emphasis on *anticipating* the popular rather than merely following the dictates of the chart – an important difference that enabled the station to retain a more contemporary image than Radio 1. Yet within months of this policy switch came yet another, prompted by an advertising slump and the first effects of the oil crisis: the music 'became sweeter and more low-key' (Mike Baron[21]) and Capital settled back into a middle-of-the-road format punctuated by chart hits.

The advent of punk-rock in 1976–7 was for Capital, as for other ILR stations, problematic, in that little such music (deliberately unsophisticated, raucous, out of keeping with standard radio fare) was deemed suitable for daytime airplay. (See Ch. 7 for a discussion of how radio treated punk.) The effect of its restriction by Capital was that younger sections of its audience were steadily alienated. Declining ratings during the late 1970s and early 1980s, which were clearly attributable to Capital's failure to keep faith with its young listenership, were nevertheless interpreted by Capital in a topsy-turvy way: deciding on a strategy of attracting *more* older listeners, especially 'housewives', Capital recruited Jo Sandilands, editor of *Honey*, as Programme Director, with a brief to effectively restyle Capital as the radio equivalent of a woman's magazine, 'appealing to a very wide audience with a bias to women'.[22] New wave and reggae elements in the schedules became marginalized still further, and the shift in music policy was complemented by changes in presenters and jingles.

But the policy switch did not work. The new wave of pirate stations in London began eating into Capital's younger evening audiences, but it was a traditional offshore pirate, Laser 558, that had the most crippling effect on Capital's pretensions to being a contemporary music station. With a powerful signal covering a large part of south-east England, a handful of American presenters, few advertisements (Laser's revenue sources were a constant mystery) a policy of continuous contemporary album music, Laser's impact was considerable. With Capital's 'housewife' patronage failing to grow as anticipated – though its original audience remained loyal – a further about-turn was effected during 1983. Claiming that the station was 'returning to its roots', Sandilands and Head of Music Tony Hale reshaped Capital's programming with a view to recapturing its lost youth audience. As Hale acknowledged, 'it took something like Laser, which was a brilliant station, playing fast and hard music to give us a good kick'.[23] New presenters were introduced (including one, Jessie Brandon, recruited from Laser), Michael Aspel gave way to David 'Kid' Jensen (recruited from Radio 1) in the mid-morning slot, and Capital launched a number of pop-oriented networking initiatives (including the *Network Chart Show*) designed to give a lead to the rest of ILR at a time when audiences generally were falling and the system's lack of national coverage was becoming a liability. In 1986 Capital began an extended experiment in splitting its AM and FM frequencies to provide different programmes – mainstream Top Forty radio on the former, and on the latter an experimental mixture of album music contrived to appeal to the affluent, compact disc-buying, young professional ('yuppie') market.[24] Although Capital labelled the new service a success, in 1987 it was revamping its AM format once again, this time with Richard Park (ex-Radio Clyde) as Head of Music in place of the now freelancing Tony Hale.[25]

Radical changes in music policy such as those made by Capital were and continue to be justified by the stations concerned on the grounds of improved audience penetration: a marked *numerical* increase in listeners ostensibly shows that the station is bettering its performance by satisfying the local public. But mere improvements in listening figures are not always of particular value in proving the worth of a station to advertisers: traditionally, advertisers are far more interested in a station's reach among *particular* consumer groups, especially high-income earners. The *demographic* make-up of the station's listenership is all-important, not its volume. Advertisers tend to deal in *specific* markets and aim to place their advertising in media that are likely to deliver the appropriate profile of consumer. Stations can theoretically exist on a low listenership if it is an affluent one, just as newspapers like *The Times* and the *Guardian* can prosper with much lower circulations than the *Sun* or the *Daily Mirror*. James Curran's analysis of advertising's role within media is relevant here:

> Advertising exerts influence through a more sophisticated process than the classic left-wing conspiracy theories would suggest. Its power is vested in its role as system of patronage subsidising the media . . . newspapers must deliver either bulk or high-spending readers to survive. It's the middle ground that suffers. The *Daily Herald* didn't die from lack of popularity; when it closed it was read by over twice as many people as the *Guardian*, *The Times* and *Financial Times*. But its readers were generally elderly and working class, the type of people who aren't useful to advertisers.[26]

The traditional difficulty for ILR has been that its brief – to be a local medium, catering for the whole community – only enables it to offer the advertiser a generalized profile of an *homogenous* audience: a station's scope for hitting the socio-economic groups most favoured by advertisers is hampered by the very terms of its IBA franchise. (The only exception to this is LBC, part of whose brief is to serve London's business community; although it has consistently attracted the lowest patronage of all ILR stations, the 'quality' of its listeners in advertisers' terms and particularly its usefulness to business-to-business advertisers ensures a consistently high level of revenue. In this respect, LBC is precisely analagous to *The Times* and the *Financial Times*). For all but LBC, to pursue a particular listenership for commercial reasons is against the spirit and the letter of the IBA Act; during the first decade of ILR's existence at least, any station doing so risked not only IBA censure but the possible withdrawal of its franchise.

But if, in theory, ILR stations are not 'allowed' to gear their programming to the young at the expense of the old, to the affluent at the expense of the low-income earners, in practice they do: stations apply carefully conceived music policies to achieve the required effect, using music not only as a marketing tool but as a means of *covert targeting*. As Tony Fish puts it, looking at ILR from across the local radio fence:

> ILR stations, their programming is dictated by the sort of demographics which are the flavour of the month of the media directors. In other words, if the media buyers want young housewives, the ILR stations will go for young housewives ... if we [BBC Radio York] went commercial, we would have to deliver the sort of demographics that the agencies wanted and they may not be the same demographics we have at the moment, which we think are right for the area. If they said that the people who are buying the products that the adverts are for are aged 20 to 35, then our station would not appeal to those 40 year olds who it probably appeals to now.[27]

An ILR station can retain the 'community' emphasis in its speech content and continue to provide a service of information and even education to the standard required by the IBA's monitors, but it is its *musical* content that determines the age profile and to a great extent the social profile of those listening. And yet the musical content of a station has never been an area in which the IBA would seek to interfere; it is one of the prime areas of programming which the IBA is professionally unable to properly assess.

A classic example of this tendency is Chiltern Radio, part-owned by Capital and one of several stations on the London periphery (its franchise area covering Bedfordshire, Buckinghamshire and North Hertfordshire) whose peak-time programmes feature exclusively Top Forty material, new releases and an average of two oldies an hour, a mixture calculated to appeal to a 15- to 34-year-old target audience (28 per cent of the population of the franchise area) but alienating, according to Chiltern's own research, to the majority of the 55+ age group, who number 21.5 per cent.[28] Strictly speaking, if ILR is failing to reach a broad cross-section of listeners, it is not meeting the requirements of its franchise. The point is not that Chiltern is necessarily falling short in its duties by not including an attractive mix of 55+ music in its daytime programmes (precisely what constitutes 55+ music is in any case debatable) but that its concentration on records *which are targeted by their manufacturers at younger consumers* inevitably leads to a bias against the older and economically less-active sections of particular communities. For a medium so anxious to put forward a caring, companionable image, this is a curious deficiency. And the discrimination isn't all one way: as Chapter 9 will attempt to show, one of the results of the emphasis within other ILR stations (Swansea Sound, for example) on the 35+ age range is that teenagers, too, become marginalized. In these cases, teenage music tends to be treated as a minority music, shunted to the mid- to late evening sidings so as not to impinge too markedly on the middle-of-the-road ambience of the daytime shows.

## Towards deregulation

But if careful selection of music is the traditional way in which ILR programmers effectively circumvent their cross-community obligations, covert circumvention has become less and less necessary as the post-1979 political climate has called the very nature of those obligations into question. Crucial here is the role of the IBA, which has been to *interpret* the provisions of the 1972 Act which set up ILR. The obligations upon the franchise-holding companies are clearly stated there, but in general terms; the IBA has considerable leeway in bringing individual stations to book if its obligations are neglected, yet the force with which the IBA exercises its policing powers depends greatly on the political and economic circumstances of the time. During the Labour government's period in office (1974–9), for example, the IBA was encouraged to toughen its stance with stations which put the commercial above the community motive. Acting directly on criticisms of ILR programming made by the government-appointed Annan Committee, the IBA's radio division insisted on the insertion of more 'meaningful speech' (as opposed to 'pop and prattle', a term used freely in the Annan Report). The result was that music fell from 55 per cent of a typical station's daytime output to 49 per cent, while the speech content correspondingly rose.[29] The two franchises awarded by the IBA during 1979 also carried the post-Annan influence. Cardiff Broadcasting (CBC) was a community-based consortium owned jointly by financial backers and the Cardiff Community Trust, which represented voluntary, charity and other social organizations. Midlands Community Radio, the holder of the Coventry franchise, was similarly constituted.

Ironically, however, the Cardiff and Coventry appointments coincided with a change of government and political atmosphere. After the Conservatives' election victory of 1979, the political will to safeguard the 'community' aspects of ILR was no longer there, and the principles of priority to local programming, broad programme schedules, cross-subsidization and a strict division between editorial and advertising content became progressively undermined. The impetus for this came from within the management boards of some of the larger ILR stations, who by the early 1980s were seeing profits and audiences decline due to competition for advertising revenue and listeners from novel, attractive media such as breakfast television and land-based pirate radio. The problem of falling revenue was particularly acute: the forty-three ILR stations' total share of national advertising revenue stood at 2.2 per cent over the fiscal year 1982–3, compared to 1.5 per cent in 1976 when twenty-four fewer stations were operational. (In 1984 the figure contracted to 2.1 per cent, in 1985 to 1.8 per cent.[30]) The IBA's original projection was that, within ten years of ILR's launch, the system would be attracting around 6 per cent of the national advertising 'cake'; indeed, plans were made for expansion of the ILR system to a maximum of seventy stations on precisely this assumption. The prohibitions in the IBA Act on sponsorship, networked output and investment in other stations were blamed by the ILR stations' trade association, the Association of Independent Radio Contractors (AIRC), for inhibiting the commercial performance of ILR to a dangerous extent, while an additional bone of contention was the way that pirate stations – subject to neither copyright fees nor fixed costs such as transmitter rental or levies on profit – were not only operating with apparent impunity from prosecution but were proliferating. As AIRC director Brian West complained:

> The competition is coming from all sides. We are not opposed in principle to competition, whether it's from the pirates or a legitimate system like community radio, but we do want to compete on fair terms. If ILR is regulated, let other forms of radio be regulated, too. And if they operate under a more relaxed system, then ILR requires parity of opportunity.[31]

The AIRC began to campaign openly for deregulation during 1983, its prime targets the Home Office and the IBA itself. It sought the relaxation of restrictions on programme content and on the volume of advertising inserted into programmes; the allowance of programme funding by commercial companies; freedom for ILR stations to target their output at particular markets rather than the whole of a local community; the end of the transmitter rental system, with stations able to buy their transmitters outright; a return to a system of rolling contracts, rather than fixed-term contracts, to give greater security of tenure; and the reduction or even removal of the profit levy, which it was acknowledged would effectively end the financial support (through redistribution of 'excess' profit) that the smaller, less profitable ILR stations enjoyed from their larger counterparts. In addition to all this, the AIRC sought to reduce overheads all round, adopting an increasingly aggressive stance in negotiations with PPL and the PRS over performance fees and complaining that the IBA's technical and engineering standards were unnecessarily high and expensive to maintain. As Radio 210 Managing Director Tony Stoller pointed out in a series of *Broadcast* articles in 1984, transmitters alone had become much cheaper to buy and much simpler to mount in the decade following ILR's arrival, hence the ease with which pirates were setting up:

> The first problem is that the IBA owns and operates the transmitters. If justified originally in a paternalistic system at a time of more complex transmitter technology, this arrangement is now obsolete. Transmitters are cheap and simple (and no longer need highly qualified engineers to operate them). Their ready availability is one of the key factors in the changing context which has brought ILR to its present *bouleversement* .... In the columns of wireless magazines you can see advertisements for a medium wave and a VHF transmitter for £1,500 each; the IBA, as transmission agency for ILR, now reckons on £200,000 for a transmitter pair.[32]

The AIRC campaign had the look of an attempt to rewrite the statute book. The IBA's initial attitude was that the terms of the Act were not negotiable, that any change in ILR's terms of reference required parliamentary approval, but against the twin background of a government more committed than any other Conservative administration this century to the free market and an industry that had clearly failed to reach anything like the commercial or programming heights expected of it, its stance altered with remarkable speed. The collapse of Centre Radio in Leicester in October 1983, following the IBA's refusal to approve the transfer of the ailing station to new ownership, sent shock waves throughout the industry, signalling as it did an abrupt about-turn in IBA policy following years of consistent benign intervention into the commercial affairs of ILR stations. In 1985 an existing franchise-holder failed to have its contract renewed for the first time: one of the oldest ILR stations, Radio Victory in Portsmouth, lost out to Ocean Sound, apparently (and the IBA has consistently reserved the right not to justify its franchise awards publicly) because of the emphasis in the latter's application on covering the Southampton area as well as Portsmouth. Other companies seeking retention of their franchises were reappointed without opposition from other consortia, the very absence of rival consortia being one sign of the general lack of commercial confidence in ILR's future at this time.

This dearth of interest, and money, prompted the IBA, during 1984, to drop all plans for developing ILR in new localities: as Peter Baldwin, Deputy Director of Radio at the IBA, told a Local Radio Association meeting, 'Cash is short. The existing companies are just not producing the all-important secondary rental which is essential to development'. In areas that bordered existing ILR station catchment areas, the IBA adopted a new policy of inviting that station to extend its coverage accordingly. With IBA approval, Radio Trent in Nottingham took both Derby and the now Centre-less Leicester under its wing, Beacon Radio in Wolverhampton expanded into the Shrewsbury and Telford areas, Radio 210 in Reading into Basingstoke and Andover, and Pennine Radio in Bradford into Huddersfield and Halifax. One of the biggest acts of empire-building was effected by Chiltern, who already had one of the largest catchment areas in population terms and studios in both Dunstable and Bedford: within five years of opening, they had absorbed the once IBA-earmarked towns of Milton Keynes, Aylesbury and Northampton, in the latter case taking over the service previously provided by a neighbouring (and ailing) ILR station, Hereward Radio. The net effect of all this was to radically reshape the ILR map, to change ILR, in the space of little more than three years, from a locally based, locally *dictated* service to a more commercially viable regional system, and all without either consultation in the areas concerned or comment in Parliament.

The switch to a regional set-up also indicated a relaxation of once sacrosanct IBA requirements regarding local financial control of the stations. With the IBA's blessing, Chiltern was one of several of the more profitable stations to make takeover bids for stations in non-neighbouring areas, along with Red Rose Radio in Preston, whose board was chaired by Owen Oyston, a leading north-western estate agent. Oyston's other media interests included stakes in cable television and local newspapers.[33] Red Rose took over Radio Aire in Leeds in 1985, then moved in to take over Gwent Broadcasting in Newport once that station had failed in its own plan to merge with neighbouring CBC in Cardiff; both Gwent and CBC were then relaunched by Red Rose as Red Dragon Radio.

As Colin Walters, Managing Director of Piccadilly Radio, commented at the time of the Radio Aire takeover:

In the eleven years since its inception our industry has seen many complex shareholding structures developed under the watchful eye of the IBA. But we've never had a courtship and seduction of this sort. The reason is that, as a government-appointed body, the IBA has insisted that 'local sound broadcasting' means locally *owned* sound broadcasting. The policy has been so rigorously enforced that local stations going to the market have even felt it necessary to warn stock purchasers in other parts of the nation that they could be forced to sell if their holdings threatened contract renewal. Yet here we are, a mere nine months after my own company took such a precaution, with a Lancashire company aiming for and likely to get as much as 90 per cent of the equity of a Yorkshire radio station. What has prompted the IBA volte-face as far as I can see is a nudge from Whitehall. The Government believes in companies acting freely in a free market and it has decided that that ethic should prevail, at least to some extent, in the world of broadcasting.[34]

Other takeovers and mergers followed in a manner that would have been unthinkable at the close of the 1970s. Wiltshire Radio and Bristol's Radio West combined to relaunch themselves in October 1985 as Great Western Radio (GWR), which in turn merged with Plymouth Sound in May 1987; Radio Tay in Dundee merged with Radio Forth in Edinburgh during 1986; while in October 1986, Newcastle's Metro Radio took over Radio Tees (covering Stockton, Darlington and Teesside) and a merger was agreed between the three major Yorkshire stations, Radio Hallam in Sheffield, Pennine in Bradford and Viking Radio in Hull. In 1987 Capital succeeded in its takeover bid for DevonAir Radio in Exeter; in early 1988, Bournemouth-based Two Counties Radio was conducting merger talks with Reading-based Radio 210.

One did not have to look far for further evidence of the IBA's willingness to regulate, as its chairman Lord Thomson euphemistically put it, with 'a lighter touch'. In November 1984 the IBA announced that ILR contractors could now vary their hours of broadcasting without having to seek permission, and that transmitter rentals would be reduced by 10 per cent. (A further 25 per cent cut was announced on the same day as Victory's failure to renew its franchise, in what appeared to be a cynical attempt to deflect criticism from within the industry.) It was on programming matters, however, that the IBA shifted most ground, again in an astonishingly short period of time. While the Authority had long encouraged a modest degree of programme-sharing between stations, usually of concerts, documentaries or artist profiles, it had never favoured national syndication of programmes because of the paramouncy of local output. During 1984, however, the Authority approved the AIRC's plans for a syndicated programme, the *Network Chart Show*, to be produced in London by Capital Radio and scheduled directly opposite Radio 1's Top Forty chart show on Sunday evenings. The programme was deliberately designed to attract *national* advertisers, as one of the commonest reasons cited by advertisers and agencies for their resistance to using ILR (and consequently for ILR's chronically low share of national advertising revenue) was its lack of national coverage, and to increase general awareness of ILR as an advertising medium. In a move indicative of the new bullishness within ILR, Capital hired one of Radio 1's highest-rated disc jockeys, David 'Kid' Jensen, to present the show and contracted the MRIB to produce a chart that was claimed to be more up-to-date than its BBC counterpart. Though there was some initial resistance from within ILR – Keith Skues, Programme Controller of Radio Hallam, raised the banner of local autonomy and told *Broadcast*, 'I don't believe local radio can be run by a committee from London'[35] – the revenue promised to the stations for simply taking the show was crucial in persuading virtually all of them to fall into line. This included LBC, despite the fact that the *Network Chart Show* was totally out of character with its almost wholly all-speech programmes and despite the fact that Capital was itself transmitting the show at the same time. As Jeff Winston wrote in a *Guardian* article in October 1984, a significant minority of London's ILR listeners were effectively disfranchised for two hours every Sunday for no other reason than commercial pragmatism.[36]

Syndication in itself was a major departure for ILR, but more radical still was the IBA's approval of sponsorship as a source of funding for such programmes. (Robert Fraser, one of the architects of the Independent Television system on which ILR was modelled, successfully argued against sponsorship as funding for ITV because it undermined the editorial independence of the programme-maker, and the principle was reaffirmed in a radio context in the 1973 IBA Act, sections 8.6 and 8.7.) The failure of ILR as a whole to increase its share of national advertising and the consequent search by ILR stations for other sources of revenue, led the AIRC to press the IBA for a relaxation of its prohibition of sponsored programmes, while another factor in the IBA's change of heart was the setting up of Channel 4 in 1982 and the freedom given to independent production companies serving the channel to seek 'co-funding' from commercial sources. This stemmed from a proposal by the Annan Committee, taken up by the 1978 White Paper on Broadcasting, that 'commercial and industrial concerns may be prepared, in return for having their names associated with particular productions, to pay some share of the costs of those productions'.[37] Cable television was another area which, following government acceptance of the recommendations of the 1980 Hunt Report, was to be funded by unrestricted sponsorship and advertising. Another significant government move saw Radio Luxembourg, prime exponents of sponsored broadcasting since the 1930s, granted a telephone landline for the first time in its history, making it possible in theory for programmes to be broadcast live from mainland Britain without the supervision of a government-appointed agency. As Tony Stoller argued in 1983, if sponsorship (however limited and however closely monitored) was to be allowed in one part of the national broadcasting map, it could not be outlawed in others:

> and so the regulators have been forced into an almost Stalinesque backward re-writing of rules. It is inelegant, probably unsatisfactory, inescapably

vague – but it is in that context that we must now develop and control this new funding source for radio.[38]

The new accommodation of sponsorship paralleled, as Stoller further pointed out, a change in attitude (and a diversion of promotional resources) towards sponsorship within the commercial world itself, brought about by dissatisfaction with the cost and effectiveness of traditional spot advertising and the promise of loosely regulated cable and satellite television. Growing commercial involvement – what in advertising is described as 'below the line' activity – in the sponsoring of sporting events and arts festivals was one indication of this.

Again it was the *Network Chart Show* which blazed the trail for outright sponsorship of ILR programmes, by means of a £400,000 per annum deal with Nestlés which *Marketing Week* described as 'the biggest sponsorship deal in broadcasting history'.[39] The deal, which still stands at the time of writing, ensures that every station taking the programme receives a percentage of that £400,000 in direct proportion to its share of overall advertising revenue. Additional revenue came to the stations from the use of chart by Channel 4's *The Chart Show* and by the cable channel Sky, and from the sale of the programme overseas. The success of the venture – and if nothing else, the show cut severely into the BBC's traditional Sunday evening supremacy in ratings – singlehandedly prompted the launch of similarly sponsored networked programmes, including an album chart show (the chart again provided by MRIB) and a US chart show, for which the producers (Piccadilly Productions, a subsidiary of Piccadilly Radio) hired yet another very familiar Radio 1 voice, Paul Gambaccini. On a local level, IBA approval was sought and given for sponsorship both of individual programmes – for example, Lasky's funding of a series of carol concerts over Christmas 1984 and the Stock Exchange's financing of *Family Money* both on LBC – and of aspects of general programming like sports coverage and advice features. Among many such deals, DHL couriers sponsored Radio City's sports bulletins, John Smith Breweries did the same for Pennine Radio, American Express sponsored BRMB's weather reports, and the Norwich Building Society put up the money for regular financial advice spots on Radio Broadland. Speaking at an advertising conference in November 1986, Capital's Managing Director, Nigel Walmsley, estimated that sponsorship was bringing between £2 million and £3 million into ILR. Bill Macdonald, Managing Director of Radio Hallam, looked forward to the day when 'we can run news bulletins presented in association with Midland Bank',[40] and his station was also one of the first to feature (in 1986) live read-to-microphone advertisements on the standard American pattern – the clearest example yet of how the distinction between editorial and advertising content could be blurred, as they required the presenter (in this case on the news and music breakfast show) to depart from his theoretically neutral role to endorse a product or service.

## An obituary for ILR?

In mid-1985 the AIRC announced in a press release that it would no longer refer to the service its members provided as Independent *Local* Radio but as Independent Radio. The reason was obvious: the AIRC was seeking to play down the parochialism of its service in favour of a more bullish, national profile, at a time when the IBA was itself floating the idea of creating a new national, commercially funded network by the end of the decade. As we have seen, ILR is in any case a medium which, because of the commercial pressure for higher revenues and systematic deregulation, has been progressively drained of its localness. The shift from local to regional centres, the concentration of ownership and influence within ILR on a few large (and mostly metropolitan) stations, the increase in the number of networked programmes and the financial pressure on less profitable stations to take them, and the growth in sponsorship by national companies – all are aspects of the same tendency. The issue of financial control of ILR stations even has its international aspect, following the IBA-ratified acquisition by the Australian media concern Darling Downs TV of major interests in LBC (58 per cent of shares), Marcher Sound in Wrexham (49 per cent), Beacon Radio (30 per cent), Radio Forth (30 per cent), and 50 per cent of shares in Independent Radio Sales, one of the two major ILR sales houses. While there was nothing new in international investors taking stakes in ILR companies – DDTV in fact acquired its ILR interests from Selkirk Communications of Canada – the ease with which the IBA approved the transaction and the known interventionist, not to say expansionist tendencies of DDTV suggested that the change would impact upon ILR as a whole in a far more significant way. Two other Australian groups also bought into ILR heavily during 1986, Linter buying 19 per cent of DevonAir in Exeter and 12 per cent of Two Counties Radio in Bournemouth and the Paul Ramsay Group buying Standard Broadcasting's 24.27 per cent stake in Capital Radio and thirteen other ILR holdings to add to its 45 per cent stake in the other major sales house, Broadcast Media Services (BMS). By early 1987, over two-thirds of ILR stations were estimated to have some degree of Australian interest at board level.[41]

That the increased militancy of the AIRC had a political effect was first evident in the favourable response to its arguments for deregulation of commercial radio in the Peacock Committee report. More significantly, it successfully persuaded the government to consider the whole area of radio separately from the financing of the BBC (investigation of which was Peacock's main brief), resulting in the Green Paper on radio that was eventually published in early 1987. The AIRC's chief proposal was that commercial radio should be taken out of the jurisdiction of the IBA and transferred to a supervisory body such as the Cable Authority, who would award franchises on the commercial merit of applications and give stations an almost free hand (to the point of allowing each free political expression) in determining programme content. The AIRC sought to make commercial radio analogous with the newspaper industry, that is subject to no political control and under no obligation to provide the 'all things to all people' service which, it was said, had been a constant impediment to commercial progress.

It should be said that not all ILR stations favoured this degree of deregulation. One of ILR's most respected figures, Jimmy Gordon of Radio Clyde, warned at the 1984 Radio Festival of deregulation leading to 'page-three broadcasting', that is a descent to the provision of lowest common denominator programmes. Whatever else, if adopted the AIRC plan would mean a complete change in the ecology of sound broadcasting in Britain and certainly the end of ILR as it was originally envisaged, that is as a public service funded by commercial sources but controlled by a public agency. This was the conclusion quite happily reached by the government itself in its 1988 proposals for what appeared to be a wholesale deregulation of radio (the BBC stations apart), one of the most dramatic of which was for the transference of control over radio from the IBA to a new Radio Authority with a far narrower range of responsibilities.

Whether deregulation really addresses the fundamental problems likely to be faced by any commercial radio system in Britain – problems related to radio's low-key presence in the advertising market – is another matter. Returning to the point made at the very start of this chapter, legal commercial radio was a late arrival on a sophisticated, television-dominated media scene and never really caught up: the failure to establish ILR as a *national* advertising medium led to indifference among the big national advertisers that was exacerbated by the failure to establish a national sales house offering air-time on all the stations. (One of the more bizarre features of ILR is that its stations are not allowed to compete directly for audiences but are expected to compete with each other for advertising.) ILR was also seriously undermined by a lack of managerial, marketing and production expertise: while editorial staff were drawn largely from BBC radio, the crucial commercial appointments were filled by marketing personnel with television backgrounds, whose outlook was conditioned by television expectations. Because of this, suggests Stoller, there was 'a fundamental mistake in the positioning of the medium. Refugees from ITV among the early radio sales-people were perhaps overaware of television issues. Had ILR been put up against the dying regional press (as the freesheets show for classified advertising) radio would have flourished, taking national display money just as it takes local'.[42] Indeed, freesheets (local newspapers distributed free by home delivery and funded entirely by advertising) offered local advertisers – the bedrock source of ILR finance – a far cheaper, more cost-effective and more 'visible' means of advertising than ILR and flourished in many areas at ILR's expense. By 1984, freesheets were estimated to be taking 5.6 times as much local advertising as ILR.[43]

Added to this, there remains a serious prejudice against radio within the advertising world. Radio advertising lacks glamour, agencies too often place radio campaigns in the hands of juniors or trainees because of television's hold on more experienced (and expensive) creative personnel, the process of buying time on stations is complicated and confusing; these are familiar complaints that help explain why radio is often used by advertisers as no more than a tactical medium, to reinforce a television campaign. Radio becomes a much more viable advertising medium at times when the cost of television air-time increases while television audiences contract. This appeared to be the cause of the marked spurt in advertising revenue that ILR as a whole enjoyed during 1986–7 – harder selling on the part of the now part-Australian-owned sales houses was claimed to be another factor, together with the £1.5 million spent on promoting British Gas privatization – yet even this seemed yet another illustration of commercial radio's continuing tendency to hang on to television's coat-tails.[44] Generally, however, in the much-quoted words of Saatchi and Saatchi media buyer Alec Kenny, speaking at the 1983 Radio Festival, ILR has 'low saliency', lacking the personality and presence required to excite the people who matter in advertisers and agencies alike. Worse, the constant airing of ILR's problems in the trade press – and the astonishing number of articles on the subject in *Marketing*, *Marketing Week*, *Admap* and *Campaign*, particularly between 1983 and 1986, make instructive reading – have served only to further undermine confidence in the medium's ability to survive.[45]

By mid-1987, there were signs of a recovery in ILR's fortunes, with revenue for the second quarter of the year up 25.8 per cent on the same period a year earlier. The consensus within the industry was that this was a much-awaited consequence of the various changes in ILR structure and practice outlined earlier; for example, a review of ILR finances by William Phillips in *Broadcast* in September 1987 attributed the new bullishness within ILR to the improved performance of the sales houses and the introduction of regional ratecards, the trimming of IBA transmitter and secondary rentals, the ending of pressure to produce labour-intensive public service programmes, and the rescue and relaunch of ailing stations by more powerful stations.[46]

The new ILR is nevertheless a very different animal from that envisaged and created in the early 1970s, and the 1988 proposals threaten to remove altogether its last structural vestiges. But the prospect of a dismantled ILR cannot simply be related to changing political fashion: the ILR ideal has fallen victim to fundamental technological, social and political change. Not only have notions of cross-subsidization, cross-community programming, local autonomy and editorial integrity become politically unfashionable in the Thatcher era, technological developments in the transmitter field and the creeping multinationalism of the media as the age of cable and satellite beckons, have undermined the very precepts under which public service broadcasting in Britain operates. Now that the consensus (and I use the term ironically) from both sides of the political divide is that ILR *as it was originally conceived* has become, or is fast becoming, moribund, the battle has begun to determine precisely what will take its place.

# Part two
# Patterns of programming

It is almost a cliché to criticize radio stations, or rather the personnel who run them, for making 'safe' choices in the music they broadcast. What constitutes a 'safe' choice depends on the nature of the station or the particular programme in question, but safety in a broadcasting context is generally a synonym for predictability, for choosing only music that matches the supposed expectations of the target audience. In this second section of the book, I want to examine these perceived expectations more closely, and in particular the assumptions upon which they are based and the mechanics involved in attempting to fulfil them.

This means looking at the 'gatekeeping' role adopted by programme producers and programme controllers and at how daytime radio is planned and executed, but the first point that needs to be made is that the gatekeepers of radio do not work in isolation from the music industry that supplies them with the records they play. However much they may profess their independence from the machinations and marketing schemes of record companies, radio's gatekeepers only select from what is made available and what record sales patterns tell them is currently popular; they are music producers in only the limited sense of commissioning and recording sessions for broadcasting, and their usual inclusion of these in evening shows rather than the better-patronized daytime programmes reflects a basic lack of faith in anything other than commercially-made, externally-provided music. This of course begs other questions. Given radio's dependence on records as the prime source of programme material, how are individual decisions made as to which are played and which ignored? What informs the decision-making process, and what is the code of professionalism to which the gatekeepers work? Does all this have an impact on what music is produced by the record companies and on how it is promoted?

Airplay policy is often seen in simplistic terms: Radio 1 or an ILR station bans a record and voices are raised for and against, proponents approving the upholding of public decency (records are usually banned on the grounds of sexual content, real or imagined) and opponents claiming unwarranted censor-ship of expression. But well-known examples of bans like 'Too Drunk to Fuck' by the Dead Kennedys (1981) and 'Relax' by Frankie Goes to Hollywood (1984) are only instructive up to a point; far more relevant is the day-to-day process by which records are selected or excluded, often for no other reason than that (in the gatekeeper's all-important opinion) the music does not match the ambience of the station or programme. To what degree this is simply a matter of musical style or of seeking to avoid the controversial or disturbing is questionable: what defines suitability for the airwaves is, in the end, far more a question of how pro-grammers judge the tolerance threshold of the listening audience itself. More than anything else, programmers fear the off switch: the skill of programming is a negative one, to ensure that the switch is never used and the dial never touched.

# 6 Don't stop the music: radio and the record industry

Radio is incredibly important. It probably does more to influence public taste than anything else . . . I'm sure there's a direct correlation between airplay and sales. Often airplay reports are of more interest than the sales charts since they're an indication of what's likely to happen.

Richard Lyttleton, International Manager, EMI Records[1]

The irony is that on the one hand the record company says that you are stealing the money out of our mouths by playing records which people will not then buy. On the other hand, the same record company gives somebody £12,500 and a BMW to go round to Capital and plug the record. Not satisfied, it also goes to the back door and supplies records to illegal outfits like the pirates of which it then professes to disapprove.

Tony Hale, former Head of Music, Capital Radio[2]

Radio stations throughout the world use records as a major source of programme material for reasons of tradition, convenience and economics: not only is music on record a proven audience-winner, it forms a cheap and ever-ready substitute for other, more expensive programme features such as live music, drama, documentaries and in-depth news coverage. But radio stations in Britain pay a double price for their dependence on what is essentially secondary programme matter. First, whatever editorial control the stations may exercise in deciding which records to play, they are inextricably embroiled in the marketing strategies (long- or short-term) of the companies originating those records: for reasons we shall explore, radio stations largely draw their selections, if not from the lists of current best-selling records, then from a pool of records that have proven their 'popularity' by selling in some numbers across record shop counters. Second, radio stations are obliged under the terms of the 1956 Copyright Act to pay the record industry, through its collection agency Phonographic Performance Limited, for the privilege of broadcasting commercially recorded material.

Ultimately, the corporate grip of the record industry on radio in Britain is of more significance than the machinations of individual record companies in securing air-time, and discussion of the relationship between the two purely in terms of the promotional process tends to miss the point. The music industry is itself dependent on radio to put its products before the public, but historically in Britain there has long been a bias in the relationship in favour of the former: the copyright laws ensure that any form of public performance of a record company's products requires not only permission but recompense, while at the same time safeguarding, at least in theory, the interests of the musicians who create the records. This is in contrast to the situation in the United States, where a tradition of mutual commercial investment between the radio and record industries stretches back to the 1920s; there, the degree of interaction between the two industries – what Barnouw calls their 'symbiotic' relationship[3] – meant that radio was never perceived as a threat by the record manufacturers and that the issue of payment for the broadcasting of records, and of limiting radio's use of them, never seriously arose. The British music industry, on the other hand, remains ambivalent, not to say schizophrenic, in its attitude to radio – demonstrating its belief in the value of airplay in the investment its companies make in promotion teams whose sole responsibility is the securing of air-time for their products, yet taking an apparently contradictory view through organizations like PPL and the British Phonographic Industry (BPI) that excessive airplay harms sales and that, in the memorable words of a former BPI chairman, 'a record played on the radio is a record sale lost'.[4]

Behind the contradiction, however, there is a consistency of objective. When the profitability of the record companies is threatened by a period of recession (as during the mid-1970s and after), so the pressure is greatest to maximize a return on investment through effective promotion; at the same time, secondary revenue sources such as radio become particularly important because they act as a bulwark against the worst effects of a shortfall in revenue from straight record or tape sales. (Whatever the publicly expressed rationale behind the music industry's posture, the record companies are essentially exploiting a legally established right for corporate revenue ends. In the final analysis, restricting airplay of records is far less important than the revenue that arises from it.) The promotion and revenue issues are therefore intimately connected, and it is instructive to note that it is only in the late 1970s and beyond – with the breaking of the BBC's monopoly on legal sound broadcasting and the moving of radio into the commercial arena – that British radio has itself seriously begun to challenge the music industry on its pursuit of revenue at the medium's expense.

## The promotional value of radio

Radio's value as a promotional medium is self-evident: if a record isn't heard, it won't sell, and even in the case of artists and groups whose records sell on the strength of their 'name' alone – the Beatles, Elvis Presley, the Rolling Stones, and even less critically fashionable bands like the Electric Light Orchestra, Queen and Wham! in recent years – radio can still be vital in establishing the fact of a record's availability. Radio fanfares a record's release and, unlike the music press, which can only provide a commentary upon it in the form of favourable or adverse editorial coverage, it has the key advantage of offering the produce itself for exposure. Compared to television and video, radio is cheap in terms of promotional resources and it has a 'sustaining' quality that the visual medium cannot match: while the impact of a television spot dissipates over a period of days, radio maintains the impact of a record by regular repetition. Finally (and most obviously), radio reaches an audience comprised at least partially of the target group of potential record buyers: listeners who use the medium not just as a source of entertainment or companionship but as a consumer's guide. Radio play is in this sense, a form of advertising; what is more, it comes 'free', although the expense of promotion usually outweighs any advantage there may be in not having to pay outright for airplay; promotional costs become dispersed into expensive (and unreliable) means of securing radio exposure, from the ubiquitous free lunch to the hiring of expert teams of independent pluggers.

Awareness of the promotional benefits of radio among record companies grew apace in the 1950s, initially in the United States, though to understand the symbiosis between the two industries there it is necessary to go back still further, to the diversification of radio networks and manufacturers (notably CBS and RCA) into music publishing and record company ownership. A dispute between the networks and the music publishers' collection agency, the American Society of Composers, Authors and Publishers (ASCAP), over fees for broadcasting use of their material resulted in the networks establishing their own rival organization, Broadcast Music Incorporated (BMI), which undertook the licensing of a vast new catalogue of material from regional sources that had hitherto been rejected by the New York-centred ASCAP. BMI's championing of songwriters in the country music field in particular helped establish Nashville as a recording and publishing centre of national importance, and widespread exposure of such material on the networks served to soften up the market for related regional styles, including rock 'n' roll.[5] The advent of rock, promoted heavily by radio stations with a view to the newly lucrative teenage market, stirred ASCAP into lobbying for a congressional investigation into the networks' financial involvement in record manufacture, on the basis of alleged violation of America's anti-trust laws. Revelations of widespread payola within radio helped confirm suspicions that rock 'n' roll had been a radio creation and led to a shift in the balance of power within radio stations, with programme controllers rather than disc jockeys assuming responsibility for the stations' total output and becoming the new target for record label promotion. It was in the post-payola atmosphere that a whole new battery of promotional techniques began to evolve, based not so much on direct financial inducements to those in charge of music selection as on the offering of 'exclusives' in the form of star interviews and endorsements.[6]

These techniques came late to Britain, where the promotion departments of the major record companies were almost wholly geared to the production of 15-minute or half-hour company showcases for Radio Luxembourg. 'Plugging' was a relatively genteel occupation often handled by department juniors and limited to fixing appointments with BBC producers who could offer, at best, the promise of a single play on *Record Roundabout* or *Pick of the Pops*. The coming of the pirates at first made no discernible difference, as the majors took a collective decision not to co-operate with the stations on the grounds that they were stealing copyright, a policy that cleared the way for the handful of new independent companies, some less scrupulous in their dealings, to establish a market presence. Tamla Motown's presence in pirate radio programming was almost entirely due to the efforts of plugger Dave Most, who kept the ships provided with Motown products – at theoretical risk to Motown's distribution deal with EMI – and cultivated professional friendships with the important disc jockeys, including the three who became most associated with black American soul music, Johnnie Walker, Emperor Rosko and Tony Blackburn.[7] By the time Radio London was launched in December 1965, however, virtually all the major labels were providing the pirate stations with copies of their latest releases.

Paradoxically, it was with the closure of the pirates and the limiting of exposure to just two outlets – BBC Radio 1 and Radio Luxembourg – that 'plugging' in Britain began to develop on US lines. In 1968 Luxembourg dropped its sponsored programmes and instead opted for live programming on the pirate model; a strip show format was introduced, featuring a large percentage of plays paid for by record companies (which tended to stand out from the rest because the issuing company was always stated). 1970 brought a further refinement in policy, with the station's management assuming the right to dictate the placing of particular records within a programme and the number of plays each could be given per evening, in deference to programme sponsors and advertisers who preferred their programmes to follow a strict, unfettered Top Forty format. The change left the way open, in theory at least, for a greater diversity of broadcast music on the station and brought the pluggers back in force to the Luxembourg offices for the first time since the early 1950s.[8]

The main focus of industry attention, however, was Radio 1. Although resented for its power to virtually make or break a record, the very fact of its near-monopoly of pop radio simplified the promotion process: pluggers were dealt with efficiently and professionally, were allocated appointments and given advance warning of the success or otherwise of their persuasion by the pinning of programme running orders to a notice board in the foyer of Egton House, Radio 1's headquarters. More importantly, as Radio 1 developed its own 'sound' and identity, so the companies began concentrating their promotional efforts on those records that matched Radio 1 producers' perceptions of their listeners' tastes – often continental or country-styled ballads by singers of the Engelbert Humperdinck/Tom Jones ilk, one-off novelties recorded by hastily assembled studio groups, or proven American hits. The introduction (in 1973) of a playlist system based on the Top Forty placings was criticized within the industry because it narrowed airplay to a fixed number of records, but it also guaranteed those records a minimum of plays and daily exposure within all of the best-patronized shows.[9] With the playlist published weekly in the trade press, to have one's company product represented in it became a status symbol for artists, management and pluggers alike:

> One record executive told me he'd rather be on the playlist with only fifteen plays than not to be on and be getting twenty plays a week. It was ludi-

crous. We were getting into a situation where it was more important to be on our playlist than being heard on the programme – a situation like the tail wagging the dog.

Teddy Warrick, Deputy Head, Radio 1, 1970–83[10]

The playlist may not have made, in Warrick's words, 'a damn bit of difference to what music was coming out of the speakers', but it provided the industry with a marketing focus and was theoretically less prone to abuse than the method of air-play selection that preceded it. Before, the concentration of influence on the individual programme producer made him a target for inducements, and a minor scandal did erupt during 1971 over favours accorded to a producer of *Family Favourites* (then transmitted on both Radios 1 and 2) and the involvement of a Radio 1 disc jockey and his producer with singer turned call-girl Janie Jones. The playlist system transformed record selection into a collective decision.

Plugging a record at Radio 1 in the early 1970s was a relatively cosy affair, handled by old hands like Dave Most, who helped promote a long run of hits for his brother Mickie's label, Rak. Rak was an example of a small, independently owned label concentrating almost exclusively on singles sales and tailoring its re-leases unequivocally to Radio 1 requirements and those record buyers in the 11 to 15 age group, a market dormant for much of the late 1960s but newly important following the successes of T. Rex, Donny Osmond, David Cassidy, Slade and others. The mini-boom in sales of singles between 1972 and 1975 con-tradicted projected industry trends (which suggested that albums aimed at a young adult market were to be the area of keenest competition), but it was mainly the independents – Rak, Bell, Magnet, UK and others – who capitalized upon it; for the majors, keen to exploit the potentially more lucrative album mar-ket and develop acts with mature, long-term appeal, ILR seemed to offer much greater promotional promise than a literally single-minded Radio 1, and a number of companies took on extra promotion staff and set up regional offices in cities where ILR stations were to be established. Their optimism was partly based on the American experience of local radio and its semi-legendary capacity for creating local hits with the potential to 'go national', and on the assumption that regional stations would automatically follow the early, comparatively adventur-ous album-based policy of Capital in London, but in all ILR was a disap-pointment. First, ILR stations pitched their music policies somewhere between Radios 1 and 2, retaining the singles bias and the Top Forty orientation; second, ILR was plagued by problems of its own that curtailed any experimentation in music policy that risked losing listeners. Third, radio advertising campaigns for new product mounted by the labels themselves proved disappointingly ineffec-tive and seemed to indicate that the average ILR listener was unlikely to be more than a casual record buyer. (In the United States, record companies are a major source of advertising revenue for the radio stations, to the point of using it as an indirect bargaining counter in persuading the stations to play their products.)

As events transpired, the ILR stations were in any case given little opportunity to demonstrate their long-term promotional worth: by 1976, with the recession and spiralling vinyl costs hitting the industry hard and the future of ILR thrown into question by the Labour government's freeze on further expansion, those record companies which had established regional teams were disbanding them. The companies subsequently concentrated their efforts on the big metropolitan stations – particularly Capital, Radio City (Liverpool), Piccadilly, BRMB (Birmingham), Radios Clyde and Forth – while providing most of the others with a 'brown envelope' service, religiously supplying new releases and promotional literature but rarely bothering to establish personal contact. At a time when the spread of 'punk-rock' was precipitating a degree of provincial pop music-making unseen in Britain since the beat group era of the early 1960s, this policy had its ironic aspect: the promotion departments began cutting their ties with the stations just when the Artists and Repertoire (A & R) departments of the same companies were becoming aware of the quality and potentiality of bands in particular local areas, and when the stations concerned were giving what proved to be some of the most successful punk and post-punk era bands their first major exposure via locally recorded radio sessions.

Even among the better-served stations the feeling persists into the 1980s that the record companies' interest in ILR extends only to dispensing product ('servicing' [sic] in music industry parlance) and to encouraging *national* sales trends at local level. The industry's trade paper, *Music Week*, features airplay data gleaned from all the ILR stations not primarily as a guide to which records might see chart action but rather as a what-to-stock guide for retailers in the stations' catchment areas. Radio 1 serves the interests of the record companies much more suitably because of its national coverage and precisely targeted music policy – and it is the industry's own sales chart, compilation of which is co-financed by the BBC, that the station uses and *Music Week* reproduces.[11] (ILR's very own chart, the Network Chart, is officially ignored by the BPI.) At the heart of this is a persistent centralism on the part of the industry that can partly be explained with reference to the British industry's role within the international music market: if that role is to provide the global (and largely American-controlled) market with internationally saleable music, it follows that local sales alone are of little significance. Put baldly, they are not really worth the effort.

## The international context

The recession experienced by the music industry from the early 1970s onwards had important ramifications for radio in Britain, but again the industry's problems were global. From the mid-1960s onwards, expectations of expansion were high, because of the growth of the US album market and the stream of British acts finding success in that market in the wake of the Beatles. Britain's domestic record market was only superficially buoyant, as the sales boom referred to earlier was of limited long-term significance. Its beneficiaries were mainly the independents, whose output was generally restricted to singles that failed to make much impact on an American market at that time uninterested in singers and groups with limited teenage appeal. The recession – precipitated by the huge rise in the price of oil, which put up manufacturing costs, and exacerbated by continuing inflation and rising unemployment – accentuated a decline in both sales of records by British-owned majors (notably the giant EMI) and domestic manufacture that had been apparent since the mid-1960s; by 1982, the size of the British record market had contracted to 6 per cent of the world market from 10 per cent a decade earlier.[12]

The effects of this were twofold. First, the British market ceased to be economic: British sales could no longer sustain the level of profitability anticipated earlier in the decade, and global success for those acts signed to British-based labels (whether British-owned or divisions of US-owned companies such as RCA, CBS, WEA and the smaller but expanding Arista and A & M) therefore became a matter of survival. Second, there was a cutback in the number of acts signed and a general 'playing safe' in the kind of acts offered contracts. This left the major companies unequipped for the proliferation of punk-rock groups to come, which quickly became identified with a new wave of small-scale independent labels philosophically unconcerned with big-money sales and American success. Although welcomed by some sections of the music press, the punk boom was disastrous for the majors in that the majority of bands were simply inappropriate for export. The Sex Pistols' experience in the United States in early 1978 proved the point, but even less strident, supposedly more 'accessible' acts like Ian Dury and Elvis Costello built up no more than cult followings abroad. The transformation in fortunes for British acts in the United States that began in 1982 was due to the intense efforts of the British divisions of the US labels, who not only chose and groomed their acts carefully but built their success on a new marketing strategy comprising video films, picture discs, special release editions of singles in 12-inch format, and other promotional paraphernalia.

As Ray Hammond, Phil Hardy and other industry-watchers have pointed out, the much-heralded 'British invasion' of the American record market from 1982 onwards (spearheaded by cable music channel MTV, which established itself by using British-made video films as cheap programming) was hardly the triumph for the home music industry portrayed in the trade press.[13] However welcome the new international demand for 'home-grown' music appeared, it in fact imposed a strait-jacket on those major UK labels with American connections. In making new signings, they were obliged to apply their attention to acts with 'transnational' appeal – that is wholesome and anodyne enough for prime-time US viewing or listening – rather than the quirky talents that had characterized the late 1970s new wave. Mainstream UK pop music became Americanized, dominated by acts (Wham!, Alison Moyet, Paul Young, Phil Collins) whose chief skill was to cheerfully replicate the two most globally acceptable US styles: soul and disco. If Britain has an importance to the world music industry in the 1980s it is as a centre of cultural production, what Hardy describes as a 'talent pool', rather than as a distinct and profitable, self-sustaining market.[14]

Britain is not only a source of talent, however, but a testing ground for that talent: artists who prove their commerciality in the British market win their chance, if signed to a major, to a career launch not just in the United States but the lucrative markets of Japan, Australasia, Canada and South America. The British divisions of the transnationals are under intense pressure to deliver the right kind of acts – musically, visually and, in a sense, attitudinally – and a run of hits in Britain brings both proof of potential and the necessary credibility. (Traditionally, or at least since the American breakthrough of the Beatles in 1964, success in Britain is a sign of pedigree to the international audience.) Getting the hits is all important, and more so than ever because of the *long-term* commercial implications; hence the massive investment involved in breaking new acts (out of all proportion to the sales generated – the real money is to be made overseas), and hence the pivotal place of radio, and particularly national radio, in promotion.

## Uses and abuses of radio

The promotion process as it involves radio can be briefly sketched, but two initial points should be made. First, promotion is concentrated on *particular* releases: the number of singles released in Britain per year continually touches the 6,000 mark, of which only a proportion will be priority items, pre-sifted for special treatment. Second, the aim of promotion is only incidentally to maximize sales; the primary purpose is *to create a climate in which sales will happen*, to boost the record sufficiently to give it a momentum of its own. This means not just getting the record played on the air but getting it accepted by a radio station as part of its playlist, thereby guaranteeing it that fixed amount of exposure mentioned earlier. (Being on the playlist has a secondary value in that it may well persuade other stations to take notice: Radio 1 was notorious in the mid-1970s for adding to its playlist non-charting records which were receiving regular plays on Capital.) Responsibility for this lies with a team of pluggers, often working independently of one another, who usually cover all possible avenues by both de-livering records personally to the stations concerned *and* sending duplicate records by mail, targeting not only the playlist compilers but individual disc jockeys, programme assistants and even secretaries; casual plays in the office and word of mouth between station staff can persuade the playlist organizer(s) to go with a particular record. Working in tandem with a co-ordinated publicity campaign – press advertising, appearances on *Whistle Test* or *The Tube*, a fabricated news story for the *Sun*'s Bizarre column – the plugger capitalizes on and helps sustain a 'buzz' around a record: if interest has been sparked *before* a plugger comes to call, half his job has already been done. Mostly, however, a plugger's job description is hard to pin down: living on his wits, cultivating con-tacts and relationships, his chief skill (and it is mainly a male preserve) lies in per-suading the broadcaster not of the quality of a record or even its capacity for sales but its suitability for the audience that the broadcaster is required to serve.

One offshoot of the growing intensity of the plugging operation has been the establishment of independent plugging companies, acting on behalf of either the record labels or (more commonly) an artist's own management. Independent pluggers have long been around in some shape or form, but their growth period was the 1970s, the new demand for their services paralleling that for other independently-functioning professionals (producers, arrangers, sleeve-design specialists, management consultants) in the shift away from the centralized, imposed decision-making that characterized the recording and marketing processes of major record companies in the pre-Beatle era. The independent plugger can act as a safety net, backing up the efforts of the label's own promotion department to ensure a record is not overlooked, but increasingly in 1980s pop he takes the prominent role, the very fact of his hiring indicating a level of commitment which, as Ray Hammond says, 'adds a great deal to the climate in which a record is first heard'.[15] Independent pluggers earn more money than their record company counterparts, take more risks and are generally more respected; many take a financial stake in the success of a record (commonly 1 per cent of sales) and the top earners – such as Ferret and Spanner, Jackie Gill, and the Sunshine Plug Company – make it a point of principle to choose the acts they promote in the time-honoured manner of theatrical agents.

Additional plugging can be provided by a more traditional source, the music publishers, the larger of which have their own teams working to the same apparent end – getting airplay for particular records – but for different motives: besides raising performance revenue (assessed, collected and distributed by the Performing Right Society), airplay leads to sales which not only bring in mechanical royalties to the publisher and composer but will prompt international exposure of the song in question. (In fact, the interest of music publishers in the success of a record can be much broader, as they also act as administrative and legal advisers and in some cases either own or are owned by record companies; the point at which publishing and recording interests diverge is finely drawn.[16])

Pressure for results leads to abuses, including the passing of cocaine to producers and disc jockeys as a trade for airplay, but the extent of this is difficult to ascertain. Ray Hammond claims it to be widespread, but names no names and cites cases in only the vaguest terms; Simon Garfield, author of *Expensive Habits*, takes the opposite line, concentrating instead on the practice of 'hyping'.[17] Hyping is based on the paradoxical notion that sales of a record will only begin to pick up once it has shown itself in the chart: if a record enters the lower reaches of the chart, it will automatically come into consideration by playlist compilers as a contender for airplay. The aim of hyping is therefore to buy sufficient quantities of the single in question from those shops designated as chart return shops and thereby achieve a chart position. The practice is not new; *Melody Maker* began a much-publicized crusade against it in 1967 by cutting its own sales chart down from a Top Fifty to a Top Thirty, thereby making the cost of 'buying' a record into the chart prohibitive. But the contraction of the singles market since the mid-1970s has made such an exercise less costly to mount, as only a relatively small number of sales (around 9,000) are required to secure that all-important chart placing. Hyping can also take the form of straightforward bribery, usually the offering of gifts or straight cash payments to dealers for entering false returns, but the efficacy of both methods depends entirely on the protagonists correctly identifying the chart shops.

Two major cases in 1980, when the Managing Director of WEA was forced to resign the chairmanship of the BPI when his company's involvement in hyping was proven, and in 1981, when an RCA field rep was found to have offered a chart shop free records in return for false entries in its sales diary, highlighted the weaknesses not so much in the system of chart compilation itself (although the then-compiler, the British Market Research Bureau, lost its contract to Gallup in 1983) as in policing possible abuses. The BPI's Code of Conduct, instituted in 1981, clarified which abuses would warrant deletion of the offending record from the chart – keying in false sales; promotional offers conditional on chart placings; promotional offers involving non-related goods; and the offering of free gifts such as T-shirts to customers. However, while a small number of records are excluded each year, the reluctance of the BPI to penalize culprit companies (usually on the grounds that renegade employees were responsible) has been marked. RCA's 'penalty' for the actions of its rep was not a fine but an instruction to pay the costs (£5,000) of the BPI investigation.[18]

Hyping is likely to be a continuing feature of record promotion as long as the system of using a sample number of shops is retained. Gallup's compilation method does incorporate a number of features designed to weed out inconsistencies and anomalies in sales, but as chart manager Godfrey Rust stresses, 'the chart doesn't judge tactics, it measures sales . . . we are the returning officer in an election'.[19] Gallup's long-term plan of setting up a completely computerized nation-wide system involving the majority of record dealers (both chain stores and independent dealers) with each keying in sales as they happen, will clearly obviate altogether the effectiveness of chart hyping: the first step towards this was taken in 1987, when a computerized scheme also enabled Gallup to offer the national sales chart to the BPI and Radio 1 at an earlier point in the week (Sunday rather than Tuesday, in time for the latter's Top Forty programme). This was in itself a response to the launch of a competing chart – ILR's Network Chart, compiled by the Media Research and Information Bureau – and the claims made for it regarding faster compilation of data. More significant in the long term, though, will be the way in which this 'alternative' chart disrupts not only the potential for hyping (to hype the MRIB chart as well as the Gallup chart means double the effort and money) but a lot of marketing assumptions. For one thing, it places new promotional importance on the ILR stations who use the chart, as its incorporation of an 'airplay factor' is a *direct* reflection (rather than a secondary reflection, as sales figures are) of promotional effectiveness.[20]

## Radio as a revenue source

The music industry's attempt to withstand the worst effects of its mid-1970s recession had other manifestations, among them the rise of the video film as a promotional aid second only in importance to radio. 'Promo' videos were first produced by British record companies for convenience value – for use by television pop programmes when artists were unavailable for live appearances – but they gradually took on a life of their own with regular screenings on children's television shows like *Multi-Coloured Swap Shop* and *Tiswas*. By the early 1980s, they were not just staple ingredients of pop shows but were also being used as 'filler' items between programmes. Compilation videocassettes, meanwhile, became steady sellers in the expanding retail video market, though the massive sales reached by Michael Jackson's *Thriller* in 1982 (200,000 within a fortnight in the United Kingdom alone) were unmatched by other releases, and the market tended to bottom out thereafter. One of the most significant aspects of cable channel MTV's opening in the United States during that same year was its demand for promo videos on an unprecedented scale, which could initially be met only by the video divisions of the British record companies; many British bands benefited directly from this unforeseen exposure, and MTV rapidly established itself as a prime promotional medium in its own right, to be serviced by US labels (and, of course, those US labels promoting artists signed by their UK subsidiaries) in a similar manner to radio. The massive investment in video films (and the setting up of special video departments within US record companies) and sundry other promotional gimmicks – the picture disc, the limited-edition 12-inch single – were widely seen as signs of profligacy when in fact they were signs of panic, and again the pattern was that these techniques became standard in the United States after what was, in effect, a period of test marketing in Britain.

The new emphasis on video (or to be more precise, on cable television and its *use* of video as a means of promotional dissemination) arguably had more of a long-term impact in the United States than in Britain, where the 'cable revolution' started hesitantly and by 1986 had shown no discernible effect on record sales. Another sign of industry difficulties was the spate of mergers and takeovers that began in the late 1970s with Polygram's purchase of Decca, although the most ambitious of all planned mergers, that between Warner Communications and Polygram, was scotched after legal manoeuvres by the two corporations' chief rival, CBS. But the clearest indication of the industry's attempt to claw back revenue to its pre-recession levels was a growing exploitation of back catalogue on the part of individual companies, together with a new emphasis at corporate level on exploitation of non-retail sources of revenue. The push for the former began, ironically, not with the companies themselves but with US-based merchandisers, notably K-Tel and Arcade, who specialized in buying in mass-produced items and advertising them on television at a bargain price. Applying this principle to record marketing, they licensed familiar 'oldies' from a variety of record labels and produced cheaply packaged albums of between twenty and twenty-four tracks each. Their success had a marked effect on record retailing in that the albums in question were mostly sold in supermarkets or chain stores, thereby beginning a trend away from independent retail; and they made record companies more aware of the potential profits to be made by unearthing their vault material, whether through issuing 'greatest hits' collections under their own label, or releasing their own compilations of recent hits specifically for a television ad campaign (sometimes in conjunction with rival companies, for example EMI and WEA's *Now That's What I Call Music* series), or by licensing their back catalogue material to mailorder specialists like Reader's Digest, who entered the pop nostalgia field in a major way during 1975 with an eight-album boxed set called *Popular Music's*

*Golden Hit Parade.* It was significant that EMI, attempting to reverse the decline in company fortunes that the success of the Beatles had masked, underwent a radical restructuring under Managing Director Peter Jamieson between 1984 and 1986 involving the separation of the company into two distinct but complementary units, one dealing with merchandising and exploitation, the other with A & R and promotion.[21]

Being primarily a singles medium in Britain, radio's involvement in these particular developments was minimal, but when it came to exploitation of secondary revenue sources – effected not on a company-by-company basis but corporately, from a position of some strength – radio found itself very much at the sharp end. The revenue source in question was the payments made by radio stations to PPL for the use of records for broadcasting purposes. The right of record companies to claim control over public performance of their material (and, if necessary, to prohibit it) was established by the Cawardine case in 1933 (see Ch. 3), following which any institutions wishing to use phonographically recorded music were required to apply for a PPL licence. We have already seen how the BBC accepted this – and the principle of *payment* for music used – almost without murmur, and the Corporation issued no formal challenge to the Copyright Act of 1956, which enshrined the principle of licensing and payment in law. Section 12 of the Act laid down that copyright in sound recordings would subsist for a period of fifty years from the year in which the recording was first published, the actual fees to be negotiated between PPL and the broadcasting institution. The basic provision of the Act, that the producer of a sound recording made for domestic consumption be recompensed for its public use, was ratified internationally by Article 12 of the International Convention for the Protection of Performers, Producers of Phonograms (sound recordings) and Broadcasting Organizations, signed in Rome in 1961. Most European nations became signatories to it and much of the work of the International Federation of Phonogram and Video Industries (IFPI) has since taken in extending the convention to countries with fledgling record industries, in order to ensure protection both of that industry's output and that of the international industry in that territory. A significant absentee from the list of signatories to the Rome Convention was the United States, where the relationship between the radio and record industries had become so intertwined that its ratification was actively opposed by both sides.[22]

For as long as the BBC retained its commitment to the employment of musicians and used records sparingly, payment to PPL was not a contentious issue: more limiting in the long term was the agreement on 'needle-time', that is restricting usage of records to a certain number of hours per week. This agreement was enforced by PPL under pressure from the Musicians Union, whose prime objective was to ensure that the BBC continued to employ its members in large numbers and did not start to use records as a substitute for live music. By the 1960s, marked increases in record sales and competition from pirate radio stations led to a new bullishness on the BBC's part in its negotiations with PPL and the MU; when Radio 1 was set up, it benefited from a slight increase in needle-time but incurred a compensatory increase in the BBC's annual payments to PPL, which were calculated on a three-yearly basis. From 1967 onwards, the BBC networks as a whole negotiated a steady rise in needle-time allocation with parallel rises in fees, and a big jump in both occurred during 1973, when Radios 1 and 2 sought similar treatment to that PPL was about to accord their coming competitor, ILR. An agreement in 1982 finally enabled Radio 1 to end its programme-sharing arrangement with Radio 2 altogether and broadcast for a total of 18 hours a day: BBC radio was granted an extra 30 hours across the networks, half of which went to Radio 1, at a total cost of £15.1 million over the three and a half years covered by the agreement.

Despite the frequent public complaints of BBC personnel, the BBC's general attitude to PPL and the MU has been accommodating. PPL's right to protect and exploit the copyright of its affiliates and that of the MU to protect its members' employment are accepted, and negotiations centre mainly on the *level* of remuneration and the amount of needle-time granted. Of these two issues, the latter is of most contention, although Johnny Beerling insists that Radio 1 would still record sessions by bands and seek out unknown, unsigned acts for its programmes even if no restrictions existed: the station would risk losing its credibility among a knowledgable, streetwise audience (especially in the evening) if it played nothing but record-company product. The only real hindrance that needle-time imposes is on Beerling's long-term plans (inherited from Derek Chinnery) to turn Radio 1 into a 24-hour station.

Locally, however, the needle-time problem is acute, despite the many ingenious attempts to overcome it. Allocated only two hours of needle-time (i.e. use of recorded material originating from PPL member companies) per day, BBC local stations are left at a considerable disadvantage to their senior network and ILR competitors. (It should be emphasized, however, that this allocation reflects BBC rather than PPL priorities; more hours could be allocated, but only at a cost to the main networks.) To make up the shortfall in music, BBC local stations rely heavily on the BBC's own bought-in library of music, the 'Radio-play' catalogue, which mostly comprises American-made recordings (often by well known artists) never intended for commercial release. These can be played free of charge and without restriction, as can UK- or US-recorded material issued on those European labels which have no PPL or IFPI association: most 'oldies' heard on BBC local radio are not the original UK releases but reissues of the same recording on German or Dutch compilation albums. Inevitably, much of what is played on BBC local radio is what in ILR or network radio would be regarded as second-choice material, though the restrictions occasionally make for interesting, not to say innovative, radio: Charlie Gillett's influential *Honky Tonk* programme on BBC Radio London from 1972 to 1979, mentioned in Chapter 4, would have been impossible to mount had the programme been excessively reliant on PPL material – a high proportion of the music played originated on specialist American labels or from specially recorded studio sessions.

If BBC radio's relationship with PPL over the years has been largely amicable, or at least non-confrontational, the same cannot be said of that between ILR and PPL. The major source of conflict here has been the agreement on needle-time and performance fees negotiated by the IBA on the ILR stations' behalf in 1972, before any ILR stations had begun operating. Because the general feeling within the music industry was that ILR was a potentially important new avenue for promotion, PPL granted the ILR stations a bigger share of needle-time than that currently enjoyed by BBC radio. The main terms of the agreement were that needle-time would be limited to 50 per cent of air-time or a maximum of 9 hours per day (to be averaged out over a 12-month period), at a cost to each station of 3 per cent of net advertising revenue rising to 7 per cent once the station had been operating for five years.[23] The ILR stations were not prepared to view the agreement so favourably, however, and sought to renegotiate it (through the AIRC) as soon as the agreement expired in October 1978. By that time, the changing climate within the music industry and disappointment over ILR's performance had combined to harden the PPL attitude against further concessions. When renegotiation began, the AIRC was actively seeking to reduce its payments to PPL while PPL was intent on increasing them. PPL's position was ostensibly based on the need to cover rising administrative costs and keep up with inflation, but an underlying factor was clearly the drop in retail sales and the consequent need to find revenue elsewhere; the ILR stations, meanwhile, against a backcloth of static advertising revenue and patchy profits, built their case on the fundamental question of the value of airplay – if the radio stations were, in effect, advertising records for free, to demand financial remuneration was unfair and penalizing.

When negotiations broke down, the AIRC took PPL to the Performing Right Tribunal (as was their right under the 1956 Copyright Act) to argue this point, but the PRT upheld the new rates demanded by PPL and imposed a new sliding scale of charges: 4 per cent of the first £750,000 net advertising revenue attracted by each station, 6 per cent of the next £750,000, 8 per cent of the next £1.5 million and 10 per cent of any remainder.[24] The AIRC's response was to put the matter before the High Court, where Justice Falconer upheld the original IBA/PPL agreement and required the PRT to state a case; after much delay, the PRT's defence of its decision was published in September 1983 and the AIRC immediately reapplied for a further High Court hearing to seek 'clarification' of certain matters. Heard in June 1984, the result of the case was not delivered until the following year, when the High Court appeared to accept an AIRC point of law that the PRT should not have considered as relevant PPL's distribution of monies to musicians and performers. By late 1986, when the PRT reported back once more, the apparently interminable tribunal and court proceedings were calculated to have cost approaching £1 million in legal fees. Under the PRT's new ruling, the ILR stations would have to pay PPL 4 per cent on the first £650,000 of net advertising revenue – indexed up from 1979 prices to £1.2 million in 1986 – and 7 per cent thereafter.[25] The question of whether the scales should be backdated was left open to further negotiation: if they were, a large station such as Capital could expect to reduce its costs by up to £300,000 per year, while other medium-to-large stations would have to pay as much as £100,000 more. PPL's reaction to the ruling was very favourable, although a report in *Broadcast* calculated that its yearly receipts could decrease by as much as £200,000. As PPL's General Manager, John Love, told the magazine, 'Overall, it's a victory for us, because it continues the principle that the rates paid by radio be substantial, not nominal, reflecting that records are a substantial part of programming'. The AIRC subsequently shifted its attack to the copyright laws themselves, lobbying for amendments to the Copyright, Patents and Designs Bill (introduced to Parliament in late 1987). These amendments, if accepted, would establish the record companies' right to 'equitable remuneration' for radio use of records while prohibiting them from restricting needle-time, and also remove copyright protection in the United Kingdom from recordings made in countries that are not signatories of the Rome Convention.

The point at issue is whether the value of airplay to the record companies out-weighs the value of the use of PPL material to the broadcasting companies, though there are complicating factors. PPL is a collectively owned organization, working on behalf of the music industry and not representing the interests of individual record companies; thus it argues that, while airplay may promote sales of *particular* discs or tapes to the benefit of *individual* companies, it in no way expands and in fact may substantially limit the total market for records. Against this, as radio stations frequently point out, there is no direct evidence of airplay actively harming sales; in 1984, when record sales in Britain increased by 14 per cent on the previous year, there were more radio stations operating than ever before. PPL's own argument is undermined by the sheer intensity of its members' promotional activities.[26] But there are inconsistencies on both sides: programme controllers claim a lack of interest in sales patterns and insist they play only those records which match their station's requirements, while at the same time stressing the promotional value of the plugs they give record company products. Clearly John Love is quite correct in saying that 'in our sound recordings we control the biggest single source of programme material for radio stations, and almost without exception that which produces the biggest audiences'; as stated at the outset of this chapter, records constitute a cheap form of programming compared to news coverage, drama and live music, none of which are as cost-effective in audience-gathering terms. And again, PPL not only acts on the record companies' behalf but in conjunction with the MU, who are the main force behind the needle-time restrictions and the enforcement of the obligation on ILR stations (enshrined in the IBA Act) to set aside 3 per cent of their net advertising revenue for the employment of musicians. Although John Morton, General Secretary of the MU, insists that 'money from records is only of secondary importance, our primary objective is that records should not remove live music',[27] the sums involved are not small: 20 per cent of PPL revenue is dis-tributed to the artists named on record labels and contracted to PPL member companies, and a further 12.5 per cent is distributed (through the MU) to the unnamed musicians who play on sessions and backing tracks, in recognition of their general contribution to the recording process.[28]

## Independents' day?

Although the music industry is constantly seeking to raise revenue from all sources, the importance of PPL revenue can be overstated, especially when one considers that nearly a third of the annual total goes to musicians and performers, and a further, albeit much smaller, proportion is absorbed in administrative costs. When PPL revenue is broken down company by company, the sums involved seem almost insignificant, but the total revenue distributed by PPL during 1985–6 – around £11 million – is best viewed alongside the overall profit (around £40 million according to BPI figures) made by the British industry from retail sales during that year.[29] Compared to several years in the 1970s and the early 1980s when the British music industry was not even in a profit situation, 1985–6 was a healthy year, but the obvious point is that revenue from secondary sources becomes most important at times of low profitability. On a more general level, the trend in the home industry and abroad in the 1980s is emphatically towards greater exploitation of rights and ownership. One of the clearest examples of this in recent years was the unilateral decision taken by the BPI to begin charging television companies for the use of promotional video films during 1986. A collection agency, Video Performances Limited (VPL), was set up on the PPL model to act on the BPI's behalf, and interestingly it was again the BBC which proved more co-operative than the commercial sector, agreeing to the principle of payment almost instantly while the makers of Channel 4's *The Tube* and *The Chart Show* simply refused to pay. The offending programmes were denied access to new promo films by the record companies (though there was some well-publicized dissent within the BPI ranks) and within months the principle of payment for use was universally, if begrudgingly, accepted within television. As with radio, the argument was that if a high-expense commercial product was to be used as a key part of broadcast entertainment – as a means of attracting an audience for a separate commercial enterprise – then the makers of that product deserved adequate remuneration for their efforts. For the BPI, it was particularly important to establish that principle while cable television, a likely user of video promos as a cheap substitute for self-originated programming, was still in its infancy in Britain.[30]

Another strategy of indirect bearing on radio is the seeking of compensation for the practice of 'home taping': the BPI claimed in 1986 that its own research indicated 'that more than six times as much music was acquired by copying than by legitimate purchase'.[31] The BPI's case was that not only were radio listeners taping records off the air rather than buying them, they were actually encouraged to do so because of the high quality of VHF stereo broadcasts. The radio stations have remained generally neutral on this issue, claiming it is outside their jurisdiction and that, because they are already paying for broadcast usage of records, they should be subject to no further penalties. In fact, the AIRC backed the BPI's demand for a levy on blank tapes in the hope that this would deflect demands for increased revenue from them. (The government's Green Paper on Copyright, published in 1981, had suggested that record companies seek extra revenue from broadcasting institutions rather than via a tape levy.[32]) In reality, the introduction of a tape levy would do no such thing: PPL's official stance is that a levy would be 'not compensation for anything but merely the recognition of a new usage right'.[33] What is clear is that the industry's renewed search for revenue is a multi-pronged assault, and that even general improvements in the level of record sales world-wide are unlikely to offset what has already been set in motion. The mid-1970s recession simply drew attention to ways and means of increasing efficiency, while technological change since that time – the advent of satellite and cable, portable transmitters, synthesizers, do-it-yourself mixing, compact discs and the inexorable trend away from vinyl records to cassette tapes – has had the twin effect of making music more accessible to all and of threatening the industry's ability to make money out of it. Exploiting copyright ownership, on a national and international scale, is one route out of this difficulty.

In challenging what I earlier referred to as the music industry's 'corporate grip' on radio, the stations lack a united voice. The BBC is cushioned, financially, from the worst effects of the industry's quest for secondary revenue because of the relative stability of its income. ILR, however, continues to feel the squeeze on its own profitability quite acutely: together with enforced expenditure on music-making and payments to the Performing Right Society – the AIRC has been in dispute with the PRS for as long as it has been with PPL, but the Performing Right Tribunal will not hear the case until the PPL matter has been fully settled – even a profitable station's music bill commonly accounts for over 10 per cent of the station's annual turnover. Out of Swansea Sound's turnover of £800,000 in 1985, for example, £100,000 was spent on music fees alone;[34] Tony Hale of Capital calculates that his station pays approximately £50 per 3.5-minute single every time it is played. While the AIRC has adopted a bullish and very public posture on the copyright and needle-time questions, the very fact that it and the BBC negotiate with PPL and the PRS separately is divisive. The suspicion lingers that BBC radio is favourably treated by PPL precisely because Radio 1 (and even Radio 2, which also uses up most of its needle-time quota during the peak daytime hours) has a greater promotional value to the record companies than ILR.

Whether under the BBC or ILR umbrella, however, radio stations in Britain have no alternative to dealing with PPL, other than dropping commercially recorded music altogether. Johnny Beerling of Radio 1 would like to see PPL concede the value of airplay by allowing free (or at least unrestricted) use of new releases during their first two to three weeks of availability, and negotiation on specific points such as this would seem to have more long-term prospect of success than any campaign to influence the shape of the Copyright Bill that the AIRC may mount. Any suggestion that stations should cut back on their use of records *per se* can be countered by reference to the late 1970s, when the amount of music on ILR fell, at the behest of the IBA, from 51 to 46 per cent of air-time and contributed to (or at the very least corresponded with) a steady decline in audience figures.[35] Replacing records with pre-recorded session music is another impractical option, because of the expense that would be incurred, though Piccadilly, Radio Hallam and several other ILR stations do include selected session recordings during daytime shows. Stations can and do circumvent the restrictions by playing PPL material but logging (on the sheets that go back to PPL) non-PPL recordings, but there are obvious risks to this: both PPL and the

PRS monitor BBC network output religiously and regularly sample, often without warning, the output of both BBC local and ILR stations. In one memorable case, BBC Radio Merseyside were challenged by PPL for under-logging their records by 73 per cent.[36]

Is it possible for radio stations to cut down on playing records issued by PPL labels, bearing in mind that a station like BBC Radio York has proved it is perfectly possible to build a successful music policy on just two hours needle-time per day? York, however, is an example of a BBC station explicitly geared to an older (35+) audience, which can afford not to concentrate too heavily on topical music: it plays a carefully selected mixture of mainly oldies (around 60 per cent of its music) and Radioplay, mostly restricting its PPL allocation to just a sprinkling from the Top Forty.[37] ILR stations have no access to Radioplay and run the risk of alienating a younger audience if they play too many former hits, though those stations which run a 24-hour service do tend to play library music (imported records of bland orchestral and instrumental music, the kind that used to accompany the test card on daytime television) during the sparsely patronized night-time hours.

It is nevertheless generally true that records released on non-PPL labels are at least likely to receive *consideration* for airplay over those on PPL labels, and this has interesting implications. Such releases appear mainly on independent labels, of which there has been a proliferation in Britain since the punk-rock associated upheaval in the economics of record-making that occurred in the late 1970s. These labels were launched as outlets for the recordings of bands who, in keeping with the punk philosophy, preferred not to deal with the major companies; most were local, small-scale, shoestring affairs run by enthusiasts, and most limited their initial production run to anything between 1,000 and 25,000 copies, which would be sold at the band's concerts or by local record dealers. The expansion in independent record-making prompted a dealer in West London, Geoff Travis of Rough Trade, to start his own mail-order service for the distribution of what was termed 'alternative' product. For the committed rock fan, such discs were the only credible source of punk and new-wave music, while the bands' management found that a place on Rough Trade's independent chart (initiated in late 1977) was an invaluable indication of their potential to any major label thinking of signing them. In the early 1980s, attempts were made to form an 'alternative' BPI in the form of the Independent Phonographic Industry, and the possibility existed that it might set up its own collection agency and offer its members' releases to BBC radio and ILR at a much cheaper rate than PPL.[38] It was a common dilemma for anyone starting an independent label whether to exploit the likelihood of greater airplay by not affiliating with PPL, or to join PPL and be guaranteed at least some level of annual revenue. That the majority of independents have chosen the latter course is indicative of the increasing incorporation of the independent sector into the mainstream industry, further evidence of which was the inclusion of representatives from the independents on the board of the BPI during 1985. Another deciding factor against non-affiliation was likely to be the attitude of the Musicians Union, which requires any commercial recording company of whatever size to sign an agreement stipulating that broadcasting use of its records will be controlled either by PPL or by the MU itself. For the long-term profitability of a company, therefore, membership of PPL is clearly in its best interests if it is to avoid dispute with the MU.

In practice, records released by the independents have tended to be regarded as too 'disruptive' (in the sense of unsettlingly unconventional) for daytime radio use and, though individual local stations have been known to give some backing to releases by independents in their locality, independents still face the problem of getting national airplay in an overcrowded and fiercely competitive promotional environment dominated by the major companies. Until its closure in late 1984, the Independent Labels Association was perhaps the single most important factor in securing airplay for independent product, as Andrew Clifton of New Leaf Records in Peterborough recalls:

> We signed to the ILA in December 1982 for £50, for which it distributed a hundred copies each of three of our singles to Radios 1 and 2, all the ILR stations, and even KNAC, Los Angeles. They followed up on airplay details, about which we could phone in and enquire each Tuesday for six weeks per record, and published an airplay chart in *Music Week*. It threw up some interesting results – one guitar-based pop band received the majority of its plays on Scottish stations whereas our heavy rock group was played far more in the north of England, especially the north-east. Hereward, our local station, rarely figured in the list. Unfortunately, smaller independent record companies like ourselves were often unable to capitalise on this regional airplay in time. Distributors used to play safe by saying 'we'll see what airplay you get on your ILA mail-out before we decide whether to distribute you'. Once they had decided and all the necessary arrangements had been made, the six weeks of ILA help were just about over. For the likes of us the ILA was an excellent idea and is missed.[39]

Since the punk era, independent releases have found a niche in the John Peel-style evening rock shows broadcast by most ILR stations, and it is in these types of programmes that New Leaf continues to enjoy the most coverage. The actual sales generated may be minimal, but such airplay serves to spread the word about a particular group, perhaps attract some press follow-up, and possibly alert the A & R head of a major record company to the group's potential.

What constitutes 'independent' or 'alternative' music cannot really be assessed in generic terms; traditionally, it has less to do with particular, established styles of rock than a certain attitude of mind, as if actually signing with an independent label is a statement of deliberate isolation from the mainstream. More usually in the 1980s, recording for an independent is an act of simple pragmatism, though radio's isolation of independent product to the evening and late-night hours serves to perpetuate the old mystique. But it is also during these evening hours that radio comes into its own and in some senses leads where the industry – and even the independents – may be loath to follow, that is in recording local bands (either in their own studios or at live gigs) and playing their efforts on air. In this, radio performs a surrogate A & R service from which a record company may well eventually benefit.

The advent of community radio (see Ch. 9) may be to the benefit of independent record companies, though one can only speculate on this point. The official PPL stance is that community stations will not be treated any differently from BBC or ILR stations on the question of fees and needle-time, and this may encourage new stations to give preferential airtime to records on labels which remain non-affiliated to PPL. There is a likelihood, too, of some ideological common ground – the rationale for the existence of each is that they kick against the mainstream – between the independent labels and the community stations. The PPL position nevertheless reflects an industry-wide suspicion (which is shared internationally) not only of new broadcasting developments but of new technology as a whole, a suspicion built on fear of losing control of its products and its markets. The attitude of the music industry as represented by the BPI, PPL and IFPI on such issues as home taping, needle-time and copyright (not to mention the introduction of digital audio tape) may seem simply reactionary, but the protectionist actions taken by the industry represent only one aspect of its attempts to adapt to quite fundamental changes in the state of the technology, in patterns of leisure, and in the domestic and world market for music. The key weapon in that attempt is a switch in emphasis from direct sales to the public to generating income through exploitation of ownership. As Simon Frith has suggested, 'for the music industry the age of manufacture is now over. Companies (and company profits) are no longer organised around making *things* but depend on the creation of *rights*'.[40] For music radio, the long-term implications are profound: not only will the promotional importance of radio in-evitably decline as the importance of selling to the public itself declines, the bal-ance in its relationship with the music manufacturers will alter irrevocably. Small wonder, then, that the focus of argument is shifting away from quarrels over needle-time and the size of payments to a questioning, on the radio industry's part, of the whole legal basis on which PPL stake their claims. One senses, looking ahead to the 1990s, that the battle lines are about to be drawn as never before.

# 7 Keepers of the castle: producers, programmers and music selection

I don't mind when people say we play wallpaper music. A lot of people spend a lot of time and money choosing the right wallpaper for their homes.

Bob Snyder, former Programme Controller, Radio Trent[1]

In earlier chapters I have touched upon the general principles guiding the use and selection of popular music by radio stations in Britain: the tendency to concentrate on the most musically familiar, the unwillingness to deviate from a selection of records based on chart placings or potential chart placings, the isolation of non-mainstream music to peripheral programmes outside the peak-time hours, the preference shown for commercially produced records over live or specially recorded music during those peak hours. These tendencies need to be examined more closely in the context of the decisions taken by those who, to use sociological terminology, are the 'gatekeepers' of radio: the programme controllers and programme producers who oversee not only what is played on the radio but the environment in which it is heard, the frequency of its playing and its positioning within programmes. They, far more than presenters, are the source of power in music radio, but the intention here and in the next chapter is not simply to equate their apparent control of radio output with a necessarily major influence over the fate of record-industry product, nor is it to pin 'responsibility' on them for the blandness and predictability of so much music programming. Rather, it is to explore how gatekeepers both represent and patrol the twin ideologies of consensus and consumer sovereignty, and to assess the end result – a pattern of programming and a style of presentation which, during the daytime hours at least, uses popular music as a barrier against tension, conflict and disruption.

First of all, we must clarify what 'gatekeeping' entails. Gatekeepers, of course, can be found in all media, and the source of the concept (and the term) is David Manning White's study of editorial practices in mid-west newspapers, *The Gatekeeper: A Case Study in the Selection of News*. White found that editors chose which stories to follow up, which to headline and which to relegate to shorter items, according to a number of different criteria: the particular editorial line (political and otherwise) of the newspaper concerned, whether the story had a local angle, qualities of 'human interest' and so on. Media gatekeepers, in White's analysis, determine not only what is mediated by technological means but the *manner*, the nuances of its communication. Later research work has concentrated on exploring the value systems and organizational constraints under which gatekeepers work, and how these are communicated and reinforced down a chain of command. Certain researchers, for example, have paid particular regard to the inculcation of notions of professionalism from seniors to juniors (most obviously, editors to reporters) and the maintenance of an editorial line – an encapsulation of a certain ideology – not so much through direct enforcement or threats of the sack as through encouraging a kind of notional independence based on self-censorship, the skill of *knowing* without having to be told which stories are acceptable and which are not.[2] This is all relevant to understanding the 'editorial' practices of music radio, because programme producers, too, are continually called upon to put their own tastes and preferences behind them in favour of a professional assessment of which music will most fit the editorial profile of their station. However, the fact that the radio gatekeeper is dependent on a commercial source – the record manufacturers – for much of his material complicates the issue, as he then becomes a mediator in their marketing strategies as well as an enactor of his own. The radio gatekeeper may appear to mediate between manufacturer and consumer, in the same way that record reviewers in newspapers do, but his *responsibilities* ultimately lie elsewhere. Radio gatekeepers have a responsibility to the public only in the vaguest sense: their primary concern is to serve the *particular* publics that the stations' managers or owners have delineated.

Precisely who, then, are the gatekeepers who make the decisions as to which music is played on British radio, and how has their role evolved? In the case of Radio 1 and Radio 2, the responsibility for music selection lies with individual programme producers, though in the former case the producer draws on a playlist predetermined by committee; within ILR, the responsibility generally lies with a single person, usually the station's programme controller or a specially appointed head of music. Differences in personnel levels mainly reflect different economies of scale, but they also reflect different traditions and priorities. For one thing, there is a strong bureaucratic tradition within the BBC which ILR stations, because of the perpetual concentration on commercial returns and cost-effective, self-sufficient operation, have largely avoided emulating. Also, the commercial imperative in ILR is to maintain a consistent musical identity throughout the prime-time hours; the emphasis is on continuity, flow, a consistent voice, to encourage listeners to stay tuned. That kind of consistency can be threatened when presenters either indulge their own musical tastes or play the same record too often, so there is a particular need in ILR for music formats to be both predetermined and policed by an individual who has the complete day-to-day output of the station in mind. Radios 1 and 2 have tended to be much 'freer' in comparison, the key difference being that, despite the sequential nature of much of their output, both networks were run until late 1987 (when policy changes, discussed later in this chapter, were introduced) as collections of connected but individually executed programmes. In traditional BBC thinking, separate programme production is a sign of quality and attention to detail, a mark of professionalism; as Johnny Beerling says, 'the most successful thing you could do on the surface of it is just play Top Forty music all day with disc jockeys like Tony Blackburn and put the thing on a format and just rotate it. We don't do that by any means. I think we try to treat the audience intelligently'.[3] Most important of all, Radios 1 and 2, unlike ILR stations, see themselves as personality stations first and foremost, their success hinging on the appeal of the disc jockeys. Producers act as stage managers to the presenters and may even choose records on the basis of whether they are 'right' for that presenter's public image. In local radio, with a few exceptions, presenters have a much more low-key role and their personalities are generally (and quite deliberately) subservient to the image of the station.

Given all this, the music choices made by gatekeepers in both national and local, BBC and commercial radio nevertheless follow a remarkably similar pattern, which self-imitation and continual aping of competitors cannot alone explain. That they share similar perceptions, a similar sense of professionalism, even a common ideology, is obvious, and I have already commented on the mobility of labour between the two systems and the degree to which ILR stations deliberately drew on BBC experience in fashioning their music policies. Historically, musical gatekeeping in British radio has been paternalistically motivated, and the legacy of this lives on.

## Producers and programming

We have already seen how the gatekeeper role evolved at the BBC with particular reference to popular music, initially through dance-band leaders who learnt the degree of acceptability of certain songs or types of music by trial and error, then via the BBC's two directors of dance music, Jack Payne and Henry Hall, who sought to lead by example. Although directly responsible to senior management for the decisions they made, both men were to some extent their own masters, interpreting a vague brief to provide tasteful, acceptable dance music in a manner calculated not to incur the displeasure of their employers – operating what was in effect a kind of self-censorship, creating music that not only matched the BBC perception of popular music as light, relaxing and 'domestic' but helped institutionalize it. Beginning in the war years, the gatekeeping function became more diffuse, less open to individualistic interpretation, as policy-making came under the jurisdiction of committees and producers assumed an almost clerical role, continually referring back any songs or records thought likely to be contentious. Out of the ensuing bureaucracy grew the two centres of popular music output, the Gramophone Department and the Popular Music Department, and a dual supply system that only outlived its usefulness once Radios 1 and 2 started and the need for programmes with a consistent network identity was established. Radio 1 in particular was not just a departure in programming terms but also in administration, as the producer's prime accountabilities shifted from supply departments to the network itself, thereby facilitating the development of a Radio 1 'house style' in presentation and a corporate policy on music selection. That policy has changed in ways both subtle and obvious over the years, but a certain Radio 1 'ideology' has been maintained throughout, to which the attitudes and working practices of its present-day gatekeepers – the network management team and, most crucially, the producers who report to them – give clues.

As Light Programme offshoots, both Radios 1 and 2 retain the vestiges of Light Programme values. Like its parent network, Radio 1 categorizes popular music as *either* easy-listening background music *or* as a culturally valid, quasi-classical music requiring isolation to the periphery of the schedules, both in deference to its assumed superiority to standard pop fare and to prevent it disrupting mainstream programming. (That the Radio 1 version of background music is different from Radio 2's interpretation of it is simply a factor of the former's dependence, for reasons we shall examine, on the record sales chart as a source of material.) The pervasiveness of Light Programme values – its populism, its domestic ambience, its commitment to the entertainment ethic – can be attributed to two factors in particular, both to do with the personnel involved. First, there has been a continuity at management level: Radio 1 has been successively headed by Robin Scott, Derek Chinnery and Johnny Beerling, all of them Light Programme trained and the latter two with technical backgrounds, having come to the BBC after service in the armed forces as technical operators. One of the most telling features of BBC radio's pre-1967 popular music output was that it was trusted to those on the technical rather than editorial side of BBC operations, in contrast to the academic editorial bias among producers on the Third Programme. A Third Programme producer, because of his 'cultural' responsibilities, was recruited on the basis of his musical know-how; Light Programme producers on the other hand might well have been musically literate (several during the 1950s and 1960s were ex-musicians with dance-bands), but they were primarily recruited on the basis of their technical expertise, administrative ability and/or their experience in radio overseas. Both the British Forces Broadcasting Service (BFBS) and the radio services of the old Commonwealth were regarded as good training grounds. While the criteria for recruiting producers have changed in the twenty years since the 1967 upheaval, the internal management structure of the two networks remains much as it was in the Light Programme days, with the respective Controllers presiding over a two-tier hierarchy of executive producers and programme producers.

The other key to Radio 1's maintenance of essentially populist values lies in the general area of producer professionalism – the way in which programme producers, working to those in executive positions, absorb and replicate those values in their daily decision-making. A good starting-point here is to develop the parallel made earlier between the selection of records for broadcasting and the selection of news items for dissemination: the process of selection in both cases calls upon the producer/journalist to exercise judgement on questions of priority, topicality and audience interest. *Professional* judgement overrides personal taste or personal politics: in newspapers, for instance, news value may be determined by requirements for sensationalism, beating the opposition in a circulation war, a certain political line, an internationalism or parochialism in outlook, the consumer orientation of the readership. Likewise in music radio, professional judgement on the acceptability of certain records to the audience overrides personal likes or dislikes, and 'entertainment value' will be similarly evaluated according to questions of how the records match the tone and ambience of the station. As John Downing writes in *The Media Machine*, 'ingraining a definition of professional excellence is the only effective mechanism for ensuring the *spontaneous* [his italics] production of acceptable items';[4] in other words, the process of selecting or discarding items, prioritizing some and underplaying others, becomes internalized to the point that no reference back to one's superiors is necessary – the house style, the editorial policy, is absorbed and justified by the individual on professional grounds. On a practical level, the news journalist is continually faced by a number of control mechanisms that have some parallels in radio: recruitment itself, whereby potential staff are judged by their past work according to how well they fit in with the editorial posture of the newspaper; short-term contracts, the insecurity engendered by which fosters a spirit of acquiescence rather than challenge; subordination of individual style to that of a house style; and of course the submission of work to editors or sub-editors.

In television and radio news there is the additional requirement, set down in the BBC Charter and the IBA Act, to 'balance' every item: the news reporter or newsreader is, in theory, a passive relater of events, neutral in his opinions and impartial in his coverage. That the notion of 'neutrality' is disingenuous probably needs little elaboration here, as there is plenty of empirical evidence to suggest that impartiality becomes synonymous with an insidious *partiality* for the notion of political 'moderation', but it is important to record that journalistic professionalism within the BBC, ITN and IRN is equated with an adherence to the neutrality ethic. And as in journalism, so in other editorial broadcasting matters: nowhere does the concept of professional neutrality – of acting as what Simon Frith calls an 'honest broker' between the record industry and the radio audience[5] – die harder than in the corridors of Radio 1's Egton House. Radio 1 depends so heavily on the sales chart – and invests a considerable sum in its compilation – because the chart is itself supposedly a neutral, dispassionate, accurate record of currently popular preferences.

**Picking the playlist**

BBC radio producers are co-ordinators and administrators, taking responsibility for budgeting, for mediating between presenters and management, for compiling PRS and PPL logging sheets, for ensuring that the programme meets the required technical standards, and for the auditioning and hiring of bands for studio sessions. Most of all, however, producers have a degree of editorial control over output that the BBC tends to publicly underplay:

It's BBC policy generally that if you employ a freelance [a presenter] whose interest is in exploiting his own talent, he is not and shouldn't need to be concerned with BBC policies. In the case of someone like Mike Read who rolls on day after day, he knows the content is going to be largely Top 40 and he's very happy to leave it to a producer to choose the running order or to listen to the hundred or so singles released during a week. The job of sifting and sorting, deciding what is good entertainment value for our market, is something the producers do. Someone has to take the responsibility.

Derek Chinnery[6]

The key phrases here are 'responsibility' and 'deciding what is good entertain-ment value for our market' (*sic*): professionalism and the sustainment of the BBC's ideology of public service (which, since the war, has meant serving up what the public is assumed to want, not what Reith and his colleagues once deemed it to be in need of) go hand in hand. Yet in seeking to define what consti-tutes 'good entertainment value' in popular music, BBC producers tend to absolve themselves of responsibility by taking the Top Forty chart as their frame of reference: the thinking is that the chart is a reflection of what people are buy-ing, therefore of what is most currently popular, therefore it is the function of a radio station with a brief to *be* popular and provide an up-to-date, pop-based service to take heed of what the chart indicates. Just as a news reporter claims to do no more than report facts, so a music radio producer claims to do no more than reflect public taste.

Many writers have pointed up the circularity of this argument, that a record is only likely to reach the sales chart after it is heard on Radio 1; frequently, the station is only playing those records that its own producers have *pre-selected* as potential chart hits, so the Top Forty is to a great extent self-fulfilling. Radio 1's own spokespeople continually contradict themselves when explaining the importance of a Top-Forty-based music policy. This is Chinnery again:

We're a popular service. Why do people listen? They want to hear their favourite music and that is represented by the charts, the one yardstick you have of the popularity of the material. . . . Those listeners who don't buy records don't know what they want to listen to until they hear it; the fact that enough people buy a record to put it into the chart, that makes it even more important that Radio 1 plays it. By playing it you are increasing its familiarity and hopefully its popularity, and people will grow to recognise it.[7]

What this amounts to is a belief in consumer sovereignty – a doctrine that of course has its own pitfalls, as consumers can only make preferences as to one product over another on the basis not only of what is available but what is pro-moted as *being* available. The choice of what to promote rests with the producers and the Radio 1 playlist is a weekly expression of their gatekeeping role.

Playlisting has a curious history at Radio 1. It was originally introduced in 1973, in anticipation of the launch of ILR, when it became clear that producers were being *too* selective in what they played from the Top Forty chart, to the point that certain chart discs were being heard too infrequently during the peak daytime hours. The playlist was brought in as a means of encouraging a uniform station identity and of ensuring that 'people who switched on at random knew exactly what sort of music they were going to hear, that is some of the top ten hits of the day at some time within the coming hour' (Derek Chinnery[8]). The playlist was limited to fifty records, three of which would be played in any half-hour, the remaining discs being the producer's own choices of either new releases or oldies; the list was arrived at in 'democratic' fashion, with producers recommending particular new releases and stating their case in open discussion at a weekly playlist meeting headed by executive producer Doreen Davies.[9] It gave Radio 1 a more cohesive sound while formalizing the station's dependence on the Top Forty, and what was remarkable about the decision to drop the list in 1979 was that it had actually become unnecessary; producers were automatically making their choices from the stance of an unstated yet assimilated corporate policy, though a number of guidelines remained, including the amount of times that the Number 1 record could be played in a week (twenty). Although portrayed in the press as a move that would give producers and presenters greater freedom of choice, it made only a marginal difference – as both Chinnery and his successor, Johnny Beerling, later admitted – to what was played. Ironically, Beerling's decision to reintroduce the playlist during 1986 was actually to *encourage* a greater diversity in Radio 1 music rather than restrict it further, the feeling being that Radio 1's sound had once again become too narrow for a national, well-patronized station. Whereas in 1973 the playlist had been introduced to ensure that the biggest selling records were regularly played, the new playlist system was mounted to prevent the *over*playing of the biggest selling records. The playlist came back after an informal series of meetings, designed to give an opportunity for evening show presenters and producers to suggest records for daytime play by marginally more left-field artists and groups, failed to achieve the desired result.[10] A formal system at least ensured that a record recommended in this way would receive a number of set plays rather than anything from one to twenty plays willy-nilly.

Radio 1's new, revised version of the playlist consisted initially of a 'front page' of fifty records guaranteed at least a dozen plays per week, comprising in the main the Top Forty 'climbers' and non-movers, a few singles 'bubbling under' the chart and likely to enter it in time, and selected new releases. In late 1987, following the appointment of Roger Lewis to the new post of Head of Music, this was modified to an 'A' list of forty priority records (grouped in fives and rotated in 30-minute blocks) and a 'B' list of twenty records played with less frequency.[11] In the United States, where playlist broadcasting was first introduced, playlists are traditionally very narrow, even at demographically defined 'specialist' stations (country music or Latin music stations in urban areas, for example), because of the intensity of the competition: the theory is that listeners will automatically switch stations once they hear a record they dislike, and that narrowing down the list of records to be played to apparent popular favourites (i.e. those that are currently selling well) limits this likelihood. By comparison, the Radio 1 playlist is bigger and broader, partly because the switch-over factor is not so important – listener loyalty to radio stations is continually highlighted in both BBC and IBA research – and partly because people listen for longer, often tuning in to complete programmes at a stretch. But the broadness is to some extent illusory, as it does not necessarily extend to any great catholicism in music selection; at its worst, a playlist of the size operated by Radio 1 may simply result in much more of the same mixture. Everything depends, inevitably, on the input of the producers who compile the playlist (and it is compiled 'fairly democratically', in Beerling's words, by a committee of producers), and one of the early problems facing Beerling's much-publicized updating of the station in 1985–6 was that the process of inculcating Radio 1 values into the practices and thinking of its producers had been almost too successful: after years of relative safety in music choices, producers were disinclined to change. Beerling tackled the problem at its root, dispensing with some of the more established producers and taking on a number of newcomers, all on a freelance basis rather than as permanent members of staff:

> Now they're not all staff producers who play it safe, we have a number of contract producers who are on a similar contract to the deejays, if slightly longer term. So they do tend to be a bit more adventurous and a bit more freewheeling with their programmes.[12]

To date, these new producers have come from both ILR and, with splendid irony, Radio 2: at the time of Beerling's appointment, the average age of Radio 1's producers was actually older than that of Radio 2's production team, while the latter's reshaping into a traditional middle-of-the-road network during 1986 left several of its producers seeking more challenging work elsewhere. In 1987 Beerling took the still more radical step (by Radio 1's standards) of reshaping the management structure of the network and moving producers from control of individual programmes to responsibility for complete programme *sequences*, which were designated as weekday mornings, weekday afternoons, evenings and weekends.

Turning to an analysis of the playlist itself, the first and most obvious point is that Radio 1's use of the Top Forty, whatever the belief in consumer sovereignty, is selective: records are not given an equal number of plays, chart positions do not automatically merit a certain ratio of airplay. Not every Top Forty record will even figure in the playlist, and the list of banned records includes those deemed salacious (Max Romeo's 'Wet Dream', Frankie Goes to Hollywood's 'Relax'), politically contentious (Paul McCartney's 'Give Ireland Back to the Irish') or offensive (the Sex Pistols' 'God Save the Queen'). These are relatively clear-cut cases, and there have been occasions when Radio 1 has been caught up in a prevailing moral panic about certain issues, notably in July 1986, when the Jesus and Mary Chain (a group treated very gingerly by radio producers anyway, by virtue of their name) issued 'Some Candy Talking' at a time when tabloid headlines were focusing on the heroin addiction and arrest on possession charges of Boy George of Culture Club. Mike Smith, at that time presenting the new release programme *Singled Out*, took the record off in mid-play and announced he would not play it on his breakfast time show because of supposed references in the song to cocaine (the 'candy' of the title). As it happened, Smith's comments split opinion within Radio 1's producers and presenters, and Johnny Beerling took the unusual step of consulting John Peel, one of the group's early champions, before finally deciding not to ban the record. The significance of the episode, however, lay in Radio 1's nervousness at the prospect of public censure if it was not at least *seen* to have considered the issue seriously; it followed hard on the heels of a Radio 1 'social action' campaign against drug addiction. (One should note, too, that suggesting the occasional record for banning is something of a convention for breakfast time disc jockeys on Radio 1: Smith's predecessor, Mike Read, was behind the ban on 'Relax'.[13])

Such episodes are, nevertheless, of only peripheral importance to Radio 1's overall airplay policy and particularly its treatment of 'disruptive' musical styles or fashions. Radio 1's management is acutely aware that banning a disc can cause more problems than it solves, in that a record's very notoriety can encourage sales; and of course there have been examples of records on highly dubious themes (Lou Reed's 'Walk on the Wild Side', for example, which contained references to transvestitism and 'giving head') being deemed acceptable simply because the playlist committee made no sense of the lyrics. Both in choosing records from the Top Forty and in selecting from each weekly batch of new single releases, producers exercise judgement based on their own perceptions of what the audience will find acceptable. There are points to be made about this selection process, both of which reflect directly on the professional backgrounds and attitudes of producers: their choices reflect a continuing, nostalgic pre-occupation with the 1960s, and they work (whatever formal attempts Beerling may make to change it) to a narrow definition of what constitutes good daytime Radio 1 music, narrow both musically and in terms of its sources – the Top Forty, the 3-minute single, new releases by established chart 'names'. There is nothing laid down, no written guidelines by which a producer will assess a disc's suitability for daytime play, and only the most intensive, sustained monitoring of the records played and the frequency of playing (a monitoring which would require pre-categorization of records into musical styles or types – a dangerous kind of pigeon-holing) would provide concrete empirical evidence of these tendencies. Rather, general observations can be made, and Radio 1's approach to the punk and new-wave music of the 1977–8 period – an important one in pop music history, if not quite the turning-point that some critics have claimed for it – proves an excellent case in point.

## The case of punk

Punk music was by nature deliberately disruptive, in the sense that it *sounded* noisy, calamitous and violent (the typical early sounds of punk were the buzz-saw drone of guitars, the relentless reworking of three chords), and in its ideology, which valued amateurism over professionalism, emotion and energy over technical perfection, anarchy over order, and maintaining closeness to 'the street' in the face of the distancing, corrupting effects of pop stardom. It was not 'entertaining' in the conventional Radio 1 sense: Johnny Beerling, speaking in 1986, explained its relative exclusion from the airwaves in exactly these terms:

'It wasn't very entertaining on the radio, it was like a lot of disco music, just not very entertaining because it was so repetitive'.[14] Punk broke the unwritten Radio 1 (and ILR) rules of good record-making, in that the music itself was too raucous for daytime listening, too dubious in the content of its lyrics, and also too 'unprofessional' in its production to stand alongside the standard pop fare of the time – Abba, Electric Light Orchestra, Dr Hook, Queen. Indeed, the reason most regularly proffered for the exclusion of punk records from daytime Radio 1 was their poor 'technical quality'. (Even John Peel's espousal of punk on his late evening shows was criticized internally because he was held by some to be wasting the station's limited VHF facility on technically appalling record productions.)

Punk posed a particular problem to Radio 1 because it was subversive, and not just in the sense of carrying anarchic lyrics. It subverted Radio 1's own criteria for playlist inclusion. While it fitted uncomfortably into the daytime shows on musical grounds, it nevertheless demanded representation there if the doctrine of consumer sovereignty was to be respected: punk was, after all, essentially a 3-minute singles form and was well represented in the Top Forty chart. It was a problematic music, but in a much different sense to that other problem form, progressive rock, in the late 1960s, when there were ready-made *technical* reasons for that music's separation from daytime output – the length of typical progressive tracks, its availability on stereophonic albums (and therefore best appreciated on VHF, which was available to Radio 1 only in the evenings and at weekends). Additionally, there were disc jockeys available (John Peel, Bob Harris, Alan Black, Pete Drummond) ready and willing to oversee the music's treatment. Progressive rock was *manageable*, in addition to which it had an intensely conservative streak, reflecting not political concerns but religious dilettantism, Tolkien-like mystical quests, astrology, the lure of the East, all the trappings of a middle-class pursuit of personal fulfilment. Progressive rock had artistic pretensions, while one of the critical poses adopted by punk supporters (including Peel) was that punk musicians, by returning to a deliberately primitivist approach, were actively rebelling against the progressive, élitist values that Radio 1 implicitly endorsed.

How, then, did Radio 1 come to terms with punk? Certain records could be banned outright, on the grounds of offensiveness; the Sex Pistols' 'God Save the Queen' was the obvious example, particularly because its release was deliberately timed to coincide with British royalty's Silver Jubilee celebrations. Most commonly, records with less contentious lyrics were played but distanced by the presenter, who would preface playing a punk disc with jokes about safety pins or gobbing or – in something of a 'rebel' Radio 1 tradition started by Tony Blackburn with his comments about Black Sabbath and heavy metal and continued by Johnnie Walker's remarks about the Bay City Rollers and David Cassidy – would priggishly announce that they had to play the records because they were popular but that didn't mean they necessarily had to like it. In *One Chord Wonders*, Dave Laing contrasts punk with disco music, which was of strictly more commercial importance during the 1977–8 period, and as a general observation it is certainly true that disco was more favoured, but the process of excluding punk by various means was not static.[15] By mid-1977 it was clear that punk was not a passing craze but the catalyst for important structural changes within the record industry itself, precipitating the growth of independent companies and recording studios and encouraging the proliferation of bands on a country-wide basis. With this acknowledgement came a steady *incorporation* – hesitant, selective – of punk into the Radio 1 playlist. The process by which 'punk' as a style and a movement mellowed into 'new wave', a more malleable and less subversive form with which the record industry could operate, has been told on several occasions and is in some respects simply a paradigm of a regular process in rock music, by which increasingly predominant, threatening styles (like rock 'n' roll itself in the United States in the mid-1950s) become tamed by record company exploitation. The media play their own crucial role in this, both by responding to record companies' own tendencies in this direction (for example, *Top of the Pops* would not agree to have the Sex Pistols in the studio for fear of a repetition of the events of their notorious appearance with Bill Grundy on the ITV programme *Today*, but Virgin's provision of a video film enabled the programme to feature 'Pretty Vacant'), and by a more general incorporation, such as by national newspapers running stories on 'my son, the punk', rendering threatening 'extremes' harmless by stressing the ordinariness of punks or their love of animals. Dick Hebdige's *Subculture: The Meaning of Style* shows how this happened in the case of punk, though one of the omissions of that book is any account of the role that radio played in the incorporation of punk into the mainstream, arguably a considerably greater role than that played either by the national press or by television.[16]

Hebdige's argument echoes that of Raymond Williams in his essay 'The Growth and Role of the Mass Media', which pointed out how media select and transform particular facets of working-class culture and offer them back to working-class audiences in neutralized form.[17] Hebdige shows how, in the case of punk, the process took a commodity form (subcultural signs converted into mass-produced objects) and an ideological form, by which deviant behaviour is labelled and redefined, transforming difference into sameness and the dangerous into a comic spectacle. To this one can add a third form, that of relegation to a quasi-artistic, quasi-élitist periphery, typified as John Peel territory, by which punk is defined as a 'meaningful' cult, with its own claims to cultish 'relevance' but irrelevant to the mass audience. One can see these three forms in action at key points in pop music history: the presentation of teenage music as a comic spectacle (typified by the *Oh Boy!* programme on ITV) in the late 1950s, the transformation of difference into sameness (for example, the emergence of Elvis Presley clones, especially Cliff Richard, who were revealed in the press as home-loving boys who sent their Mums flowers every Mother's Day), then the invention of a cultural category (progressive rock) towards the end of the 1960s. The spread of all-day music radio since that time simply accelerated these processes: punk's true heyday was very short-lived, not so much because of industry exploitation (and the willingness of certain punk groups to submit to it) but because of the intensity of (usually distortative) media coverage. Punk became 'new wave' as Johnny Rotten of the Sex Pistols' comic sense became noticed by the press and punk fashions spread to the department stores, and the very fact of its assimilation by other media – particularly television – made a similar assimilation of it by Radio 1 not only inevitable but necessary if the network was to maintain a degree of credibility with a young listenership.

Credibility is an important concept here, as perhaps the most important legacy of punk was *attitudinal*: it undermined pop music's love affair with technology for its own sake by presenting a new set of values, re-establishing rock 'n' roll virtues and returning pop to its (albeit romanticized) roots as a subversive, rebel music with teen appeal and racial/class connotations. It readjusted the critical perspective on pop to a profound degree: the post-punk consensus automatically favoured the independent over the mainstream, the small label over the major company, the 'new, young' band over the ageing dinosaur, the primitive over the cultured, do-it-yourself over-passive acceptance. Similarly, acceptance or rejection of the punk ethos (if not of punk music itself) became a yardstick by which the credibility of Radio 1's disc jockeys and producers was judged, if only by the music press. 1977 in particular was a vital year for the network, when its disc jockeys began either pinning their credibility to the mast by picking the latest independent releases as Records of the Week or setting themselves against punk altogether. It was the year in which several of the older presenters took the opportunity to move from Radio 1 (including Noel Edmonds, Tony Blackburn, and Rosko) and some of the others, notably Simon Bates and Andy Peebles, declared their new faith. This did not mean any overnight change in Radio 1's musical identity and certainly no sudden accommodation of Peel-proselytized records, but in a small yet significant way, punk had the indirect effect of refocusing Radio 1's attention on the *music*. The post-punk period saw a subtle change in the disc jockey stereotype, from the egotistical supermarket opener of tradition to figures, perhaps equally self-obsessed, who made a virtue of their interest in the music *as* music. Post-1977 Radio 1 personnel prided themselves in their awareness; they wore their hipness on their sleeves. What undermined their sense of awareness – the eagerness with which they sought to persuade their listeners that they were themselves part of the scene – was that their use of the music, their championing of post-punk pop, was ultimately as unthinking and as uncritical in its own way as Tony Blackburn's automatic championing of Tamla Motown output had been in the early 1970s. Perhaps more importantly, the enthusiasm of presenters such as Simon Bates and Peter Powell for independent label releases was not necessarily matched by their producers, whose sense of conservatism was informed both by a more traditional view of pop and by the requirement of the network, as defined by the management team, to deliberately centre on mainstream tastes at times of peak listening.

Radio 1 lived far more comfortably with the aftermath of punk – the transition from punk to 'new wave' mentioned earlier – than with punk itself. There was a certain irony in this, as one of the characteristics of post-punk pop was a far greater, far more vocal and visible politicization of the music than punk had witnessed. This extended to chart music; the polemical records of mixed black and white groups like the Specials AKA ('Too Much Too Young', 'Ghost Town'), Selecter ('Too Much Pressure'), the Beat ('Stand Down Margaret') and UB40 ('One in Ten') were aimed quite deliberately at the musical mainstream represented by Radio 1 and the Top Forty, to spread the anti-unemployment, anti-racist, anti-Thatcher message to as wide an audience as possible. As Jim Brown, drummer with UB40 put it, 'a dance band is a package with which to sell your politics':[18] if punk was openly confrontational, post-punk music (of the 1978 to 1981 period at least) was more insidiously challenging, offering subtle, usually non-specific but often barbed political comment clothed in innocuous pop-ska colours. That Radio 1's playlist compilers rarely saw fit to actively exclude such records showed the success of the strategy, though this was arguably one of the few times in British pop history when non-broadcasting factors had the most direct bearing on sales and opinion, particularly the music press (which universally endorsed the 2 Tone stance) and the crucial impact that the groups had on audiences on several intensive tours of British pop venues. Post-punk music did not *appear* to disrupt standard Radio 1 notions of pop as listenable dance music, it even carried musical connotations of those 1960s pop styles (Motown, soul, ska, beat music) so beloved of the pirates; but it followed what Elvis Costello once defined as 'the golden rule of subversive pop . . . don't say it's subversive'. The other distinctive feature of post-punk music was its source on independent labels: Radio 1 found itself dealing with a succession of mostly completely new companies, some (like 2 Tone, whose roster included the Specials and Selecter) run by musicians themselves, who actively sought airplay (as earlier album-based independents like Virgin and Charisma had generally not done) on daytime radio. That a large amount of the output of independent labels very quickly became characterized by radio (ILR as well as Radio 1) as 'indie music' was arguably one of the failures of the post-punk years, typical of a standard process by which any music which does not fit the criteria for non-disruptive daytime fare becomes confined to the élitist margins of the airwaves. At least in part because of Radio 1 policy on seeing daytime and evening audiences as diametrically different, 'indie music' became invested with post-1967 progressive values, a negation of what punk initially represented.

## Daytime use and 'suitability'

Radio 1's playlist is devised purely for daytime use: it governs around 50 per cent of the total musical output of the station over any given week and is not effective after 7 p.m. on weekdays or at any time at weekends. Programmes at these times are the responsibility of a separate production team headed by Stuart Grundy, and we shall return later in the book to the kind of values these programmes embody. It is the apparent exclusion from, or rationing of certain records within the daytime 'strip' shows that concerns us here. What makes one type of record suitable for daytime play and another not?

'Suitability' is primarily determined by the producer's perceptions of the requirements and expectations of his programme's audience. 'Indie music' is classified by Radio 1 as youth (and even more specifically, as student) music: Johnny Beerling's rationale for its low profile during the daytime hours is that the youth audience is not listening at that time: the majority of young people will either be in full-time education or at work. Daytime programmes are geared, so the rationale has it, to the majority audience and to their daytime activities:

> The people listening to us during the day are using us as background . . . during the day, we're consciously catering for people, the majority of whom are perhaps working, so listening to Radio 1 is a secondary activity, a background to what they're doing. People sometimes say it's just audible wallpaper and mean it cynically, but it's probably a fair description at that time of day.
>
> Derek Chinnery[19]

But if the majority audience for the daytime programmes is an older one (and BBC research confirms the median age of a Radio 1 listener as 25), why then does the network persist in drawing the major part of its daytime output from the Top Forty chart – from singles generally (but not exclusively) marketed at, and mainly bought by, a young, *pre*-student clientele? The network's official argument is that chart music has a much broader appeal than its sales figures and the apparent narrowness of its market suggests, but the only evidence for this is the success of Radio 1 itself; the policy is self-fulfilling. A wiser conclusion to draw is that Radio 1 is trapped in a tradition of its own making: having started in 1967 from the premise that 'pop radio', pirate style, could appeal beyond the immediate teenage audience, and having largely kept that original audience as the network grew older, Radio 1 still finds itself having to justify itself as a pop network without age limits. It is, in Chinnery's words, 'a music network first and a young person's network second': it is in the very nature of Radio 1 daytime policy to divorce pop from its place in youth culture, to cater particularly for an older audience brought up on pop but no longer part of the culture which buys it or helps fashion it.

Writing in *The Sociology of Rock* in 1976, Simon Frith suggested that Radio 1 uses pop 'in a context that drains it of its significance as youth music and transforms it into an all-purpose musak. The BBC is not concerned with rock as a cultural form; its interest is confined to the music's inoffensive ability to soothe, cheer and comfort a mass audience'.[20] But Radio 2 producers exercise very similar criteria in selecting from the Top Forty; the point is that the chart is absolutely central to Radio 1 ideology in a way it is not to Radio 2, that pop music actually defines the network's *personality*. What Radio 1 effectively does is fashion programmes and select music according to its own definition not of 'youth culture' but of a permanent, traditional *pop* culture to which anybody of the post-1967 generation is admitted. Pop, in Radio 1 terms, is both unchanging in appeal yet ephemeral in character, constant in its inconstancy; its 'youthful' aspects are important because they give it an identity, but Radio 1 defines pop not just as a youth music *per se* but also as the music of youth remembered. This is why oldies – past hit records – play such a prominent part in daytime programmes: not only do they offer a kind of living nostalgia, they help to cement the continuity between pop of the past and pop of the present and in so doing reassure the older listener of his or her continued inclusion in the Radio 1 community. This also explains the continued presence of a 1960s sensibility in the selection of individual records for the playlist: producers of the daytime shows will favour discs which they know will strike an emotional chord with their age-defined listenership, be they straight reissues or new recordings of old-time hits or records redolent of once-popular artists or styles. Not that simple re-creation of former hits is any guarantee of selection; discrimination can work the other way, as in the case of Dr and the Medics' 1986 revival of 'Spirit in the Sky', formerly a Number 1 for Norman Greenbaum. It was rejected almost unanimously by Radio 1 producers on a point of principle, because it was a note-for-note retread of the original rather than a reinterpretation; it picked up sales after screenings of the accompanying promotional video on Saturday morning children's programmes and was introduced to the playlist only once it had charted.

All this implies that Radio 1's music selection is innately, unerringly conservative, both in the range and in the retrospective quality of the music played. As we have seen, many of the constraints on Radio 1 are self-imposed, and its very success has tended to negate any pressure to change either the basic format or the network's organizational procedures and conventions. Apologists might also argue that the conservatism of Radio 1 is matched by that of the music industry itself, that in the key area of newly released material its gatekeepers can only make their choices from what the record companies make available, and that if industry output is uninteresting or lacks originality, radio can only reflect that. But this begs the question of to what extent records are released with Radio 1 airplay in mind and fashioned to meet the requirements of its gatekeepers. Alan Durant, for example, contends that the very process of playlisting not only forces music-makers into a musical strait-jacket defined by the playlist but that musical idioms 'develop both directly and indirectly in reflection of constraints of airtime'.[21] A further point is that Radio 1 has a self-defined myopia when it comes to selecting from the commercially recorded material available, drawing almost wholly on singles for its daytime output and only fitfully on album tracks – a tendency that, after two decades of the network's existence, no longer necessarily suits record industry strategy. When given the opportunity to speak to music radio practitioners at the 1986 Music Radio Conference in London, both Peter Jamieson of EMI and Rob Dickens of WEA argued against the prevalence of the 'singles mentality' in Radio 1 on the grounds that it denied the radio audience the full range and quality of the industry's product. Interestingly, the reason offered by both Radio 1 and ILR gatekeepers at the conference for the preference towards singles was purely practical, that the pressures of daily broadcasting are such that no time exists to even hear the number of albums released each week, let alone select suitable tracks from them. Probably the real reason, however, is more philosophical than practical: a nervousness at departing from tried-and-trusted broadcasting formulas, which also shows in the general reluctance to feature live or pre-recorded music (from sessions that stations themselves record under MU agreements) during the peak-time hours. Session music breaks the flow of sequentially programmed records, because it cannot match the technical standards of excellence of record company product and because the artists concerned are generally not Top Forty-oriented performers;

the cost of continually hiring Top Forty 'names' for session work would be prohibitive even for Radio 1. Even Radio 2, which uses more BBC-recorded studio material than any of the other networks and is obliged to do so because of long-standing MU agreements, prioritizes commercially recorded music by relegating the majority of in-house orchestral and big-band sessions to the non-peak hours of 7 p.m. to 7 a.m. The narrowness of playlists and the exclusion or otherwise of particular idioms from standard daytime fare are symptoms of a more general conservatism, at the heart of which is an almost thumb-sucking dependence on the security of the commercially produced record.

## Music selection in ILR

I noted earlier how the music policies of ILR stations are, if not directly influenced by those of Radio 1, at least fashioned with those of their largest competitor in mind. And the influence has not been all one way: Radio 1's change, mentioned earlier, from individually produced programmes to complete sequences incorporating up to three formerly distinct programmes, was clearly influenced by conventional ILR practice. But if the mechanics are similar, there are clear differences in perspective that impact on the process of selection. The producers of Radio 1's daytime shows select their music according to its assumed appeal to a mass listenership, big audiences being necessary to justify both the continuance of the network and the continued apportioning to it of part of the licence fee. ILR programme-makers, however, are less interested in big audiences *per se* than in reaching specific, demographically defined audiences of most interest to advertisers. ILR's targets are sharper, better defined, commercially logical, to the point that any BBC-like over-reliance on consumer sovereignty (as embodied by the Top Forty chart) is superfluous. This does not mean that ILR gatekeepers ignore the chart or that they do not replicate many of the conservative tendencies exhibited by Radio 1, but rather that they can afford to pick and choose from what is commercially available in a much more openly manipulative way, homing in on particular target groups and basing their choices on an upfront, coolly professional appraisal of the acceptability of certain records to those groups.

Music selection at Radio 1 is quasi-democratic: everyone puts in his or her twopence worth, the playlist is compiled on the basis of a majority vote, producers work within its guidelines. Radio 1's playlist is mulled over, discussed, by twelve good men and true; ILR playlisting, though often incorporating some input from presenters, is dictatorial, in that the choices of programme controllers and heads of music are imposed from above. This concentration of power allows the commercial imperative to remain supreme: programme controllers devise and manage a format into which commercials fit neatly and unobtrusively, and which (depending on the station) either simply outlines or unequivocally dictates how the ingredients of the format – the weather checks, news bulletins, travel information, advice spots, the records – should frame the commercials within any given hour. Records are not chosen to match the commercials, but they are quite deliberately chosen to match the personalities, life-styles and tastes of the listeners at whom the commercials are aimed. Selecting the music in ILR is therefore very much a marketing skill – and an individual, specialist skill at that – requiring not only a feel for the tastes of the public or a knowledge of the business but an ability to interpret and fulfil advertisers' requirements. The special nature of the gatekeeping role in ILR is that he or she mediates not between the record makers and the public but between the *advertiser* and the public.

A head of music in ILR takes charge not just of the selection of individual records for broadcasting but of creating and maintaining a steady, consistent musical identity for the station; the latter inevitably informs the former. Consistency is vital: listeners tune in to particular radio stations for emotional as well as practical reasons, because the style or sound or tone of voice suits them, and variability in the musical 'signature' of the station can break the sense of familiarity or rapport. On a more mundane, workaday level, because listening to the radio is in the main a secondary activity and because the whole pattern of the radio day is built around the structure, pace and rhythms of the working-day, ILR gatekeepers cannot afford to let through any music that would jar in the context in which it is heard. Tony Hale, when Head of Music at Capital, stated that he based his selections for the breakfast programme on the image of 'a man in Bromley shaving in front of his mirror at 6.50 a.m. . . . he doesn't want heavy metal or anything too loud like hard rock, but music that will ease him awake and prepare him for another day at the office'. The ILR gatekeeper must not only choose the 'right' music but programme it effectively, and the playlist provides the mechanics to do so.

The structure and make-up of the playlist varies from station to station, though the uniformity in outlook is remarkable. Some examples give the flavour. Radio Hallam's playlist consists of the entire local Top Fifty, forty new releases and selected tracks from five featured albums. Swansea Sound, on its own admittance an 'MOR-ish station' with a median listening age of 38, has a playlist of sixty drawn from 'the more tuneful' records of the chart and the most 'MOR'-like of the new releases. Radio 210 in Reading, offering 'good listening music turning more poppy for the breakfast and late drive time programmes', has a playlist of between sixty and seventy, divided, as is common practice in ILR, into an A and B list, the former including current singles and the latter a mixture of new releases and non-needletime records. Capital, which as the first music-based ILR station had a pivotal role in influencing the playlisting procedures of stations in general, had a record list of sixty-five during Tony Hale's reign as Head of Music that consisted of

> five climbers, twenty on what we call the A [list], twenty on the B, and twenty Capital extras. The climbers are records we feel very strongly about – not necessarily by famous names, just tunes that have impressed us. 'A' records are hits, or well-known songs, or recordings by very well-known acts . . . the B list is for records that we hope will be successful by newer acts. The extras lists new records that perhaps aren't suitable for all times of day, plus some hits that are on the way down, plus novelty records or discs

that perhaps do best with just a few plays per week. We have a 'rotation' for the daytime shows; all this means is that a grid with letters and numbers tells you, if you're producing a daily show, which climbers, A list and B list records you can play in a particular hour.[22]

The playlist is changed weekly at all stations and the turnover in records is commonly in the region of 25 per cent; the average length of stay on a playlist is between four and six weeks, though compilers sometimes keep particular records on a lot longer when their sales remain abnormally high over a long period. Stevie Wonder's 'I Just Called to Say I Love You' in 1984 and Chris de Burgh's 'The Lady in Red' in 1986 were two such records. Capital institutionalized this process by adding a separate section to the playlist of 'replay' hits, to which the relevant tracks would be apportioned after six weeks. For stations with a cultivated middle-of-the-road ambience, 'replay' hits can be a lifeblood: County Sound in Guildford, for instance, has 'a D list which is made up of the former major records on our main playlist, and we play them rather than something new and obscure. It makes the station sound more familiar'.[23]

The ILR gatekeeper's primary consideration in deciding what goes into his station's playlist is its general suitability for the target audience, which might be young and upwardly mobile in the case of Capital or considerably older in profile and with a large percentage of the economically less active (pensioners and the unemployed) in the case of Swansea Sound. Quasi-local factors can colour the choices made: Downtown Radio in Belfast, for example, plays a large proportion of country music because of the strong following for it in Northern Ireland, while Radio Hallam in Sheffield is one of several stations to build their playlist on local record sales, drawing on a chart compiled from the returns of a number of retailers in the city and on weekly 'dipstick' surveys (by stopping people in the street) of reactions to current records. The idea here is apparently to seek confirmation that the choices made and the playlisting strategy already effected by the station are broadly correct, not to invite real local involvement in the process of choosing the music. Where stations do invite 'participation' in the process, it is usually on the basis of telephone votes for a handful of pre-selected new releases – a scheme which, when operated by Capital in its first year, was open to abuse by record companies. (It became part of record industry legend that it was pointless to try ringing record labels around 5 p.m. on a Friday evening because the switchboards were always jammed with staff members placing their 'votes' for their own company's releases.) Generally, local stations' acknowledgement of local tastes does not extend to promoting locally *made* music during the daytime hours: although stations do record a large amount of work by local musicians (and are obliged to do so because of national agreements with the Musicians Union), this is rarely heard during mainstream programmes. This is because it is either not polished enough, technically, to sit comfortably alongside commercially recorded product, or because the style of music (and stations record anything from local choirs and youth orchestras to synthesizer bands and *a cappella* quartets) is deemed unsuitable for the daytime context. But even when locally-made music is available on record, for example through releases on local record labels, there is still a marked reluctance to include it in the playlist: playlist compilers justify this on the grounds that, however large and loyal the local following of a band, it will only constitute a minuscule proportion of the station's audience and a smaller proportion still of those listening during the day.

Playlist compilers in ILR – and those, where playlists exist, in BBC local radio – take their selections from national rather than local sources for reasons of history, competition and simple inertia. ILR's reliance on nationally available records is primarily a matter of convention, dating from a time (the early and mid-1970s) when hardly any local record companies existed; despite their proliferation since the late 1970s, the local labels have struggled for a hearing on radio because of difficulties in distribution and in combating the big-money promotional efforts of their major label competitors. Competition between stations also works against local music: because they form the main competition in virtually every ILR area, the selections that Radios 1 and 2 make (from mainly national labels, for a national audience) have an obvious impact on what an ILR station is likely to choose for its audience, if only in the sense of a general favouring of current chart material. Gatekeepers also react to an insidious kind of peer group pressure, adding records they had overlooked to the playlist or ignoring others on the strength of what other ILR stations may be playing; each week, *Music Week* publishes precise details of what the ILR stations are playing and how often. Finally, there is the question of having to streamline choices out of physical necessity: it is not physically possible to listen to every record released each week, and a large proportion of records in the playlist are so chosen because they are records by familiar, reliable names whose suitability for radio play has been proven in the past. External and internal pressures such as these are enough to ensure that even heads of music sympathetic to local music are unlikely to give it preferential treatment.

The main common ground between the BBC stations and ILR is the dependence of each on sales charts as a guide to airplay and a basis of the playlist, though *which* chart is another question. The BBC shares copyright on the Gallup chart with the BPI and *Music Week*, but in practice ILR stations have continually drawn on it (and, in pre-Gallup years, the chart compiled by BMRB) without referring to it on air. Playlist compilers have to have a front page of current hits to build the rest of the playlist around, and for some years a placing in the BBC-sponsored chart was the only realistic definition of a hit. This began to change in 1984 with the start of the *Network Chart Show*, produced by Capital for simultaneous live transmission by virtually all the stations in the ILR system and scheduled directly against the BBC's own *Top Forty* show. Although the show represented only two hours of the ILR week, it had ramifications for music programming throughout the whole of ILR: because of the programme's success in not only establishing the concept of a credible 'alternative' chart but giving it a high public profile, it introduced and effectively imposed on theoretically autonomous stations new *national* criteria for the selection of individual records. The haphazard and unspoken reliance on the BBC chart was replaced by an almost obligatory dependence on (or, at the very least, reference to) its alternative, and one consequence was the almost immediate redundancy of local sales charts and local chart shows. Meanwhile, claims that music selection in ILR would at least become more 'sales-led' – echoing the Radio 1 belief in the sovereignty of the consumer – could be countered by reference to the methods used by the Media Research and Information Bureau (MRIB) to compile the Network Chart. Although MRIB worked from a sample of 300 retail shops and processed the data with greater speed than Gallup – giving the impression that its chart was always a week ahead of the latter – they also incorporated an 'airplay factor' based on the weekly playlists of the ILR stations. The AIRC's programming committee, in nominal charge of the chart, stated that 'this extra ingredient will account for up to 10 per cent effect on movements up and down the chart',[24] but the real effect was that the chart became potentially self-fulfilling. A record currently enjoying big sales could have its status in the chart either undermined or artificially boosted according to the attitude taken to it by playlist compilers: the chart position attained by a record becomes less a reflection of sales in the marketplace, more of the *frequency* with which that record is played.

The concentration on charts as a guide to what is played does, however, obscure a debate within ILR as to the relative importance of sales in dictating air-play. As far back as 1976, Bob Snyder of Radio Trent commented:

> We've never based our music policy on the sales chart for the simple reason that record purchasers are only a small proportion of the public and it would be foolish to base a station's programming intended for all the public on the demands of a minority. I don't believe the charts are accurate anyway . . . it's all so pointless to just play discs that have already sold well. The last way to promote a record here is to tell me that it's going to sell a million copies. I don't care, I want to know whether it'll sound good on the radio.[25]

Tim Blackmore, former Radio 1 producer and subsequently Head of Programmes at Capital, echoed these sentiments at the Edinburgh Radio Festival in 1982, pointing out that sales figures at a local level were meaningless:

> When you realise that a Top 10 record could have sold as few as 100,000 copies and then find out that 20 per cent of national sales are in an area that approximates to the Capital Radio coverage area, it doesn't take an Einstein to see that only 20,000 of our potential audience bought it. That means that some 12 million of our potential audience didn't and I don't like that ratio as a basis for programme judgements.[26]

This theme was pursued further by Robin Valk, Head of Music at BRMB in Birmingham, speaking at the 1985 Music Radio Conference, who issued a two-pronged attack on the 'lemming-like inclination to rush to the security of the Top 40' and the overuse of such records in programming: 'saturation play turns the right records into wrong ones'. He contrasted the industry's desire for a quick turnaround of hits – which its very emphasis on chart placings and statistics in general contrived to encourage – with the innate conservatism of the listening audience and pointed out not just the minimal sales required for chart success but their variability. Taking the Christmas 1984 period as an example, he demonstrated how the Number 1 record, 'Do They Know It's Christmas' by Band Aid, sold 750,000 nationally in the week prior to Christmas and 30,000 locally; two weeks into the new year, 'I Want to Know What Love Is' by Foreigner was at Number 1 with a national sale of 86,000 and a local sale of just 3,500. And while a Bronski Beat record stood at Number 30 in the chart during Christmas week on national sales of 15,900, its local sales peaked at just 630 – hardly enough to automatically warrant a place on any playlist. The lower one went down the chart, the more meaningless the placings became: even at national level, differences from one chart position to another reflected differences in sales of just a few thousand.[27]

Valk's comments amounted to a call to use the chart far more selectively, but at moments of 'crisis' this happens anyway; ILR's almost universal cold-shouldering of punk was one example. Punk was initially frozen out of ILR playlists purely because its reputation went before it: this was most marked in provincial stations geographically distanced from the punk subculture itself, where knowledge of punk was derived from the media in general. The Sex Pistols' TV interview with Bill Grundy in December 1976 set in motion an undignified scramble among the stations to make their dissociation from punk public. At Radio Hallam, the board of directors became involved, expressing concern over the number of punk-type discs in the chart and backing Head of Music Beverley Chubb's decision to simply ignore most of them: to make up the shortfall, more oldies were introduced into the playlist. But the long-term effect of punk was to make the Top Forty chart an uncertain and faintly dangerous source of ILR music, as David Thomas of Swansea Sound remembers:

> In the late 1970s, when punk music became popular with younger people, it was difficult to match the aspirations of 15 to 24 year olds with the aspirations of 35 plusses, because the Sex Pistols, Stranglers or the Clash were very popular with 15 to 20 year olds, and it's very difficult to persuade people of 40 to 50 or even younger that they want to listen to it. That's when Radio 1 did pick up more of the younger listeners than we would have liked because they did play a great deal of that sort of music, and we weren't doing so, not only us but Independent Radio generally, because it would have driven away a lot of the rest of our listeners. At least that was the fear at the time, I'm not sure it would have done but one has to go by one's instincts at the time. Now things are rather more melodious – Wham!, Culture Club, they're more accessible across a range of ages, I think.[28]

### Beyond homogeneity

ILR programmers make their selection decisions on commercial grounds: their hostility to punk stemmed from its alienatory effect on the audience they wished to attract and the potentially adverse effect its inclusion might have on advertising sales. I have argued elsewhere that ILR's neglect of punk and new wave led, albeit indirectly, to a loss of credibility among younger audiences: at a time when pop music was opening up in a participatory sense, with new bands proliferating and new venues and recording outlets (studios as well as labels) springing up to service them, local radio in particular retreated into itself, clinging on more than ever to the musically tried and trusted and leaving the door wide open for pirate radio stations like Laser and a rejuvenated Radio Caroline to cater for the youth sector. When ILR belatedly woke up to the drain on listeners, its attempts to capture lost ground took two forms – a radical reshaping of the evening fare to take into account young tastes (the departure of Capital's 'progressive' expert Nicky Horne and his subsequent replacement by ex-punk Gary Crowley was symbolic in this respect) and an injection of new presenters and Laser-like presentation and promotion techniques to create the impression of streetwise contemporariness. As often as not, however, stations found themselves caught between two stools, attracting back a large part of the youth audience yet failing to gain listeners from the hard-core 25 to 45 age group.

Here in the late-1980s, radio gatekeepers increasingly find themselves wrestling with an ever-growing, ever-ageing audience made up of many different musical communities. The old homogeneity – or what the programmers always assumed was a homogeneity – of tastes began breaking down around the time that punk made its breakthrough, and one solution (strengthened, of course, by commercial considerations) has been for ILR stations to narrow their demographics still further: Capital's split frequency experiment of 1986, aimed unashamedly at London's compact-disc buying 'yuppies', was an attempt at just this. The AIRC's antipathy towards community radio was based on the fear that small-scale stations would exploit the potential of 'narrowcasting' before a deregulated ILR had the chance to take the concept further. But picking a musical community and sticking with it implies a certain kind of usage of music by that community – that the audience will use the music as a focus rather than as background, as a source of aesthetic pleasure rather than of neatly programmed, astutely chosen musical wallpaper. The majority of radio listeners, if research by the radio stations is to be believed, do not use the medium in this primary sense but as a domestic utility, offering information and entertainment as a soundtrack to workaday activities, and the skill of the radio gatekeeper is not only to select the appropriate music for that soundtrack but to programme it in a manner that matches the pace and rhythms of the working-day. The very process of running records together in a pre-determined sequence is an attempt to impose a sense of harmony on the listener's emotions. The programmer not only sifts and sorts, he *constructs* a kind of temporary reality out of available musical resources. In the next chapter we must focus on what that 'reality' is and how it can be constructed.

# 8 Mother's little helper: programmes, personalities and the working day

While ILR stations vary in the amount of music they programme, each one carefully structures its output over the day to create a mood in keeping with that of the audience. No-one takes kindly to a rowdy awakening, nor do they want to be lulled back to sleep — something bright but not raucous is the order of the day. Later, when most people are busy either in the home or perhaps at work, a little up-tempo music can give an extra lift to the workload.

*Television and Radio 1980* (IBA Handbook)[1]

Turning on popular radio is often prompted by a listener's need to create an atmosphere different from the one he or she is already immersed in — the stillness of an empty house for a housewife, the closed environment of the work place, the monotony of the rhythm of the road. Stations like Radio 1 and 2 provide that atmosphere.

Steve Wright, Radio 1 presenter[2]

In studying radio output, it is largely meaningless to consider individual programmes in isolation. So much radio criticism of the kind favoured by daily or Sunday newspapers is of limited value because it is based on a very selective listening to self-contained broadcasts, usually of plays and documentaries and usually emanating from Radios 3 and 4. Not only does this tend to perpetuate the élitist and reactionary assumption that the only worthwhile radio is that which follows what might be called traditional Home Service norms, it also misses the significance of how radio is *used* by the majority of its audience and how broadcasters respond and adapt to that usage. Radio is not a primary medium of either entertainment or information in the sense that television is — that is to say, requiring some degree of focused attention — and neither is there much evidence in any of the extensive research work undertaken by the BBC, the IBA and commercial concerns that listeners continually comb the dial in channel-hopping fashion, switching from programme to programme, restlessly searching for diversion or stimulation. As Derek Bloom, former Chief Executive of the Radio Marketing Bureau, has succinctly put it, 'television is a medium in which entertainment is pursued, radio is one in which it is accepted'.[3]

It was the realization by radio stations around the globe, from the early 1950s onwards, that radio had become a medium of secondary importance to television that shifted the emphasis from individually constructed programmes to 'programming' of a sequential nature. Sequential programming – literally the running of news, music or other programme features in sequence, usually across 3- or 4-hour blocks or strips – offered the listener a continuous, predictable format designed to complement his or her activities; it implicitly accepted that the audience was tuning in and out irregularly, that listening was fundamentally casual. The practical advantages for radio stations were that such programming was easy to mount, plan and sustain, was relatively cheap to produce, and offered spot advertisers and sponsors a more flexible environment for their messages. Sequential programming came to Britain via pirate radio and was developed most intensively by Radios 1 and 2, but the concept was later adopted experimentally (and controversially) by Radio 4: *The Colour Supplement* on Sundays, *Rollercoaster* on Thursday mornings and *Pirate Radio 4* for children on Saturday afternoons were all collections of disparate feature items presided over by one or more link-persons. The approach was even adopted by breakfast-time and daytime television (9 a.m. to 4 p.m.), tellingly, the only times of day when television takes on the utilitarian characteristics of radio, when it is assumed that viewers (because of the primacy of paid work or domestic chores) will give programmes only intermittent and desultory attention.

The point of the kind of sequential radio operated by Radios 1 and 2, BBC local radio and ILR is that it dovetails with our lives, and it is this essential functionalism that I want to explore in this chapter: the way radio, and music radio in particular, is geared to not just the tastes but the daily activities and the life-style patterns of those listening, and how these considerations determine the way in which radio *speaks* to its audience through the personalities it employs. The major part of the research effort in ILR in particular is to find out precisely not just what the listenership constitutes in terms of social class, age and gender – the prime concerns of advertisers – but the minutiae of how those listeners organize their day, as an aid to the stations' own programming process. (BBC and ILR-sponsored research should not, of course, be regarded uncritically: there are enough disputes over methodology between the BBC Research Department and its various counterparts in commercial radio to question the validity of either's findings, particularly regarding 'ratings', and one has to bear in mind that the publication of research data is in part a public relations exercise, designed to inspire confidence in the station. But we are not concerned here with inter-station rivalry, rather with the way in which the stations' own research not only illuminates but *defines* the programming decisions they make. In this chapter, I've drawn freely on commercial research where it concerns audience usage rather than comparative scales of patronage, because it is here that commercial researchers can most genuinely claim professional disinterest.)

There is, however, much more to the question of radio's functionalism than the assumption that the medium simply acts as a background, a musical backcloth to everyday life: the intimate connection between the standard daytime radio sequences and the notion of a fairly fixed, universal working-day needs some examination, raising as it does a number of important, related questions about radio's role in reinforcing societal attitudes towards both work itself and the place of women within it; radio is notorious for its preoccupation with the 'housewife' stereotype. Radio brings order and regimentation to the working-day and uses music both as a buffer against the boredom, repetition and depersonalizing aspects of work (and domestic work in particular) *and* as an emotional trigger, as a means of locking in to the memories, aspirations and fantasies of a largely domestically-tied listenership. What is said between the records, the very style of presentation adopted – the preponderance of 'pop and prattle' on the airwaves, to use the Annan Committee's critical phrase – reflects the same concerns.

## A home service

What sets radio apart from other media is its ready availability, its ubiquitousness – not just in the outside world of shops, work and places of leisure but within the physical boundaries of the home: a July 1973 survey conducted by Research Surveys of Great Britain found that the average UK home had 2.7 sets that were listened to mainly in the kitchen (53 per cent penetration) and the bedroom (55 per cent).[4] Home use of radio far outweighs patronage in non-domestic situations, and perhaps the biggest myths surround in-car usage: in-car listening is constantly quoted by programme controllers and producers as determining particular programme features (most obviously, regular traffic reports from either the AA or RAC or specially hired spotter planes), but both ILR and BBC research findings continually question its significance. A 1984 paper prepared for Capital Radio, for instance, found that only 15 per cent of its sample of listeners had the radio turned on while driving to work.[5] Stations stick with their battery of road reports, however, because they create an *impression* of pace, mobility and activity which both suits the station's self-image and gives the listener an illusion of service.[6] They make the station *seem* indispensable, and they punctuate programming at times of day (6 a.m. to 9 a.m., 4 p.m. to 7 p.m.) when the station perceives its 'social' function as one of getting workers to and from their places of work.

Traffic bulletins (and the whole paraphernalia of weather checks, airline news and bus and train information that provide similar punctuation) have an essentially cosmetic use, but it is the effectiveness with which they not only establish but actively patrol a domestic routine that is important. The relevance of the information imparted doesn't really matter, the predictability of its placing within the programme does. (I can remember as a 12 year old once getting up as my father and brother prepared for work and switching over to Radio 2's other frequency when the shipping forecast came on; despite its total irrelevance to their situation, the effect of its absence was to disrupt their entire routine, and they were not amused.) Even advertisements can have the same function. Harrods, for instance, for some years styled its 'early morning call' commercials in the manner of standard ILR information features, complete with jingle, and placed them at precisely the same time every morning on LBC and Capital, between a live travel information sequence and the 8 a.m. news.

The early morning routine, as marked out by the breakfast-time sequences, is worth looking at in some detail. Breakfast time is the most patronized slot in radio, and the time-sequence usually occupied by the station's most experienced and affable presenter. In terms of securing an audience for the station for the rest of the day, the breakfast show is crucial, not only because it carries promotional trailers for forthcoming programmes but because of the audience's conservative listening habits: listeners tend to stay with whichever station they were last tuned to. (Tony Fish of BBC Radio York argues that some ILR stations carry on broadcasting into the night, even when it is not obviously cost-effective, because late-night listeners tuning in to the station and finding only a signal would automatically retune to a competitor; the risk is that listeners would then not bother to tune back in time for the morning. BBC local stations, he maintains, have a built-in advantage in that they carry Radio 2's programming once they go off the air, thereby keeping the audience for the following morning.[7]) According to BBC research, radio's peak audience tunes in between 7.30 a.m. and 8.15 a.m. and numbers 27 per cent of the total population (around 14 million); not only Radios 1 and 2 but Radios 3 and 4 also enjoy their biggest audiences at this time.[8] The radio audience is also at its most homogenous in terms of age, gender and social class at this time, attracting a roughly equal balance of men and women and a cross-section of listeners running the gamut from schoolchildren to pensioners. Their need, as Capital's research defines it, is for programming that 'increases physiological arousal, facilitating wakefulness, giving brief information and encouraging cheerfulness',[9] and Radio 1's Derek Chinnery has spoken of there being 'a constant awareness that people are getting up, on the move, doing things and going out . . . there's a changing audience all the time. No one listens for perhaps more than half an hour'.[10]

Breakfast radio for the work- or school-bound is a relatively recent development in radio history, dating from the changes in Light Programme schedules activated in 1957 but taking off in a major way with the inception of Radio 1 (the first traffic jingles on BBC radio were those heard seven minutes into Tony Blackburn's very first Radio 1 show) and the subsequent advent of ILR. Indeed, breakfast radio has in some senses been the salvation of local radio, as the ability of a station to capitalize on local information – on traffic conditions in the high street, on which schools are closed during a midwinter freeze-up – during the breakfast hours gives it a major advantage over national competitors. It was the sheer localness of the service that enabled ILR and BBC local radio to withstand the arrival of breakfast television with relative ease, and one of the most interesting features of the latter was the way in which both the ITV and BBC programmes deliberately aped the breakfast radio format, mixing short interviews, morning paper reviews and items of light relief with constant time checks, traffic information (regional as opposed to local), brief news bulletins and the odd music video.

Not only the content but the style and tone of breakfast radio is geared to the idea of a preparation for work, offering a burst of friendly cheer prior to the tensions and pressures of the grindstone, a *bridge* between the private and public worlds, between the hours of leisure and labour. Radio's function is in this respect socially approved – unlike breakfast television, which still faces charges of social irresponsibility from some quarters for showing videos and children's cartoons when the children should be getting ready for school, for *confusing* the private and public worlds. Breakfast radio also acts as a subtle but potent reinforcing agent, not only in the mundane sense of constantly reminding and even nagging the listener to get a move on but in reinforcing the work ethic itself: stations accentuate the divisions between home-time and work-time by changing their programming patterns and musical signature between 9 a.m. and 9.30 a.m., and it is standard radio practice to feature more job vacancies for the unemployed during the breakfast hours than at any other time of day, the implication being that it is the early bird, those least keen on the state of being jobless, who will catch the worm. (Such recruitment advertising as there is in ILR – and it tends to be obviated by the willingness of stations to give free vacancy announcements as a 'community service' – is similarly rarely placed during standard working hours, for the obvious reason that the ideal job candidates will already be gainfully employed.)

The work aspect informs the whole of radio's daytime hours, but not necessarily in the sense of providing a backcloth to paid working activity. BBC and IBA research indicates a modest use of radio in offices, garages, doctors' and dentists' waiting-rooms, shops (though for the 'benefit' of shoppers rather than staff) and factories, but whether radio is actually *allowed* in working situations is very much down to the policy of individual employers. The days of organized rediffusion of existing radio services ended with the 1950s, though use of Muzak (specially recorded background music) in factories was widespread by the 1960s.[11] More significant in an industrial context have been the various attempts by employers at running their own mock radio stations, notably EMI Records in Hayes, Middlesex, and United Biscuits, whose 'network' was operated in the late 1960s to mid-1970s by a consultancy called Sound Developments and based in Osterley, West London. Their transmissions, styled in the pirate/Radio 1 fashion but with safety announcements replacing commercials and trailers, went out to a largely female workforce of 20,000 at five UB factories. UBN took its news bulletins from the Press Association and ran a 24-hour service, catering for three 8-hour shifts. UBN was a vital recruiting ground for ILR presenters in the early 1970s, and it is easy to trace back much of the sexism of local radio presentation – the patronizing tone adopted towards what is perceived to be a mainly female listenership – to their industrial background. We will return to the UBN sexism factor later in the chapter, but a further point on the industrial use of radio (or pseudo-radio) is that music in the workplace has traditionally been imposed upon workers rather than fought for, primarily a benefit to the employer rather than the employee: astutely paced music is simultaneously an aid to a steady level of production and a source of pacification.

Nevertheless, it would be easy to overemphasize the use of radio in working situations and the extent to which radio stations take note of that use in programme planning. Reception of radio in offices and factories is too diffuse to be measured with precise accuracy, and radio institutions have undertaken no systematic research into radio listening in a work context since the 1950s. Even the BBC's own exhaustive *Daily Life in the 80s* research, while detailing all manner of daily activities by viewers and listeners, chose simply to record the fact that radio was available in a work situation (to 6 per cent of the 25–44 population, for example) rather than attempt to delineate the occupations or working environments of those listening. The whole historical emphasis in British radio has been on private rather than communal usage, and much of the impact of the factory-oriented *Music While You Work* during the war lay in its isolation to two half-hour segments during the working-day: had the same principle been applied across the whole of the day, it would have been taken for granted and its morale-raising potency would have been diminished. The use of radio in working situations is incidental to the domestic targets at which all British music radio stations aim their post-breakfast time output, and even when radio practitioners do speak of working listeners it is rarely in terms of occupations oriented towards mass production and most often in terms of independent, one-man occupations providing some kind of domestic service,

> Whether it's the plumber who comes to fix your sink and has a radio on the floor beside him or the mechanic in a workshop or a commercial traveller driving up the M1 in his car . . . whatever, that's the sort of activity that's going on, and Radio 1 is really in a sense a background to that.
>
> Derek Chinnery[12]

Radio *frames* the working-day, it does not impose or impinge upon it. It smooths the way to work in the morning, it provides a pacy, cheerful interlude during the middle of the day – the lunchtime programmes being aimed, as at breakfast time, at a broad audience of listeners at home, workers and schoolchildren in their lunch breaks – and it offers a musical backcloth to the return journey home during the so-called 'drive-time' hours of 4 p.m. to 7 p.m. Given the low amount of in-car listening recorded by researchers, 'drive-time' is a dubious concept, and even news of train cancellations or bus delays – imparted with the same intensity that characterizes the early morning shows – can be of little use to returning commuters when so few of them have access to a radio set at their place of work.[13] That drive-time is inappropriate to the British radio context (it originated in the United States, where more than one in three radio listeners are car radio users) is appreciated best by Radio 1, who after 4.30 p.m. offer two hours of chart and album music aimed unequivocally at returning schoolchildren. But throughout BBC radio and ILR there is a universal decline in patronage from 2 p.m. onwards, and most stations attempt to minimize that decline by reverting to the 'strengths' of breakfast-time output, by playing a broad mix of music for a similarly homogenous audience and providing a 'community service' of sorts by means of traffic information and extended local news. The difference between morning and drive-time programmes lies mainly in their tone: the latter are less urgent, the music is more 'relaxing', 'helping the listener to unwind after a hard day's work', as Tony Hale put it while Head of Music at Capital.[14]

But if early morning, lunchtime and early evening sequences are fashioned with the 'worker' in mind, going away from and coming back to his castle, what of the hours in between? Work may be referred to, presenters may feature regular dedication spots for workplaces, phone-in participants may ring in from their work numbers, and local stations may run periodic outside broadcasts from local factories for promotional purposes, but there is an unmistakable sense in which daytime listeners are regarded as a different community – a community of *domestic*, housebound workers. The connections between radio and work in the literal (expenditure of energy, the application of effort) as opposed to employment sense are most clearly and significantly seen in the domestic context, where 'work' means housework, is unpaid and is carried out mainly by women.

## Housewives' choice?

The housewife is of course particularly central to BBC radio mythology. The idea of a diligent, houseproud, housebound wife running a household and taking on the day-to-day responsibility of bringing up children dates in BBC terms from the immediate post-war period and was for many years encapsulated in the Light Programme's *Housewives Choice*, heard on every working day (including Saturday mornings) between 9 a.m. (later 8.30 a.m.) and 9.55 a.m. Sandwiched neatly between taking the children to school and going shopping, when housework activities were confined to the kitchen (washing up after breakfast) and the living room where the radio was commonly housed (polishing the furniture), the programme was very much a product of post-war thinking, designed as a kind of recognition of or even reward to the female populace for giving up their wartime occupations in the munitions factories and service industries and returning to an almost wholly domestic role. The post-war years saw considerable development of women's media in general, with the same network also starting a daily *Woman's Hour* and the launching of a number of new women's magazines – *Housewife, Women's Mirror* – giving a similar mixture of consumer advice (deemed important in a time of austerity, when rationing necessitated economical use of resources), romantic fiction, practical features such as recipes or cleaning suggestions, human-interest articles and advice on personal matters. They reinforced the notion that housework was 'women's work' by offering endless suggestions as to how to lighten the housework load and cope with the attendant pressures. Above all, such magazines offered their readers reassurance that their renewed peacetime role as housewife and mother was both necessary and valued; rebellion against these 'norms' (i.e. refusing to accept a subordinate role to the man, either within or outside the family) was characterized as undermining the fabric of family life.[15]

The characteristics of housework in modern industrialized society are defined in Ann Oakley's study, *Housewife*, as:

> (1) its exclusive allocation to women rather than adults of both sexes; (2) its association with economic dependence, i.e. with the dependent role of the woman in modern marriage; (3) its status as non-work – or its opposition to

'real', i.e. economically productive work, and (4) its primacy to women, that is, its priority over other roles.[16]

One of the most consistent features in popular culture's portrayal of, and catering for, the housewife is the manner in which each of these points is transformed into a positive aspect, delighting in the exclusivity of the role and emphasizing the importance of the woman in the context of the family – as the one who binds family relationships together, who keeps the family afloat in a practical and emotional sense. The importance of housework is never belittled, but rather revered and exclusified: for men to undertake domestic chores is an incursion into female territory, and one of the clichés of housewifery is that men are hopeless at housework. The most highly circulated women's magazines, even in the modestly liberated 1980s, still follow this line: their ideological strength comes from the fact that they are edited and written largely *by* women, that they do not have the air of a dispensed sexism.

Analogies between women's periodicals and programmes on radio aimed at women are instructive, up to a point. Commercially, the impetus is the same, to provide entertainment of a kind assumed to be of most interest to the home-tied woman and thereby create an editorial environment in which advertisers will want to promote products of traditional bearing on the female purse. When Capital Radio altered its programming in 1983 with a view to mining more finely the housewife audience in which its advertisers professed most interest, it hired the editor of *Honey*, Jo Sandilands, for the purpose. Editorially, there are obvious parallels between radio and traditional women's magazine journalism: mid-morning programmes in local radio are traditionally the home of the 'guest expert' – someone brought in to the studio once a week to give advice on a specific household topic, often keep-fit on a Monday ('to get us all in trim for the week ahead'), consumer matters on a Thursday ('to give a helping hand *vis-à-vis* the weekend shopping') and more practical matters (do-it-yourself, gardening) on a Friday, 'with a weekend of leisure in mind'.[17] The expert is usually someone representing local officialdom, for example the director of the local Citizens Advice Bureau, the chairman of the local gardening club, a local GP, officials from the local inland revenue office or small claims court. Then there is the radio agony column, a vein of programming first tapped by Capital in the mid-1970s in the form of an evening phone-in but now a regular feature of daytime programmes throughout local radio; most of radio's agony aunts and uncles are in fact writers on emotional or sexual topics (Claire Rayner, Anna Raeburn, Philip Hodson) who first made their name in magazine journalism. Phone-ins in general are little more than letters pages of the air, beloved of local radio because they combine cheapness of programme matter – the only cost incurred is use of the telephone facility, callers usually bearing the cost of the calls themselves – with the appearance of giving listeners 'access' to the airwaves.

However, daytime radio departs from the women's magazine approach in two ways. First, radio offers more than just a commentary on or a practical guide to domestic tasks: looking beyond the factual content of daytime radio, it is the message inherent in the entertainment provided – the seemingly inconsequential chat, the lyrics of the records played, the requests and dedications honoured, the relationship of the (male) presenter to the audience – that betrays radio's true perception of and attitude towards the female listener. Second, and related to this, radio is overwhelmingly a male domain, in which women have traditionally found difficulty in winning acceptance either as producers or as presenters and in which marketing principles – identifying a market for a product (in this case a radio programme) and fashioning that product to meet the perceived 'needs' of that market – remain prevalent even at supposedly 'public service' stations. The 'market' for daytime (post-9 a.m.) radio that stations have identified to their satisfaction is the woman at home, but is this traditional perception in fact correct?

The evidence of BBC and IBA research is that 'housewives' (using Ann Oakley's definition of a housewife as, effectively, a female houseworker) no longer (if they ever did) constitute a huge proportion of the daytime radio audience. During the hours of 9 a.m. to 12.30 a.m., 66 per cent of the audience is estimated to be female, 44 per cent male (IBA).[18] The BBC's *Daily Life in the 1980s* shows that 21 per cent of the female population with access to a radio set is listening at 10 a.m., 16 per cent at midday; comparative figures for male listening are 16 per cent at 10 a.m. and 19 per cent at midday.[19] While there is a clear female bias earlier in the morning, it is hardly enough to justify gender-specific programming. But much more pernicious than the simple attempt to translate a female bias in listenership into 'female programming' is the tendency to stereotype that listenership as housewives alone – and, worse, the tendency to stereotype housewives as passive home-makers with limited imaginations:

> We [Essex Radio] call our average listener Doreen. She lives in Basildon. Doreen isn't stupid but she's only listening with half an ear, and doesn't necessarily understand 'long words'. That doesn't mean that we treat her like a fool but that we make certain she understands first time, because when listening to radio you can't re-read what's just been said as you can in a newspaper. Her husband Bill is treated in the same way.[20]

In programme plans submitted to the IBA prior to the awarding of the London ILR franchises in 1973, Capital Radio pontificated with breathtakingly pompous certainty on women's interests and emotional 'needs':

> In constructing programmes to appeal to women (and to a large extent women as housewives) two things have been borne in mind. The first is that there is a very wide area of overlap between programmes that might be called 'general interest' and subjects that are also of deep interest to *some* men, but not of automatic interest to *all* men. . . . Lively programming in these areas ought to mean that not only would the housewife not turn off the programme – assuming she could rid her hands of flour quickly enough – but that a man punching the buttons of his car radio might find his attention caught. . . . The second thing is that there are certain fundamentals that women enjoy. Women are sentimental, or they care deeply about emotions. . . . They are escapists, or they are not sufficiently cold-blooded to enjoy drama which, if taken seriously, would represent alarm and despondency.[21]

This was, in Anne Karpf's words, 'a masterpiece of doublethink. It categorizes and stereotypes women in the crudest and most traditional way . . . but at the same time attempts to soften its impact with approvingly unctuous and apparently flattering alternative explanations'.[22] Such stereotypes have been forcefully challenged in a study by Helen Baehr and Michele Ryan, *Shut Up and Listen!*, which confronts the issue of the treatment of women in and by ILR by reference to the latter's experiences as a producer with CBC in Cardiff in 1981–2. They point out the lack of real research into 'the needs and interests of women listeners' and comment on the

> remarkably universal profile of 'the housewife' in the minds and hearts of ILR programme makers [from which] a very specific picture of the housewife can be built up: she is young, or at any rate 'young at heart'; she is married; she is part of the nuclear family, with husband (out at work) and children (in school); she does not work outside the home; she does all the housework; she is satisfied at being at home; she is generally content.[23]

Quoting figures documented by the Equal Opportunities Commission, they show that these kinds of perceptions have no real basis in fact. Britain's workforce comprises 15.6 million men and 10.4 million women; only 5 per cent of households follow the so-called average family pattern of a husband at work, a wife at home and two children; 62 per cent of married women are either working or actively looking for employment.[24] What Baehr and Ryan do not explain, however, is quite why ILR management teams should persist with the stereotype: can it be put down simply to the prejudice of male management, is it simple ignorance of the changing socio-economic fabric of Britain, or a pandering to the stereotypes beloved of the advertising world on which ILR depends for its commercial survival? It is clear that, for the radio stations, maintaining such a limited perception of the daytime audience is a matter not just of tradition or convenience but of deliberate policy. This, for example, is an ILR programme controller writing in the IBA's official quarterly, *Independent Broadcasting*, in 1984:

> When I joined Mercia Sound in Coventry, prior to going on air in 1980, I discussed the format of my programme – which was 9.30 a.m. until 1 p.m. – with my Programme Controller. He gave me a clear, if broad, outline of what he wanted and left me to it. From our discussions, I gathered he wanted to go for the housewives. And so we did. But people kept saying, 'there's 20 per cent unemployment in Coventry – shouldn't you be catering for the male listener at that time of day?' The Head of Music at the time was at the end of his tether with me, because I would insist on playing Mario Lanza or Mantovani next to Slade or Shakin' Stevens. But I remained totally sexist in a pro-female way, and it worked. The increase in the JICRAR [Joint Industry Committee for Radio Audience Research] figure was quite appreciable. We aimed for a particular segment of the audience, our assessment of the potential was apparently right, and we got results.[25]

The assumption that particular artists have automatic feminine appeal, that it is actually possible to be both 'totally sexist' and pro-female, that 'results' matter more than devising ways to meet the needs of the whole listening community, all indicate the nature, if not the origins, of ILR's housewife preoccupation.

Such attitudes are not, of course, confined to ILR: Britain's version of commercial radio was constructed in the light of BBC experience. I have commented elsewhere on how Radio 1 placed its faith in a mass audience of housewives during its early years, and that tendency has persisted. Speaking in 1977, Derek Chinnery described the average female listener to the network as 'this dreaded housewife figure who I think of as someone who, perhaps last year or two years ago, was a secretary working for a firm, who is now married and has a child. She wants music that will keep her happy and on the move'.[26] At that time, David Hamilton, presenter of the mid-afternoon show, still felt able to reprimand a listener who had written in to complain that his 'keep young and beautiful' spot (featuring beauty tips sent in by listeners) was patronizing and sexist with the remark that it was 'only a bit of fun'; he described his own image of his typical listener as 'a housewife, young or young at heart. She's probably on her own virtually all day. She's bored with the routine of housework and with her own company and for her I'm the slightly cheeky romantic visitor'.[27]

The preoccupation remains – Johnny Beerling referred in a 1986 interview to Simon Bates (Radio 1's 9 a.m. to 11.30 a.m. presenter) 'targeting to people listening in their own houses – that has to be generically housewives'.[28] This is despite the fact that Radio 1's image of its housewife listeners has modified over the years, there being no way that Bates for one would revert to the recipe features that Jimmy Young made his trademark between 1967 and 1973, or to features like the 'tiny tots spot' (a children's record played 'to give you mums a moment to put your feet up') which Young's mid-morning successor, Tony Blackburn, made a particularly patronizing part of his programme. Similarly the current occupant of the mid-afternoon programme, Steve Wright, would regard it as an offence to his professional standing to have to present such overtly sexist features as Hamilton's beauty tips or his predecessor Terry Wogan's 'fight the flab' exercise spot. Indeed, Radio 2 – home of Wogan, Young and Hamilton since the mid- to late 1970s – has fostered and perpetuated many of the traditional sexist perceptions in a much more overt manner. But we are to some extent talking of generational differences here: Radio 2 speaks to an audience both older in profile than Radio 1 and conservative in more than just the musical sense. It is characteristic of the Jimmy Young approach to women's programmes to emphasize domesticity in a material sense – the concentration on consumer affairs, the questioning of political guests on economic matters as they affect 'the family budget' (and Jimmy Young is Margaret Thatcher's favourite interviewer precisely because of this bias) – while the Radio 1 approach is more openly acknowledging of the fact that women have sexual lives, sexual banter and innuendo (and an apparent obsession with the sexual lives of the famous) being one of the chief characteristics of the Steve Wright show in particular. What has changed is simply the degree of permissiveness within daytime radio: Radio 1 attempts to speak to a supposedly more 'liberated' female, but the underlying attitudes remain. Looking at the style of presentation adopted, the speech content, the music chosen and the manner of its programming, daytime pop radio (including much of ILR) perpetuates a superficially more contemporary version of the old stereotype – woman as not only inherently domestic but romantically inclined to the point of obsessiveness.

## Women's programming?

Rosalind Coward, in an essay in *Female Desire: Women's Sexuality Today*, has identified 'sexual desire, attraction and love' as the chief themes not only of the music featured in daytime radio but of the major part of disc jockey chatter.[29] She shows how the features of a typical daytime show – the dedications of records to loved ones, slots like Capital's 'top six' feature in which listeners ring in with their personal selection of favourite records, even the horoscopes that only half-jokingly promise romantic encounters – are all geared to the romantic lives of women; both the music played and its framing by the presenter encourages listeners towards an appreciation of popular music for its *emotional* value, that is to associate the popular records of today and yesterday either with specific memories of particular emotional moments (a first kiss, a blind date, a summer romance) or with a more generalized nostalgia for a pre-nuptial past. 'Daytime radio', she writes, 'works to validate the choices which women have made. The phase of their lives when they went to parties, experienced their carnival of emotions, is treated nostalgically as part of a comfortable personal history . . . [it] tells women who are isolated and at home, and possibly very fed up, that the choices which they made were OK'. Dorothy Hobson, in a study of women's uses of daytime radio, similarly suggests that it 'can be seen . . . as providing women with a musical reminder of their leisure activities before they married' and also as a 'substitute for the real world of music and discos which they have lost'.[30] What daytime radio attempts to offer to women is escapism, but not just the mundane escape from tedium or the rut of housework: at its most effective, it also *engages* the listener in a manner which critics of the assumed blandness (i.e. *lack* of engagement) of radio programming often fail to fully appreciate. Contemporary radio does not *simply* act as a barrier against boredom or as a setter of time boundaries for the day, it also peddles fantasy of a deliberately modest, yet still powerful kind. A very subtle form of oppression is at work here.

Simon Bates's Radio 1 show provides excellent examples of the tendencies identified by Coward and Hobson, particularly the constant assumption that nostalgia – the rooting of musical meaning in memory or evocative value, not in straight musical appreciation – is an intrinsically 'feminine' concern. Bates has a daily spot called 'Our Tune', for which listeners are invited to pick a record associated with particularly strong memories of an event, person or time: according to a feature in the *Sun*, 'up to 500 letters pour in each week from listeners revealing a secret sadness they haven't shared with their nearest and dearest'.[31] A piece of lush orchestral music played gently under Bates's voice sets the tone for a story of personal upset or tragedy – a child born to a father shortly to die of cancer, a marriage that both sets of parents said would never work and didn't – that acts as a prelude to the song in question. It is sentimental theatre, deftly done, and can be undeniably moving at times, but it is of course deeply manipulative: the stories (or rather, Bates's telling of them – he rarely quotes direct from the letters) evoke sympathy or even empathy while providing reassurance. They suggest to the listener that she is not alone, or that her own situation may not be so bad after all. Above all, Bates offers a kind of temporary *resolution* to what are often fairly universal and time-honoured situations: a listener's letter is rarely featured which does not carry some implicit moral or message, even if the ending is a sad one. 'Our Tune' is admittedly a very special example of the kind of emotional stage management that is endemic to daytime radio, but in essence it is no more than an extended dedication spot, in which the customary baring of feelings for lovers, family or friends takes on an almost confessional aspect.

Another regular feature of the Bates programme is the 'golden hour' of oldies, divided into two 30-minute sections covering a selected year. The fact that virtually the only extended slot for oldies on Radio 1 should be within a show targeted primarily at housewives is revealing. Bates's technique is to frame records from the year in question with the headline news of the time, cleverly juxtaposing the world-shattering with the parochial, 'silly season' news stories with brief accounts of political upheavals or distant wars and a flurry of statistics on prices, tax rates, television ownership or cinema-going. Although Bates – a Radio 2 newsreader-cum-continuity announcer before he became a Radio 1 presenter – has perfected a cool, measured, even faintly ironic delivery, the effect of this constant juxtaposition is to reduce every event referred to down to the same level of nostalgic, romanticized trivia, a uniting of personal and public history under the same cosy umbrella. It *packages* the past in a manageable, undemanding way.

Bates is a self-confessed populist, and his programme betrays an alarming tendency not so much to talk down to his (apparently) mainly female audience as to assume of them a limited range of expectations and interests. His stock-in-trade is gossip about show business personalities, usually from the pop, film or television worlds, studiously gleaned from the pages of the tabloid press or from his own 'researches'; he features pre-recorded interviews (often 'exclusives', extensively trailed in the *Radio Times* and in other Radio 1 programmes) which gently probe the life-styles of the stars in the manner of a Sunday supplement article, but one continually senses that he imposes deliberate constraints on his questioning in deference to his audience; that he can be an intelligent and incisive commentator on events is evident from his occasional programme-making for Radio 4, notably compiling and presenting *Pick of the Week*. Certainly he and his producer generally avoid the worst excesses of *outright* sexism that characterize the programmes of many of his competitors on other stations. Elsewhere, indeed, mid-morning presenters parade their populism by taking ostentatious delight in patronizing their listeners and, occasionally, their guests. A woman ringing in to take part in a phone-in competition is sent up unmercifully because the milkman happens to call for his money at the same time ('you mean you're paying *him*, darling?'); another competition contestant is 'reassured', after telling the presenter that she is 'only a housewife', that 'housewives do a marvellous job – tell your husband I said that and perhaps he'll drop you an extra quid in the housekeeping'; a woman from the Citizens Advice Bureau (invited on to a programme to discuss returning defective goods) is asked if she has done her ironing yet 'because there's lovely weather forecast and you don't want to be stuck behind an ironing board all weekend, do you?'[32] Then there is the self-parodic figure of Tony Blackburn, who has 'progressed' from preaching to women listeners to his 9 a.m. to 12 midday Radio 1 show about the perils of adultery and how divorce actions hit the husband hardest, to running a daily morning programme on BBC Radio London in which women are invited to indulge in sexual flirtation with him over the air. ('Have I got a 12-incher for you today, ladies ... how about if I call round and kiss you in all those important places?'[33]) Blackburn's portrayal of sexual excess as harmless macho fun needs little comment: it is precisely the 'page-three broadcasting' of which Radio Clyde boss Jimmy Gordon warned in 1984, writ large.[34]

## Jockeying for position: the male preserve

Dorothy Hobson describes Blackburn (in his mid-1970s guise) as representing 'an extreme form of the reinforcement of the dominant ideology of domesticity of the housebound listeners of Radio 1'.[35] What the presenter says, the tone of voice he adopts, the attitude he strikes all articulate that ideology in subtle ways, 'he' being the operative pronoun. While women are coming to play a more active role in radio presentation, particularly at local level, the mid-morning show remains an almost exclusively male preserve throughout national and local radio. The low ratio of women on the presentation side of radio is itself a reflection of the prevailing daytime radio perception of the woman as housewife, and the usual reason forwarded by station executives as to why women do not occupy the mid-morning slots is that such an apparent contradiction of that perception might alienate the listening audience. 'If a girl in some studio in London starts talking about getting your washing and ironing done, you're going to resent it', Doreen Davies, Executive Producer at Radio 1 until her retirement in 1987, has said: 'It just sounds personal to another woman. It's different if Tony Blackburn says it; that's just light-hearted'.[36]

But why should *any* presenter, male or female, necessarily have to talk about housework anyway? The fear of station managers is possibly not so much the question of causing resentment as the implicit calling into question of the listener's own role as a domestic labourer: the conventional ILR perception of the woman-as-housewife is reinforced by the advertisements themselves, which invariably feature women as housewives and/or mothers while depicting men in positions of authority. The voiceover in radio advertising is itself an almost wholly male domain, because male voices are traditionally seen by agencies and their clients as carrying authority and influence. There is an unspoken fear, too, that the placing of a woman in radio prime time might *create* expectations among the female audience. This is precisely the argument *for* more women at prime time put forward by a number of the women who are already established (albeit in non-prime-time shows, like Radio 1's Anne Nightingale and Janice Long) as radio voices: one clear way to get more female voices heard on radio, to encourage new talent to come forward, is to provide role models. Of course, there is something backhanded about this, echoes of the woman having to prove herself in what is accepted to be a man's world, to be accepted in effect as an honorary male. An alternative way forward is mapped out in the pages of *Shut Up and Listen!*, where Baehr and Ryan suggest that it is the very nature of 'women's programming' in radio (patriarchal, imposed, limiting and limited) that requires changing by pressure from women listeners themselves.[37]

Sexism within radio runs deep. Senior male staff even refer to their stations in 'feminine' terms: 'Capital is the woman who is ageing, used to be beautiful and has to wear heavy make-up to cover the cracks', Tom Hunter, head of publicity at LBC in London, has opined in the pages of *Broadcast*, 'whereas LBC is the undiscovered beauty who has been living at home with her mother'.[38] Would-be women presenters have to counter a number of ingrained and rarely questioned prejudices: the belief among programme controllers that a woman would limit herself to talking about traditional women's concerns, the belief that high voices do not carry authority (Nightingale and Long, it is pointed out, have deep, husky voices), the feeling that women are somehow not assertive or ambitious enough to take the top spots in radio, the feeling that those women who are ambitious and assertive will be detected as such by the audience and disliked as the 'pushy woman' of male myth. Speaking at the Radio Festival in 1984, Red Rose Radio's managing director, Keith Macklin, came up with a further variation (and prompted a furious reaction from women in the audience) when he suggested that women presenters 'always sound as if they're metaphorically putting on make-up'. Though Baehr and Ryan found some general enthusiasm among programme controllers for recruiting more women, the common argument was that women simply do not see radio as a potential career and, unless some kind of tokenism is operated, men will invariably be granted the plum jobs because of greater radio experience. Meanwhile, IBA-sponsored research into public attitudes to women on radio is not encouraging: among the findings of a 1984 study into listener's perceptions of presenters in general was the belief that 'few women are as well equipped as men to handle humour in public . . . comparatively few female voices are conducive to relaxed listening', though reactions to established women presenters in two of the areas covered by the survey (County Sound in Guildford, Piccadilly in Manchester) was positive.[39]

In Baehr and Ryan's book, the Controller of Invicta Radio, Michael Bukht (who had the same position at Capital in its early years before taking up a position with the National Broadcasting School), suggests that women are more capable of handling the 'meaningful speech' element of ILR content than music-based shows. Accepting that Bukht's definition of 'capability' means the skill with which women presenters can replicate the customary tone of voice or the cultivated macho presence of male music presenters, he has a point: the very presence of a female voice on daytime radio does alter the nature of the rapport with women listeners, as it draws on an essentially asexual intimacy rather than exploiting the sexual potential (albeit entirely in fantasy) of the relationship between the male presenter and his female flock – a relationship Doreen Davies likens to 'having a male friend in the house while the husband's away without the obvious repercussions'.[40] Davies also suggests that prejudice against women within music radio may also be a reflection of that against women in the music industry itself, where it is only in recent years that women have come to be accepted in a major way as musicians in their own right rather than simply as singers or as glamorous figureheads, and where women have traditionally played an important backroom role (as press officers and personal assistants) yet have been largely excluded from positions of influence in management and A & R. Perhaps more significantly, if music radio is, as Baehr and Ryan describe ILR, 'a medium dominated by male producers and female consumers', then traditionally the same has been true of pop music production itself. Indeed, the traditional contemptuousness shown not only by producers but by media commentators and critics towards the tastes of female record buyers in their teens mirrors and *anticipates* that of radio gatekeepers towards women in general and housewives in particular.

## Presenters: the Redcoat mentality

The daytime presenter is in the front line of the maintenance of radio's domestic ideology, and it is appropriate, finally, to examine that role a little more closely. Presenters (the term 'disc jockey' has fallen out of fashion in recent years) are the cheery, matey, companionable voice of music radio – the important *personal* link between station and audience, their role combining that of entertainer, counsellor, professional Everyman and permanent PR man. With the presenter lies the responsibility for forging and keeping a relationship with the listeners, in the course of which (depending on whether he is on local or national radio) he may have to act not only as a full-time record spinner but as an interviewer of the great and good, as an expert on the day's news, as a fascinated questioner on everything from antiques to veterinary bills, and as a source of perpetual good humour and repartee. Combining elements of straightforward announcing, reporting, news reading and stand-up comedy, the contemporary disc jockey is (especially at local level) a broadcasting jack-of-all-trades floating uneasily between the two worlds of show business and radio journalism.

What he is not required to be, paradoxically, is a music enthusiast. Indeed, one of the most striking features of the disc jockey's role in the context of a station's *business* – the actual process of music selection, the formulation of marketing strategies – is how minor it is; as I showed in Chapter 7, the producer, programme controller or head of music is the source of real power and influence in music radio. Except in the case of some stations (BBC locals and ILR) where some senior presenters also double as producers for specialist evening shows, the presenter is employed primarily for his voice, his technical ability (if only at the mundane level of operating a turntable and not talking over the vocals of records or 'crashing' the commercials[41]) and his personality. A disc jockey, as critic David Hepworth wrote of Jimmy Savile, doesn't 'do', he *is*,[42] which in turn encourages the development of a 'star' mentality. The employment of presenters on freelance contracts – standard practice at Radios 1 and 2 and among the larger metropolitan ILR stations – rather than as members of staff accentuates this, and music radio has long been a stepping stone to a career in television (Terry Wogan, Kenny Everett, Noel Edmonds, Mike Smith, Gloria Hunniford, Timmy Mallett and Mike Read all made the transition with relative ease).[43]

Historically, disc jockeys stand at the end of an evolutionary line that began with the BBC announcer-cum-newsreader, who framed the beginning and close of programmes with scripted pieces of information delivered dispassionately in clipped BBC English. Two further traditions of radio presentation developed in tandem: the expert, typified by Christopher Stone, who spoke articulately and knowledgeably of his subject; and the compere, whose function was to inject a sense of showmanship and glamour into the broadcasts of variety acts and dance-bands. Luxembourg's policy of allowing its post-war disc jockeys to ad lib was not adopted by the BBC until the early 1960s (Jimmy Young credits his late-night Saturday show for the Popular Music Department, which began in 1963, as the first Light Programme music show to dispense with a pre-approved script), but the standard Light Programme approach to presentation generally followed the cosy, intimate manner established during the war. 'Disc jockey' itself was an American term (derived from the way radio presenters 'rode' selected records into the best-selling record chart), and I mentioned in Chapter 3 how presentation in US radio changed with the coming of rock 'n' roll, switching from the easy-going, soft-centred approach of *Make Believe Ballroom* to the frenetic, rapid-fire delivery copied by white presenters from disc jockeys on black stations. This style came to Britain via pirate radio, where the adoption of a fake American 'mid-Atlantic' accent became almost obligatory, but it is important to note that the pirate disc jockeys had few American role models: a handful of the pirate recruits had experience in commercial radio overseas (including BFBS), but most were young amateurs who based their style on what they *imagined* that of the average American disc jockey to be. The pirate factor apart, British 'disc jockeying' developed in line with the Luxembourg mode: the BBC's first disc jockeys were largely ex-Luxembourg men like David Jacobs, Pete Murray and Brian Matthew, avuncular figures who were meant to act as go-betweens, trusted by the adult establishment but benign and sympathetic enough to be accepted by teenage listeners. This approach was successfully absorbed into television: *Juke Box Jury, Thank Your Lucky Stars, Ready Steady Go!* and *Top of the Pops* all had professional front men drawn from the Light Programme-Luxembourg axis.

One of the paradoxes of pirate radio was that while the amount of air-time allocated to the jockeys (sometimes up to five hours at a stretch) and the concentration on listener feedback (letters, competitions, dedications) encour-aged disc jockeys to think of themselves as stars, or at least as public figures with a following, the general entertainment and fashion milieu of the mid-1960s – and particularly its population by apparently working-class figures like the Beatles, Mary Quant, David Bailey, Twiggy – inspired a kind of cultivated 'ordinariness' in manner, typified by the exaggerated provinciality of Kenny Everett and Dave Lee Travis. Radio 1 took the notion of disc-jockey-as-star still further, dispensing with individual programme titles (*Easy Beat, Saturday Club* and *Pick of the Pops* all changed title within two years or were dispensed with altogether) in favour of just the presenter's name in the *Radio Times* listings, but again qualities of chumminess and first-name affability were regarded as paramount. The double effect was to encourage the idea that 'disc jockeying' could be a serious career, or at least a means of entry into the wider show business world, and to stereotype the function and personality of a music radio presenter in a very

The inevitable result of this was a cloning effect, accentuated by the paucity of outlets for the would-be disc jockey between 1967 and 1973. Only Radio 1 and Luxembourg provided role models, and only Radio 1 and Luxembourg offered job opportunities: the awkward Light Programme/pirate radio hybrid style of presentation favoured by both stations became self-perpetuating. The stations even drew on each other for suitable presenters: as Derek Chinnery later approvingly remarked, 'people who worked on Luxembourg were very conscious of broadcasting nationally, and the fact that they were living abroad anyway broadened their experience',[44] and both Noel Edmonds and Paul Burnett came to Radio 1 via this route. In the absence of other outlets, those intent on a jockeying career developed their 'trade' generally on a semi-professional basis; the standard pattern was for the aspirant jockey to set up a disco roadshow, at its simplest a set of dance records, a stereo system and PA and accompanying light show, and establish it locally, as entertainment for parties, wedding receptions, school dances or college functions. The other main outlet, mentioned earlier, was the industrial station, and UBN was particularly vital here because not only did it recruit presenters, it also trained them in broadcasting technique and practice. Unsurprisingly, as local radio expanded in the 1970s and experienced presenters became thin on the ground, UBN was a prime source of microphone 'talent': Capital's Graham Dene was UBN's head of training in the early 1970s, and Roger Scott (Capital) and Tony Gillham (BBC Radio Bedfordshire, ex-Mercia Sound and Chiltern) were just two others who came through the UBN ranks. Equally, because UBN presenters were trained in the art of speaking to a captive, mainly female workforce – jollying them along, reassuring them of the value of their work, making great play of being a male in an all-female world – they were ideal for recruitment to positions in daytime ILR, where the 'housewife' was pursued as a commercial imperative. In the end, what UBN contributed to British radio was a number of highly professional, apparently imperturbable presenters with astonishingly similar styles and even voices – presenters who in some cases moved on to management positions, presenters whose sense of good radio practice (essentially, what to say and how to say it) was formed within a particularly functional broadcasting discipline and clearly continues to be informed by it. This is not to say that the patronization of women that is so much a part of daytime radio can be wholly blamed on certain ex-UBN presenters, but rather that the UBN legacy has become diffused throughout local radio in particular as they themselves have become role models. Ironically, it is the cloning of disc jockeys in the Roger Scott/Graham Dene mould that – even allowing for the vast expansion in radio since the mid-1970s and the consequent increase in the number of professional disc jockeys applying for radio jobs – causes Radio 1 chief Johnny Beerling to complain of the difficulty in finding suitable voices for the station:

> Too many people who aspire to work in radio base what they do on existing characters and don't try to create anything unique. . . . On BBC local radio, the severe limitation of needletime precludes the presentation of more than a few hours per day of music radio. On ILR, most managers play it safe so as not to offend either advertisers or listeners. Hence blandness and a very incestuous style of DJ-ing.[45]

Beerling suggests that one of the lessons of 1960s pirate radio was that disc jockeys blossom in an unregulated environment, and he looks to future, similarly unregulated community radio to produce more 'original' talent. (Radio 1 has already had some success in recruiting disc jockeys direct from contemporary pirate stations – Dixie Peach, Ranking Miss P. – for weekend and evening slots.) But sources of disc jockey talent are few, and what might be seen as a potentially munificent source of new presenters – night-clubs and discos, where DJs have perfected the US-born arts of scratching and 'disco mixing' – Beerling rejects out of hand, insisting that the disciplines of club jockeying (playing to the crowd) and radio broadcasting (suggesting a one-to-one relationship with the listener) are entirely different. Whatever his criticisms of ILR and BBC local radio, it is from such stations that Radio 1 has drawn five out of its eight current weekday presenters.

As the top of the career pyramid in radio presenting, Radio 1 has its own influence on disc jockeying at every level. I have stressed at several points in this book how important the influence of Radio 1 has been on the shape and content of British radio since 1967, the point being that all would-be competitors aim to attract broadly the same audience. It is the *values* of Radio 1 broadcasting that have been most doggedly absorbed, especially by commercial radio, and the outcome is a very standard, irredeemably egotistical, monotonously upbeat style of presentation. David Hepworth's comments on the career pattern of the typical Radio 1 disc jockey are apposite here:

> Most of them get into the job early, running the school disco, judging knobbly knees competitions, choreographing the hokey cokey at weddings, eventually graduating to local radio. Through this school they acquire a Redcoat mentality which manifests itself in a single-minded dedication to getting everyone to cheer up, as though a listening audience who weren't permanently wreathed in beatific smiles were a slight on their professional capabilities.[46]

The other key training ground for would-be jockeys that Hepworth could have mentioned, hospital radio, inspires a similar disposition: playing records for bed-confined patients, hospital jockeys develop a vein of jolly patter optimistically aimed at alleviating pain, boredom and the hardship of enforced separation from family and friends. The rules are carefully kept: no constant reminders of the reasons why people are there, no mentions of illnesses by name, no loud music in deference to the older patients, but plenty of dedications to show that people are not forgotten. It is within hospital radio that future radio professionals learn the art of dispensing a kind of aural balm to a largely captive audience; it is within hospital radio that they learn the standard radio definition of service to the community, which is to reflect sympathetically, uncontroversially and selectively the most positive aspects of community life.

Daytime disc jockeys, and daytime radio as a whole, fulfil the primary function of entertainment which, as Richard Dyer suggests, is to 'provide escape ... show business operates in full awareness of the unpleasantness of most people's lives: it is built into its definition of its job that it must provide an alternative to the world of work and of general drudgery and depression'.[47] Dyer describes the mechanisms by which entertainment achieves this as *obliteration, contrast* and *incorporation*, and in radio these are easy to trace. Music radio obliterates the nasty and discomfiting by means of simple exclusion – the gatekeeping function described in the previous chapter – and by celebrating fantasy and romance in its stead. Where music radio does 'acknowledge the existence of the real world', it contrasts that reality against 'the warmth of the immediate moment': music radio glories in an insulatory kind of good-time camaraderie, marshalled by the disc jockey and reinforced by the paraphernalia of listener response – competitions, phone-in requests, outside broadcasts. The cleverest disc jockeys encourage the listener to feel special, even unique, yet simultaneously one of a community of listeners with common interests, tastes and emotions. Finally, music radio puts forward an alternative, eternally positive world-view by selective incorporation of 'elements of the real world' into its programming; it 'tries to deny that the world is, after all, so bad' by emphasizing, most commonly, the comic side of life and feeding off other media (television, newspapers, cinema) for confirmation of the alternative scenario it favours.

Presenters shoulder the main responsibility for the success of music radio *as entertainment*, and like any entertainers they fall prey to delusions of grandeur, to an exaggerated view of their own importance at the very least. The most overbearing sees his audience as a community of listeners united around *him*, and the tell-tale signs are an overdefensiveness in interviews, an inordinate stress on the size of his programme's postbag, and a cultivated anti-intellectualism. But if disc jockeys are entertainers, they are also salesmen, '*selling* sincerity' in Emperor Rosko's telling phrase[48] in a commercial (ILR, Radio Luxembourg) or pseudo-commercial (Radio 1) environment. Disc jockeys sell themselves and sell their station; they record voiceovers for radio and television commercials; one of the increasingly important training grounds for disc jockeys is the in-shop studio to be found at chain stores like Top Shop, where bright UBN-type voices nudge customers towards bargain offers or new-to-shop lines between bursts of Stevie Wonder and Billy Ocean and custom-made jingles. The commercial world, not radio itself, provides the best-known disc jockeys with their main source of income; radio fame enables them to build a much more lucrative career making personal appearances, opening supermarkets or running their own roadshow.

Inevitably, daytime radio gets the disc jockeys it deserves, who justify its simplistic populism by extolling it as a prime example of consumer-led service – responsive, responsible, reflective of and owing its existence to a customer consensus. It is an attitude born of the self-preservative spirit that runs right through radio, a peculiar mixture of cynicism and defensiveness: only in the poorly patronized evenings and at odd spots on the weekend, when television supersedes radio as the main source of entertainment and the medium's mythical consensus magically fragments into a host of 'minority' communities of tastes or interest, is the populist grip allowed to relent. Keith Belcher, a disillusioned former Programmme Controller of Southern Sound in Brighton, has perhaps put it best:

> By and large, radio's a pleasant, passive medium produced to interest some non-existent majority. Is it me, or is it all immensely boring? A procession of strip-show presenters, nationwide or corner-shop, plodding on day after day tucked behind the thumb-sucking security of the Top 40 and Frank Sinatra. Nothing startling, nothing dangerous, nothing memorable.[49]

# 9 Late in the evening: minorities and specialisms in music radio

Let's not be seduced by any unhealthy longing to be credible to the minority, or popular with the denizens of that mythical Tin Pan Alley. In broad terms we need to maximise our audience, not to drive it away by being musically élitist, or playing to the *Time Out* gallery.

Simon Bates, Radio 1 presenter[1]

When Simon Bates made the above remarks in an article just prior to the 1986 Music Radio Conference, John Peel was moved to riposte that they constituted 'as eloquent a plea for cultural fascism as I've ever heard in my life'.[2] Bates and Peel are two of Radio 1's most established and longest-serving presenters; Peel is in fact the network's only survivor from its original 1967 DJ line-up. Their audiences are loyal and long-standing, but they operate from entirely opposite poles of the music radio spectrum. Bates is the arch-populist, delighted to be entertaining an audience second only in size to that of the breakfast show with music chosen by a producer and patter derived at least partly from a judicious reading of the *Sun* and the *Mirror*; Peel is Radio 1's resident guardian of self-chosen alternative musics, a holder of a late-night ghetto slot who talks affirmatively of the Reithian principles of encouraging audiences to discriminate in their listening and of bringing the more difficult and demanding to their attention. In his own way, each represents a different pole of BBC traditionalism, and there is no doubt who can feel the most secure; rumours of Peel's impending removal have circulated for years, and Johnny Beerling has warned that any switch in funding for Radio 1 from the licence fee to advertising would almost certainly mean pressure for more 'popular' programming and consequently no place for Peel in the evening line-up. But this is to simplify matters: Peel, and what he represents in the sense of giving alternative voices a hearing and upholding the right of 'minorities' to space on the airwaves, acts not only as a bastion against 'cultural fascism' but as a built-in bringer of credibility to a network that would otherwise be seen as having no 'serious' purpose at all. However hostile Bates and Peel may be towards each other in musical attitude, they need each other: a wholly 'popular' Radio 1 could not justify continual public funding without some kind of intellectual credibility behind it, while programmes of the Peel variety would never reach the air but for what is effectively subsidization by the daytime shows.

What is true for Radio 1 is also true for commercial radio: although ILR stations do not depend on public funds, their survival does depend on honouring their franchises and meeting with the approval of the IBA, which in turn means producing programmes for 'public service' reasons for minority audiences. Station executives talk of winning 'brownie points' from the IBA for their minority coverage, though ILR defines 'minorities' not just in terms of followers for particular 'non-popular' musics but as a series of special-interest groups – ethnic minorities, children and the elderly among them. Behind all such programming lie paternalistic assumptions about the 'duty' of broadcasting to cater for all, but within radio as a whole that duty has long been approached in a strictly pragmatic, not to say cynical way: creating a separate stream of minority programming enables the broadcaster to remove from mainstream programming anything that might question or threaten the majority consensus, while conferring a limited legitimacy on the minorities concerned. It is as if the minorities are expected to trade their right to be heard for the knowledge that few outside those minorities are likely to hear them anyway. The scheduling of minority programmes apart from standard majority fare is acknowledgement of this: because tradition and research dictate that the biggest audiences tune in during the daytime hours, radio stations aim their daytime fare at what I quoted Keith Belcher as calling (in the previous chapter) 'a mythical consensus', leaving the barely listened-to evening hours as a repository for the alternative and the worthy.

In a sense, such programmes *are* no more than conscience slots, designed with the specific purpose of enhancing a station's public service profile, but they carry other implications. The granting of air-time to minorities denotes a prior process of selection and prioritization: *which* minorities gain the allocation, how are their needs assessed and by whom? Why are certain specialist programmes run on a shoestring budget – sometimes on the strict understanding that they do not eat into the station's precious needle-time allocation – while others make healthy use of specially recorded sessions or out-of-studio recordings (local classical concerts, for example)? And how effective are the programmes in reflecting, fairly and comprehensively, the requirements of their supposed target audience? In this final chapter, I want to try to answer some of these questions and explore 'alternative' programming in its wider sense, that is the attempts by those working *outside* mainstream radio to broaden not only the range of choice available to listeners but the scope of radio (and particularly music radio) itself. This takes us into the area of contemporary radio piracy and proposed community radio, which its advocates believe has the potential to strike at the heart of the contrived daytime/night-time dichotomy of popular radio and, perhaps more significantly, subvert the very definition of radio professionalism by making a priority of listener involvement in the programme-making process. Certainly, as more frequencies become available and it becomes politically expedient for government to allow much greater expansion of the radio medium than hitherto, as the radio audience is increasingly perceived (by administrators as well as practitioners) as a collection of individual communities rather than a single homogenous listenership, and as (crucially) the emphasis in advertising and business switches from mass marketing to demographically defined target marketing, so radio ostensibly aimed at minorities – young people, women, blacks, non-English speakers, as well as minority music lovers – comes to assume a greater importance. But as community radio assumes at least some of the programming areas that are currently the province of night-time (and weekend) radio, so popular radio also becomes free to pursue with greater diligence than ever the audience maximization of which Simon Bates speaks so highly. Is the paradox of community radio that it actually strengthens the hand of the populists, turning national music radio in particular into a Top Forty or easy-listening playground and pushing the minorities further back into the radio ghetto?

## Programming for youth?

Derek Chinnery has succinctly defined the function of Radio 1 as 'to cater for the available audience', and we have already seen how the daytime output of the network changes with each perceived shift in the demographic make-up of the audience.[3] The placing of minority programmes in the evening hours is, if Radio 1's official line is to be accepted, simply a reflection of the fact that listening figures decline dramatically from 7 p.m. onwards, leaving a residue of young and *committed* listeners who tune in to the network in deliberate preference to watching television:

> The majority of people watch television in the evenings and don't listen to the radio. You ask yourself who is *likely* to be listening to the radio in the evening, and particularly to pop and rock music. The age group is going to be lower, largely young people ... I think the distinction is that the listener is more likely to be taking what we do seriously in the sense that they're more attentive.[4]

Research commissioned by Radio Luxembourg into evening patronage of radio has indicated that Radio 1's audience does indeed drop sharply after 7.30 p.m., from 2.2 million to less than 500,000, but there are some interesting assumptions in Chinnery's statement.[5] Television's senior relationship to radio is unques-tioned, and there are more trailers on daytime Radios 1 and 2 for forthcoming BBC television programmes than for the networks' own evening shows; daytime radio and night-time television are assumed to share the same basic audience. But even if one accepts that the listening profile of the evening audience is considerably younger than that during the day – and the teenage audience does have a traditionally low patronage of television – there are spurious grounds for assuming both that the audience is automatically more 'attentive' and that their musical wants fall into the nebulous category of 'serious' non-Top-Forty music which forms the core of the various evening programmes. (Radio Luxembourg, with the youngest audience profile – 71 per cent under 35 years – of any UK station, assesses the requirements of its audience quite differently; it continues to play straight Top Forty pop music in the early to mid-evening as it has done for twenty years.[6]) Above all, Chinnery's comments suggest (oddly for a radio station cultivating a young image) that youth is itself perceived as a minority audience, and it explicitly accepts that there are internal qualitative distinctions within pop music which require honouring.

Radio 1's image of the after-7.30 p.m. listener is in fact very specific. Essentially, he or she is depicted as a school or college student and the programmes as a background to homework or study; the implication is that the programmes act as a stimulus to and as a reward for study, and they act as occasional vehicles for the station's various 'social action' campaigns, among them spots designed to give advice on choosing GCE or GCSE subjects, university or polytechnic applications or general career prospects. Johnny Beerling suggests:

> If I'm right, and there is a certain amount of guesswork involved, the audience that's listening is a student audience and it is the youngsters who are either doing their homework or don't have any money to go out. Lots of youngsters today, because of the unemployment situation, haven't got the money to buy the latest video or album by fairly obscure bands, so it's part of Radio 1's public service duty to try and provide that missing musical education for them. That's what Peel and Kershaw, Vance and Peebles, all of those people, do, I think.[7]

Such 'educational' notions underpin much of the evening and weekend output, not only in the sense of assuming in the listener a certain degree of (or willingness to achieve) intellectual attainment, but also in the sense of providing programes of educative value. In the past these have included documentaries on hard news stories such as heroin abuse and the migration of unemployed young people from the provinces to London, but usually the Radio 1 documentary has taken the standard form of a musician's profile (*Simon and Garfunkel Together and Alone, The Beach Boys Story, The John Lennon Tapes*), often based on extended interviews, or an illustrated musical account of a particular phase in pop history (*Hitsville USA*, about Tamla Motown, *From Punk to Present, The Story of Pop* itself). The Executive Producer in charge of evening and weekend output at Radio 1 is Stuart Grundy, who in the 1970s initiated, produced and presented many such series.

The problem with the majority of the evening output is that it reflects a fundamentally middle-class usage and *interpretation* of pop music; that is, to paraphrase Simon Frith, pop is regarded not simply as an accompaniment to leisure (which he defines as the standard use of rock by working-class youth) but as a focus of leisure.[8] Andrew Weiner has described the 'progressive rock' of the late 1960s as 'enshrining and propagating middle-class values and aspirations: creativity, individuality, intellectuality',[9] and I commented in Chapter 4 on Radio 1's role in carving out an intellectual identity for that music among students and sixth-formers in particular. While there may be little stylistic link between what passed for progressive rock and the music now played on Janice Long's show or John Peel's, the values are similar: presenter and listeners alike thrive on their sense of isolation from the plebeian hordes who buy Top Forty records; records emanating from independent labels are described as such to emphasize their separateness from (and superiority to) the products of the mainstream record industry; didacticism is revered, anything with less than serious intent criticized as value-*less*. Frith has further described student-oriented rock as taking on

> an ideological purpose that's rarely needed in working class culture. . . . Higher education gives access to culture as well as to knowledge, and 'free-time' activities are, in fact, part of a wider learning experience. Leisure concerns art as well as entertainment and in so far as students learn the conventions of traditional high culture, rock may get dragged into the argument, to be given intellectual and aesthetic justification and not just casually enjoyed. Students' tastes become significant, as does their ability to argue their tastes; music is used as a source of value.[10]

It is the notion that rock has cultural value that Radio 1 so diligently reflects and legitimizes outside the daytime hours. Even the pop documentaries follow the standard 'progressive' interpretation of pop history, plotting the careers of musicians in terms of ill-defined artistic development, beginning with his or her influences and ending with the influence he or she has had on others. But that cultural value is limited to middle-class concerns – music as an expression of individual creativity, music as art, music as statement, music as inherently meaningful – and is generally accepted uncritically. Evening programmes may be aimed at a discriminating listener, but the comments of Long and Peel are almost always wholly affirmative: the spoken links between the records aim to inform rather than provoke, and (though this is less true in Peel's case) they tend to assume a consensus of opinion among the listeners in the same way that daytime presenters assume a consensus of taste among theirs.

All this amounts to a narrow perspective on youth and youth culture. It locates the listener in the home (or the equivalent of home – hall of residence, bedsit, student house), in solitary activity, and in a curious way it ignores the possibility that young people can be social animals. There is a little more acknowledgement of the latter in the weekend schedules, when Radio 1 offers programmes such as Dixie Peach's *Midnight Runner Show* and Robbie Vincent's eponymous show, both of which highlight American (and sometimes British) soul music and attempt to simulate some of the excitement of a club or disco night out. Soul music's following among white working-class teenagers is traditional, with particularly strong local pockets in the East Midlands, the North-West and London, where Vincent's weekly Radio London show was one of the few regular outlets for soul on radio anywhere in Britain during the 1970s; his Radio 1 show offers the same mixture of gig news, new releases and club mixes, information from the United States and the occasional live interview with a visiting personality, all delivered in affectedly laconic style and aimed firmly at a streetwise cognoscenti. These shows apart, the exposure that Radio 1 gives to black music seems pitiful, especially when compared with the attempts by Capital and Radio London to make soul-cum-funk the very basis of their respective playlists in the mid-1980s and to convey at least some sense of the music's dance-floor strengths. (The competition between the two stations has been intense in this regard: late in 1986, Radio London poached Capital's resident evening presenter, Gary Crowley, to help launch the nightly *Nite FM*, which was to major on what producer Tom Brown described as the main elements of 'club music' – soul, jazz-funk, hip-hop and electro-funk.[11] Controller Johnny Beerling's view is that the club scene has little to offer radio, either in the sense of providing suitable music or of providing suitable disc jockeys: 'disco DJs don't understand the medium of radio, have little in common with their broadcasting colleagues and care about either even less'.[12] If anything, Radio 1 takes a more purist attitude to black music as a whole, stopping short at defining it solely (as the Radio London approach tends to do) as a source of entertainment for hedonistic young whites. Although Radio 1 has been fiercely criticized for its coverage of black music, it has been mainly on the grounds that it does not play enough and that it is too fearful of placing it in the daytime shows, rather than the manner or style of its presentation when it *is* featured. Reggae, for instance, is allocated just one hour-long show per week, *The Ranking Miss P.* at 11 p.m. on Sunday, and there is at least a sense with her that she is not prepared to compromise either the style or the content of her show (both largely unchanged from her days on the pirate station DBC) for the sake of white listeners.

## 'Ratings by day, reputation by night'

That Radio 1 takes its non-prime-time programming very seriously is obvious from the resources devoted to it; for one thing, the evening and weekend programmes were, until September 1988, the only shows carried on stereo VHF. BBC radio is obliged because of its relationship with the Musicians Union to record a set minimum number of hours of music each week and it is as a matter of policy that Radio 1 allocates its proportion exclusively to the evening and weekend shows. There is an element of convenience about this; BBC-made recordings, however well made, could never match the technical precision of 'produced' records and so would fit uneasily (and perhaps off-puttingly) alongside them in the audience-maximizing daytime shows; but fundamentally the network sees its patronage of the offbeat or specialized as an expression of its public service obligation. Johnny Beerling:

> Our task [in 1967] wasn't just to capitalise on the popularity of music, but to discover new talent, to create new areas of interest and to better inform our listeners about their own and other cultures. If occasionally we stepped outside the accepted guidelines of taste and popularity, that didn't matter, if by doing so we were able to lead our audience down paths they might never have discovered and incidentally enhanced their musical appreciation.[13]

The reality is that Radio 1 has only ever put these principles into practice in off-peak parts of its programming, never across the whole of it: the network has never had any interest in allowing the offbeat to cross over. Those bands or artists who have crossed over to the mainstream after initial sponsorship by John Peel have done so because of their own adaptability, not because Radio 1 introduced them direct to a mainstream daytime audience. Radio 1 has traditionally defined its 'public service' function not as enhancing the musical appreciation of the majority but as continuing to please a minority cognoscenti which is to some extent its own creation. This particular 'minority' music has virtually no defining characteristic other than its oppositional or 'alternative' nature, and the artists or bands that Radio 1 hires for sessions are mainly those who fit this category – 'indie' bands, to use standard 1980s rock terminology, who, even if they do not actually record for independent labels, strike the right detached, insular, disinterested posture. Radio 1 devotes around 5,000 hours of studio time per year to recording special sessions, but there is a distinct bias towards the indie-type acts and a marked failure to record more than a token amount of reggae, soul or heavy metal. When Radio 1 does give extended live or session coverage to the latter styles – beyond the usual weekly shows – it is usually as part of a special outside broadcast event like the Knebworth Festival or the 1986 Caribbean Focus (which some cynics suggested was covered by the network only because of the proven success of Capital's annual sponsorship of one of the main black music events of the year, the Sunsplash Festival).

The apparent indie fixation is in part a legacy of John Peel's espousal of punk in 1976–7, when he and producer John Walters departed from the customary policy of acting on record company suggestions for suitable session bands to go into London's punk venues and hire any acts they felt worthy of national exposure. Peel's was the first radio show anywhere in Britain to acknowledge the growth of the punk subculture, and his patronage of particular bands was instrumental in securing them recording contracts; a little later, as the do-it-yourself spirit of punk was absorbed by numerous new bands in the provinces, Peel began playing demonstration recordings sent in by the bands and granted session time to the best of them. As the economics of music-making underwent a sea-change (if not quite a revolution) with the advent of cheap synthesizer and fuzz box technology and the rapid expansion of the independent sector, so indie music became almost a separate genre in itself, with exposure on Peel's programme (usually of an independently made, often self-financed release) sought by all. The promise of almost direct access to the airwaves, circumventing the standard career procedure of having to work with managers, agents, promoters and impersonal record companies before making any headway, gave Peel an unparalleled degree of credibility within independent circles, and Radio 1 has to a great extent basked in the reflected glory ever since, even if management attitudes have seemed ambivalent at times. Derek Chinnery:

> There is a joke that a band with a clever name stands the best chance of get-ting a session, but I promise you that's not true. You can go around clubs if you're auditioning, but it must be very difficult to distance yourself from the atmosphere of a club. John told me he listened to 500 cassettes last weekend – an accumulation of material over a number of weeks – but I can't see how you can retain your objectivity with that amount of material.

There are just so many bands around now – every lad in school wants to play a guitar, be in a group.[14]

But attempts by others to absorb the play-anything Peel principle simply resulted in the establishment of a new stereotype as restrictive as that which Peel has consistently reacted against, with 'play anything' coming to mean anything in the indie mould, preferably with some kind of record company backing behind it; Peel is still the only presenter in national radio prepared to give air-time to complete unknowns. (Typically, Peel has lately reacted against such stereotyping by testing the tolerance of his listeners even further with his enthusiasm for hip-hop, Nigerian juju, reggae and British-made soul.) Evening-show presenters and producers may not be beholden to a playlist but they operate a selectivity as precise and as calculating as that of their daytime counterparts: the prime determinant of airplay is their finely tuned anticipation of the target listener-ship's tolerance threshold. The difference with Peel is that he is less concerned with retaining his constituency than with persuading the listener to look beyond what may be the narrowness of his or her own tastes: like other supposedly 'specialist' presenters – such as rock 'n' roll aficianados Charlie Gillett and Stuart Coleman on BBC Radio London, whose shows evolved into something very different from that envisaged by the station; jazz specialist Peter Clayton, presenter of *Album Time* on Radio 2 – Peel outgrew the confines of his brief a long time ago to pursue a genuine musical eclecticism.

Frances Line of Radio 2 spoke for both of BBC radio's popular music stations when she described her network's objective as one of securing 'ratings by day, reputation by night'.[15] Like Radio 1, Radio 2 uses its evening shows as vehicles for specially recorded material, including that featuring the BBC's own in-house orchestras. Its night-time priorities are slightly different from those of Radio 1, however, in that its responsibilities, though broader, are much more tightly defined in musical terms. Whereas Radio 1 has had to select its specialist categories from an internally defined sense of a pop (post-rock 'n' roll) tradition, Radio 2's sense of popular music tradition necessarily goes back much further, and it is obliged to keep faith with followers of musics not only of particular vintages but of particular regional appeal (brass bands, Celtic folk music) and religious aspect (inspirational music, hymns). Radio 2 in fact acts as a safe house for all those limited-appeal (yet culturally 'valid') musics which were inherited from the Light Programme but are deemed unsuitable for daytime use, and a resolute, ever-watchful army of musical conservators (in the shape of preservation societies, vintage music clubs, appreciation societies, the church lobby and various other well-organized pressure groups) ensure that that situation is maintained. Radio 2 has never dropped coverage of any music for which it has a known, established, if numerically very low following, yet the range of its specialist coverage has grown since the mid-1970s to accommodate what was once Radio 1 territory – jazz, country, folk and rhythm and blues, all of which had a distinctly ageing profile as that decade went on. (The consequences of this for Radio 1 have been, first, that even its supposedly more considered specialist programmes lose sight of the important contributions of peripheral styles to the pop heritage, even in its most narrow post-rock 'n' roll sense; and that when resurgences of interest do occur and have a significant impact on pop culture, as happened with British jazz in the mid-1980s, Radio 1 is not at all equipped to deal with it.)

Radio 2 attempts to cater for its minorities in evening sequences of shows devoted to related (or at least non-disparate) styles or periods – dance-bands, swing and jazz on Monday, orchestral music on Tuesday, folk, traditional and brass-band music on Wednesday, country and rhythm and blues on Thursday, 1930s nostalgia and what the BBC used to classify as light music (operetta, parlour music, light classics) on Friday. On Saturday and Sunday the retrospective mood is maintained through programmes seemingly aimed at particular age groups – *Sounds of the 60s* for 1960s pop fans (and one-time Radio 1 listeners?), Charlie Chester's Sunday afternoon show (which includes information on such issues as pension rights, travel-pass provisions and the dangers of hypothermia) for senior citizens – which collectively give the network an image of somewhat somnolent dutifulness. There is little sense of missionary zeal in any of these programmes, though Peter Clayton and Benny Green are masters of the art of making the obscure and unusual (for Radio 2) acceptable by framing it in an anecdotal, informative, see-what-you-think way. Their presenters and producers appreciate that attempting to broaden horizons is probably the last thing that any diehard buff really wants. What comes over most when listening to Radio 2 in the evenings is, rather, a sense of regressive insularity. Radio 2 is, nevertheless, quite possibly the closest that we have in this country to (legal) community-of-taste radio at the present time.

## Minority interests and local radio

Radios 1 and 2 cater for musical minorities: local stations, whether BBC or ILR, have to determine their minority coverage in terms of locally defined communities of interest, though the effect is the same – anything that the station is expected to cover and yet might interfere with the breezy wholesomeness of the daytime programmes (because it induces boredom, antagonism or discomfort in the 'typical' listener) is transferred to times when listening figures are low. So the 6.30 to 9.30 p.m. slot becomes a ghetto for programming aimed both at ethnic groups within the locality and at various sectional interests, 'a relegation to the second division', as one programme-maker in BBC local radio has called it, compounded by the low level of funding usually allocated to the programmes by the stations concerned. Funding for ethnic programmes within BBC local radio comes from the station's education budget and responsibility for them has traditionally rested with education producers, some seconded from teaching positions in schools or adult education colleges, and very few of whom are actually drawn from the ethnic groups concerned. Although Michael Barton, the BBC's Controller of Local Radio, talks bravely of ethnic programmes as 'access broadcasting' – 'we say to the community: here is an opportunity to make a programme. If you would like to get a team together we will give you as much professional help as we can, usually through an education producer but not exclusively. They are in the same category as religious programming' – there is an unmistakable sense of dispensed liberal favour about the programmes which result.[16] At times of financial stringency, as BBC local radio experienced in the late 1970s and early 1980s, minority programmes are the first to feel the effect. Radio London found itself in the middle of a major crisis when *Black Londoners*, a weekday programme on black issues presented by Alex Pascall, lost two of its production team due to station cutbacks in 1984. It is also true that many stations would be unable to mount such programmes at all but for supplementation of their budget by outside groups like the Commission for Racial Equality or local authorities. Radio Leicester, for instance, runs a two-hour weekly programme for its Afro-Caribbean community called *Talking Blues* on an £8,000 grant from the CRE; two separate grants to a value of £20,000 from the City Council and the County Council fund the Asian serial *Kahane Apne Apne*.[17]

Mike Shaft, formerly Head of Music at Piccadilly Radio, describes ethnic broadcasting as falling into three categories: educational programmes aimed at 'helping minorities, particularly Asians, to improve their English and to adapt successfully to the British way of life'; documentaries whose prime function 'is to educate whites about non-whites'; and straight music shows.[18] The latter two categories have a crossover intention, though possibly the only occasion when white listeners deliberately tune in to the documentary or magazine-type programmes is for score flashes when the local soccer team is playing an away match. With music shows, stations can make a conscious effort to break out of ethnic boundaries: Capital is a particular believer in developing programming along these lines, its Saturday night reggae show *Roots Rockers* having enjoyed a sizeable listenership among young whites almost since its inception, but its treatment of minority musics is selective. Music of Afro-Caribbean or indigenous black origin may have a fairly high profile within programmes as a whole, but Asian music has no comparable status, and while Capital can claim in its franchise reapplication to be particularly concerned with 'helping youngsters adjust, the second generation immigrants who so often feel odd man out, torn between rival cultures', no programme has yet been devised with the tastes of young Asians in mind.[19] (To call young blacks and Asians 'second generation immigrants' is in any case appallingly careless – if they feel torn between cultures it is precisely because of inaccurate and insensitive descriptions like that.) In fairness to Capital, it does also offer one of the most original and outward-looking specialist shows in British radio, *City Beats*, in which Charlie Gillett plays popular music (much of it never heard in Britain) from around the world.

The reggae show is a standard feature of ILR programming, and virtually every local station in the country runs its own country, jazz, soul and folk programmes, often presented by local enthusiasts armed with gig guides, news culled from the specialist press and the odd white label record. One of the more bizarre facets of ILR is the common presence at the microphone of the station's chairman or managing director (usually early on Sunday mornings) introducing a classical music programme. Programme budgets are low because of the unwillingness of advertisers to buy offpeak spots, needle-time is restricted, and what advertising is placed during the shows can make for a disturbing juxtaposition with the music played: around 90 per cent of all radio advertisements carry some musical accompaniment, which simply grates within a specialist music environment. Charlie Gillett was so concerned during 1986 about the intrusion of commercials with Top-Forty-like soundtracks into *City Beats* that he spoke of approaching agencies personally with a view to either attracting advertising more sympathetic to the programme's ambience (travel companies, publishers) or adapting their commercials with the programme in mind.[20] The emphasis on country, jazz and folk in particular stems from ILR's historical preoccupation with aping Radio 2's specialist coverage, and any local flavour they have is variable. Stations do co-sponsor local events (e.g. the Nottingham Festival Jazz Week, covered by Radio Trent, and the Wimborne Folk Festival, from which Two Counties Radio in Bournemouth mounts annual live coverage), but such once-a-year coverage generally reflects the station's concern for visibility in the locality rather than an on-going concern for local music-making in these specialist areas. The funding for one-off events like these comes from the station's promotional budget and from the 3 per cent of advertising revenue that it is required to be set aside for locally recorded music under the terms of its franchise. As networking of programmes becomes more commonplace, there are already suggestions that stations should drop their weekly specialist music coverage in favour of sponsored, centrally produced specialist shows (with local opt-outs for gig information and local news), presented by a nationally-known name, which would then compete directly with the established and well-funded shows broadcast by Radio 2.

If the majority of ILR's specialist coverage is determined in the light of either Radio 2 experience (in the case of music shows) or BBC local radio (in the case of ethnic ventures), in one key area it takes its cue from Radio 1. In recognizing the following for pop music as a minority community in its own right, ILR stations use that music as the basis for a separate stream of youth programming in which they can, at the same time, demonstrate their social commitment. Virtually every local station has its own 'youth show', offering a local representation of youth culture built around music, leisure and concern for social issues, sometimes involving some degree of listener participation in the production of the programme itself. The 'social action' orientation of some of these programmes is partly a consequence of their funding by outside organizations and their co-production or presentation by youth workers or members of youth-related community groups: in an extensive report on *Young People and Local Radio*, resulting from a project undertaken in conjunction with the National Youth Bureau, Neville Cheetham listed twenty such 'youth' programmes, some with some kind of direct community back-up. These included Severn Sound's *Club 388*, broadcast in association with the National Association of Youth Clubs; Radio Tees' *Street Level*, with a 'know your rights' feature provided by the National Council for Civil Liberties; and Beacon Radio's *1922 Show*, which featured a telephone 'help-line' manned by two women recruited through the Manpower Services Commission's Community Enterprise Programme.[21] The MSC's involvement in local broadcasting has been sporadic but significant; it cosponsored a major study of broadcasting's treatment of and attempts to cater for young people, *Broadcasting and Youth*, in 1979, and one of the recommendations of that report was that a 'Young Adult Unit' should be set up:

> a central organisation to bring together on a working basis those who are concerned to help young people in association with the media . . . to help stimulate collaboration and co-ordinate action between the media and young adults; provide channels of communication between the two; and especially help formulate and present young adults' needs to all concerned.[22]

While there is still little co-ordination at national level between the radio institutions and the various youth organizations, at local level the collaboration has become more marked: during International Youth Year (1985), for instance, various stations undertook initiatives in conjunction with local Youth Services and the IYY Radio Project, and some of the school children and students who took part in the resulting programmes were (as the IBA's *Television and Radio 1986* proudly noted) later taken on by the stations as permanent staff.[23]

Unlike BBC local radio stations, ILR stations do not have education producers as such – one exception is Beacon, whose post is part-funded by Wolverhampton's local education authority – and Cheetham notes the reluctance among their staff to take the principle of 'access' beyond publicizing youth-oriented events or playing demos by up-and-coming local bands in the allocated youth slots. But there are problems inherent in regarding young people as a separate community-within-a-community, not the least of which is the tendency to assume a consensus of attitude and interest among everyone aged 12 to 21. The selection of music in youth programmes on ILR can reflect this, being the one particular area for which the presenter or producer (who is usually slightly older than the audience) always takes individual responsibility; listener input on the music is restricted to comment from 'pop juries' on new releases, not to the process of selection itself. The other difficulty is that young people tend to be seen as a social problem in themselves, which is precisely how the state of youth has been seen by the media since the moral panic over juvenile delinquency in the 1950s. If there is a kind of corporate philosophy behind these 'youth programmes' it is to present young people in a positive light, both to themselves and to the adult world, and to provide a kind of general guidance to the perils of being young, hence the concentration on issues such as unemployment, drug abuse and AIDS and the general emphasis on advice-giving and problem-solving. They are mounted in a liberal spirit, and old-fashioned paternalism runs right through them.

Looking more closely at the music in youth-oriented ILR shows – bearing in mind that most stations supplement the conventional all-purpose youth show with other programmes of music defined as having specific youth appeal – it tends to fall into one of two broad categories, either non-chart music of a Janice Long/John Peel kind or club music of the kind outlined earlier. ILR, like Radio 1, honours 'indie' pop, though its support was belated: while Radio 1 was perhaps fortunate to be able to extend its broadcasting hours into the early weekday evening (bridging the once yawning gap between 6.30 p.m., when the network was forced to share programmes with Radio 2, and John Peel at 10 p.m.) just at the time when the independent movement was gaining credence, ILR's coverage was limited to isolated programmes like a late-night Charlie Gillett show on Capital. More characteristic of ILR evening programming was another Capital show, Nicky Horne's *Your Mother Wouldn't Like It*, which centred mainly on album tracks by established British and American bands of the pre-punk era. Horne's mid-evening sequence was eventually taken over by a far more streetwise character, ex-punk Gary Crowley. The main point about ILR's evening rock shows (and 'rock' is the word most commonly used by station managers to describe them) is that they are very much individualistic affairs, presented and put together by local would-be John Peels, in which station management take no particular interest: the presenters are employed to provide a music show of appeal to young people and are left to interpret that brief as they think fit. This is not so true of the big metropolitan stations (Capital, BRMB and Piccadilly in particular), which have a younger profile in musical terms to start with and have a generally keener sense of the range of 'minority' tastes on the periphery of pop. The club shows, meanwhile, are typical Friday and Saturday night features which, as on Radio 1, attempt to dovetail with the leisure activities (as opposed to working or studying activities) of young people: 'we're trying to catch them before they go out to the discos', as David Thomas of Swansea Sound puts it.[24]

The most obvious parallel with Radio 1's non-mainstream coverage is the putting of resources into recording sessions or live concerts, which ILR stations have to undertake as part of their franchise agreement. The stipulation was originally made by the IBA as a compensatory gesture towards the Musicians Union, whose members were theoretically deprived of employment by the stations' commitment to an all-record format; the fixing of the 'live music' fund at 3 per cent of each station's net advertising revenue was a recognition of the role musicians played (directly, through their presence on records) in the financial success of the station. In addition, where ILR stations become liable for secondary rental (which, before the terms were revised by the IBA, was an extra levy payable to the Authority when station profits exceeded £60,000, or 5 per cent of income), the MU is granted an allocation from the monies received. Rather surprisingly for an industry which complains almost constantly of the burdens on expenditure that result from regulatory requirements, this particular obligation is rarely cited as a contentious issue, and stations can fairly claim to regularly exceed the 3 per cent stipulation. The reason for this is that in-house or outside broadcast recording brings its own benefits to the stations in terms of prestige and, in some cases, extra revenue: concerts by bands of international stature can be packaged for sale to American or European radio concerns. The prestige comes from the raised profile of the station within the relevant community of listeners: this can mean pop fans, who will feel more loyalty to a station if it is seen to have its finger on the pulse of local tastes, or it can mean classical concert-goers – sponsoring an orchestra (as Capital does with the Wren Orchestra, and Swansea Sound with the Swansea Sound Sinfonia), and having its name associated with the 'cultural' night-life of a locality can help immeasurably to establish a cultured image for a station that may be crucial when the time comes for franchise renewal. Concert tapes are also endlessly reusable, at minimal cost – 24-hour stations rely heavily on them as time-fillers.

Of most interest is the use of the great majority of this specially-recorded material in a specialist context. Its general exclusion from daytime use (though Capital and Hallam do play live tracks by chart artists in their afternoon shows) suggests a fear of upsetting the casual listener's (presumed) expectations of chart records of a high technical quality; its concentration into the evening hours suggests a marking out of the material for a more *dedicated* listening clientele and with it a 'cultural' usage: if stations did lend their financial resources simply to building up a library of non-needle-time music, it would be seen as a self-interested measure of no cultural value at all. Why, then, should stations spend a large part of their recording budget on pop bands who may be relatively unknown even locally? Partly it is a question of maintaining credibility among a young and knowledgeable listenership. Partly it is down to cheapness and convenience: established bands come expensive and may refuse to record in unfamiliar and relatively primitive studios. Partly it is the expectation that a band, once known, will carry the image of its radio patron with it. If the station's involvement in promoting young bands can be dramatized in some way, so much the better: this is the thinking behind the various talent contests arranged by stations across the country – Metro Radio's *Track to the Top* and Essex Radio's *Band Search '85*, for example, though as a general rule the station's ability to make promotional capital out of the existence of local groups depends entirely on the foresight and inside knowledge of the local scene demonstrated by the station's resident youth-slot disc jockey. In some areas, this is spot on, in others simply appalling. Andrew Clifton, Manager of New Leaf Records in Cambridgeshire and a one-time contributor to Radio Cambridgeshire's *The Rock Show*, remembers Hereward Radio's rather comic attempts to come to terms with local pop music-making around 1984–5:

> Most groups in the area play heavy rock/metal/R & B or punk/new wave/alternative music, and there are some excellent reggae bands. Programmes specialising in these forms were short and short-lived. Most of the Hereward DJs also work in discos so the specialist soul/disco programme survived. One or two of the DJs did show interest in the local scene but what contribution they could make depended on what programme they were assigned to. There were attempts at gig guides but often as not venues were playing at bands! In mid-1985 the Key Theatre, across the car park from Hereward, put on a week-long festival. Hereward were supposedly co-promoting it, but they hardly mentioned it. Then, following the success of their teenage rock band competition in 1984, Central TV decided to organise a second in 1985, with the finalists being winners of rounds held by each of the Midlands ILR stations. This certainly meant that Hereward would have to take more interest. Tellingly, it was apparent that they did not even realise that the 1984 winners were from Hereward country.[25]

But even when stations can demonstrate an awareness of the vitality of local scenes, it can still be argued that their perspective on local music-making is limited. When Hereward invited entries for the local heats of the Central TV competition Clifton describes, the Peterborough Unemployed Musicians Co-operative threatened to petition the station over its belief that certain types of music were to be excluded no matter what the merits of the bands. Where the ILR approach to 'specialist' music falls down is not only in its narrow definition of what constitutes a specialism but, paradoxically, in the essential populism of the choices which stations make; in many cases, the very representation of particular specialist interests within the evening or weekend output is, if not exactly a response to popular demand, then a response to well-organized, numerically strong lobby groups. When it comes to allocation of resources, pragmatism and long-term benefit inevitably colour the decisions of any commercial operator working within the public service field.

## Piracy and community radio

To assume that all communities of taste and interest can be served adequately and fairly within the existing two-tier system of radio is naïve; limited outlets and limited air-time, quite apart from the editorial parameters imposed both from within and without the radio institutions, render it impractical. So-called 'specialist' and/or minority output on British radio therefore depends on the exercise of editorial selectivity, choosing the communities most 'deserving' of sectional coverage, a process which can come dangerously close to a granting of 'rights'. Those editorial decisions are exercised only in indirect acknowledge-ment of public consultation, the machinery for which is in any case suspect. Both BBC local radio and ILR insist that note is always taken of criticisms or comments on minority programming received via their respective local advisory councils, which are made up of unelected representatives from the various public services in the locality (teachers, doctors, police, local councillors) and have a brief to ensure that the whole spectrum of community life in the area is reflected in the programmes transmitted.[26] The inadequacy of this system of consultation has been commented upon many times, and the failure of local radio in particular to fully respond to the needs, both general and specific, of its communities and to involve them at the editorial and presentation level – that is, in what both the BBC and the IBA regard as *professional* capacities – has given increasing impetus to the campaign for some kind of alternative radio system, a possible third tier, in which those groups which are at present effectively disfranchised, in broadcast-ing terms, would have the opportunity to make their voices heard.

Community radio is, at the time of writing, a concept – in fact several interlocking concepts – rather than a reality, but my interest here is in its potential impact both on existing specialist music communities and on the specialist music policy of the established stations. Accepting the proposition (which some sections of the community lobby fiercely dispute, as we shall see) that the precursors of community radio – or at least the catalysts for the placing of community radio on the political agenda – were the numerous unlicensed stations that sprang up in metropolitan areas between the late 1970s and the mid-1980s, some of that potential has already been demonstrated: the vastly increased coverage of soul music and other black music forms like jazz-funk and hip-hop by Capital and BBC Radio London was a clear response to the apparent popularity of London-based pirate stations like black music specialists Solar and Horizon. But it is arguable whether the pirates really represent anyone other than themselves, and most equate narrowing their output down to a particular, neglected style or sound with 'spotting a gap in the market' (Charles Turner, Manager of Manchester pirate station KFM); the commercial potential of low-cost, small business radio is what excites. And while the ILR stations in particular, through their trade association the AIRC, complain publicly of the pirates' 'theft' of frequencies and copyrights and of the ineffectual action taken against them, the very success of the pirates in operating profitably in an unregulated framework serves to demonstrate their own case for deregulation: as Brian West, Director of the AIRC, has long pointed out, the AIRC's argument against a third tier of radio has not been on the basis that competition would harm ILR's commercial standing, but that any competition should be on the same terms – that is, that ILR should also benefit from relaxed programming obligations and from the opportunity to own its own transmitters.[27]

Some background to the community radio campaign and the growth in radio piracy is useful here. For the former, the Annan Committee report of 1977 was a major focus: an umbrella group of interested parties, the Community Communications Group (COMCOM), was constituted early that year with the task of responding to the report, and it backed the proposal for a Local Broadcasting Authority under which locally accountable radio could be nurtured. Although the LBA suggestion was rejected by the Government, COMCOM was encouraged by the IBA's decision (clearly Annan-influenced) to award ILR franchises to community-based groups in Cardiff and Coventry, and in 1978 it proposed to the Select Committee on Nationalized Industries that 'a new sector of autonomous, non-profit, community-based local radio – one that is *not* dependent on advertising' be set up.[28] The Home Office Local Radio Working Party discussed the proposal in lukewarm terms, but it was in the 1980s that the campaign grew apace, as the extent of the availability of frequencies (previously denied by the Home Office) became apparent and the Greater London Council, through its GLC Radio Forum, took a major interest in the establishment of active community radio workshops in the capital. The Community Radio Association was formed in 1983.[29]

The proliferation of land-based pirates from the late 1970s onwards was partly traceable to the outlawing of the offshore pirate stations in 1967, which led to the formation of a number of groups (notably the Free Radio Association) dedicated to 'freeing' the airwaves for anyone with the money and enthusiasm to set up their own transmitter and play music. These groups in turn spawned a trade in information regarding transmitter technology, the construction and purchase of which became both easier and cheaper as the 1970s went on. A further development was the disco cult of the late 1970s, instigated in part by the film *Saturday Night Fever* but drawing on a long-standing but relatively dormant and unsung following for black music among white teenagers; the only existing black music pirate, Radio Invicta (not to be confused with the later ILR station of similar name) capitalized on the new interest and was soon joined by London Weekend Radio (LWR), JFM and Horizon.

A 1979 article in *Time Out* by Lennie Michaels identified the new pirates as belonging to any one of five different categories: the would-be disc jockeys for whom 'pirating on the airwaves can be the ultimate in liking the sound of your own voice'; 'techfreaks', whose love of the technology tends to outweigh any interest in programme content; 'music missionaries' intent on bringing their own tastes in the obscure or unknown to a wider public; believers in 'community access', who argue that 'radio technology can put members of a locality in touch with each other and have a transforming effect on the political process'; and those with political interests (like the left-wing Our Radio and the right-wing Radio Enoch) which echo Che Guevara's belief that 'radio is a factor of extraordinary importance . . . It explains, teaches, fires, and fixes the future positions of both friends and enemies'.[30] As action by the Radio Interference Department (later the Radio Investigation Service) became noticeably selective (aimed mainly at the political stations) and the financial risks involved in unlicensed broadcasting diminished (because any confiscated equipment could be quickly and cheaply replaced), so the stations began to operate quite openly, to the extent of publicizing their frequencies and advertising for staff. Radio Jackie in South London, which had been broadcasting in some form since 1969, even opened its own shop and enlisted the on-air help of its local Tory MP (later a minister), Angela Rumbold. Most took any advertising that was going: *Time Out* publisher Tony Elliott, in what was perceived as a symbolic gesture of solidarity, announced early in 1984 that he would drop advertising on ILR in favour of the pirates.

A full list of all the pirate stations operating in Britain at this time, let alone an account of their ownership details and the various programming approaches adopted, would be almost impossible to compile, though John Hind and Stephen Mosco's *Rebel Radio: The Full Story of British Pirate Radio* describes at length a number of the more 'visible' and influential broadcasters.[31] Certainly there was more than an element of hyperbole about the whole pirate boom, typified by articles in the *Mail on Sunday* and *Sunday Express* which took the pirates' claims of high public patronage at face value.[32] (There was even one such article on the Media Page of the *Guardian* based on supposedly 'official' IBA figures showing Solar Radio to be capturing 6 per cent of weekend listeners in London as opposed to Capital's 3 per cent: the figures were an elaborate hoax on IBA notepaper.[33]) Even accounting for the apparent resurgence of a newly seaborne Radio Caroline and the arrival in the North Sea of a rival ship, Laser 558, claims that the pirates were drawing listeners away in droves from the established legal stations were inevitably exaggerated: JICRAR's 1984 survey found that listening to stations other than the BBC networks and locals, ILR and Luxembourg stood at 2.2 per cent – just 0.1 per cent higher than in the pre-pirate days of 1977.[34] Besides the pirates, that figure also included the BBC World Service, foreign broadcasters and out-of-area ILR stations. But such cross-country figures hid the localized appeal of the pirates, at its strongest in parts of London, Manchester and Birmingham, while ethnic stations like London Greek Radio and its rival offshoot The Voice of the Immigrant, both based in North London, could fairly claim that they were reaching audiences – Greek and Greek Cypriot, with a high proportion of non-English speaking elderly people – who but for their existence would not tune in to radio at all.[35] It was possibly the impact of stations such as these (and a walk down the main streets of Harringay or Palmers Green, with the sound of one or other of the two Greek stations coming from almost every Greek-owned shop, testified to that impact) which led the government, in 1985, to announce a tentative experiment in what was labelled 'community radio'. This followed a crackdown on piracy through a strengthening of the Telecommunications Act – which led to the shutdowns of Horizon, Skyline Radio, JFM and LWR in October 1984 – and the first case of court action by an ILR station (Radio Mercury in Reigate) against a pirate (Radio Jackie) in its locality.

The announcement of the experiment seemed designed to undermine the position of the pirates by apparently giving the more serious operators a chance to prove themselves worthy of legalisation. Several pirates did indeed stop broadcasting as an immediate gesture of good faith. Sunshine Radio in Shropshire even handed over its transmitters to the Department of Trade and Industry (which was responsible for investigating airwave piracy) for safe-keeping while it prepared its application, but the real surprise was the huge number of groups which applied to broadcast in one (or in some cases several) of the twenty-one locations selected by the Home Office.[36] The invitation for applications specified that there would be one of two types of licence on offer, depending on the locality – for small and large 'neighbourhood' stations broadcasting over a 5-kilometre or 'substantially higher radius' (how high was not specified) and providing cross-community programming, and for 'community-of-interest' stations covering a 10-kilometre radius and catering for audiences linked by a shared interest across several localities. Regarding programme content, the guidelines to applicants specified only that community radio should 'broaden the diversity of consumer choice' and be 'distinct in character', and they made clear that 'applications which mirror the most popular programming elements of existing radio services are unlikely to be successful'.[37] A total of 245 groups applied, sixty-four of them for just one community-of-interest licence (North London). The latter included groups representing British Greek Community Radio, Radio Krishna, London Greek Radio, Turkish Community Radio, Irish Community Radio, the Confederation of Indian Organizations, the UK Turkish Islamic Trust, the Arab Broadcasting Company, London Asian Radio, the West Indian Leadership Council, Cypriot Community Radio, Italian Community Radio, the Board of Deputies of British Jews and Greek Community Radio, alongside non-ethnic groupings like International Jazz Club Radio (with Ronnie Scott as its chairman and Anthony Hopkins and Spike Milligan on its steering committee), London Arts and Music Radio, ICA Radio and the Broadcasting Projects Group. The sheer weight of numbers and diversity of the applications underlined the severe limitations of the experiment;

in this particular case, the advisory panel charged with recommending a group for the licence award effectively had to choose between ethnic communities or be seen to ignore them altogether.[38] Once the problems not only of selection but of monitoring and assessing the successful groups became clear, together with the ethnic and political (and apparently anti-Tory) interests of the applicants, the experiment was abruptly curtailed before even a single licence had been awarded. Even one of the members of the Home Office panel, Bevan Jones (also the Chairman of the Community Radio Association) was moved to call the abandonment of the experiment 'outrageous and quite possibly racist, as well as being deceitful ... it's particularly damaging for ethnic minority groups and highlights again the Government's scant regard for these sections of the community'.[39]

The Home Office insisted the abandonment was only a postponement pending a government Green Paper on the whole future of radio, and indeed the resulting consultative document, *Radio: Choices and Opportunities*, mapped out (albeit in very imprecise terms) a scenario for the development of community radio that was broadly welcomed by most interested parties.[40] But the ambivalence shown by the government towards community radio mirrors an internal debate within the wider 'alternative radio' lobby itself. Conservative philosophy, especially during the Thatcher era, favours the operation of a free market in broadcasting as elsewhere, and the three main architects of the government proposals on community radio (Leon Brittan, David Mellor and Douglas Hurd) see its development in these terms. Any station would be permissible so long as it kept within bounds of decency and good taste and paid its way. This dovetails with what the majority of the pirates have campaigned for – to programme as they like, legally, but with no interference – but only partly with the concept of non-paternalistic, non-commercial, democratically controlled and locally owned access radio developed by the various community radio pressure groups since the 1970s. The implication in the Green Paper is that both perceptions of radio are tenable and can live together: community radio is regarded as a measure of deregulation throughout, and one of the consequences of deregulation would be a station's freedom to choose, without pressure, its own editorial posture and its own scheme of ownership and control. But the antagonism between the two factions runs deep. In 1985, prior to the announcement of the community radio experiment, members of the pirate lobby distanced themselves from the Community Radio Association by forming their own campaigning umbrella group, the Campaign for Successful Radio; in 1986, following the experiment's abandonment, some of its members established the Association of Small Independent Radio Stations (ASIRS) as what appeared to be a pirate counterpart to the AIRC. Ironically, this action simply appeared to confirm the prevalent AIRC view, stated by Piccadilly Radio's Colin Walters in *Marketing Week*, that community radio protagonists were primarily interested in establishing unrestrained, low-cost commercial radio via the back door:

Some, particularly the smaller ILR stations, have found advertising hard to come by and it's more than likely that some community stations will have the same problems. But, unlike ILR stations, the community stations have the massive advantage of having their costs almost entirely under *their* control. It is this freedom from official stricture that has prompted all the current wave of enthusiasm.[41]

Some community-of-interest stations, it was pointed out, would be the same size as or possibly even larger than existing ILR stations: as David Thomas of Swansea Sound remarked, 'we might be interested in becoming a community station ourselves if they can negotiate better terms, especially with the music royalty bodies. Perhaps we would want to be part of that system rather than the one we're in now'.[42]

## Music for the community?

Whatever shape community radio does eventually take, music, or more precisely the cost of music, is likely to be a central issue. The pirate stations could run on such low overheads only because they paid nothing for the music they used: while some made an effort to pay token sums to the PRS and PPL in an attempt to gain respectability, none was accepted by the respective organizations because it would have appeared to condone illegality. Community stations, even those that use music only minimally, will be required to negotiate a scale of payments with the copyright agencies, and there is little to indicate that PPL in particular will be any more amenable to the newcomers than it has been to the ILR stations, particularly if advertising does become the stations' main source of funding. (A new trade association for prospective community radio contractors, the Association for Broadcasting Development – stated objective: 'to ensure continuous music stations become a reality' – began negotiations with PPL in late 1987 with a view to achieving double the allocation of needle-time granted to ILR stations in return for a higher percentage of advertising revenue. Figures quoted in *Broadcast* suggested 10 per cent of advertising revenue for 20 hours a day of PPL-registered recorded music.)[43]

It is possible that specialist music stations may be able to exist without playing any PPL-registered material at all, and some community radio groups have already suggested giving a major proportion of air-time to live music; here again, however, live music is costly, and the Musicians Union is unlikely to countenance its members playing live or recording for the stations without at least the same level of remuneration as the ILR stations are at present providing. Generally speaking, too, the union attitude to community radio is not particularly favourable: the NUJ's broadcasting organizer, John Foster, is suspicious that 'so-called community broadcasting is in fact broadcasting on the cheap', and the experience of local radio (BBC and ILR) suggests that when money is short, stations depend overly, especially in minority or social action programmes, on unpaid contributions by volunteers.[44]

Some kind of community radio has to come: the frequencies (though not unlimited) will be there after changes to the VHF band due in 1990, the technology is there, the political will appears to be there, the personnel are ready – probably the major consequence of the aborted experiment was that alliances were formed, expertise was shared, training mounted, all of which must find an outlet. The chief criticism of community radio is that it may ghettoize the very audience it seeks to speak to and cater for, because the presence of such an alternative service will encourage the mainstream stations to relax their minority coverage still further; however, since the main reason for a community radio station's existence is likely to be the inadequate coverage of that community by BBC radio and ILR – to take one example, it had never occurred to any of the three London stations to mount programmes for the Greek community prior to the appearance of London Greek Radio, despite the presence of 200,000 Greeks and Greek Cypriots in the city – then this is perhaps not as major an issue as it might appear. The other argument, and a classic liberal one, is that the loss of such minority programmes as do exist on mainstream radio would decrease the opportunities different communities have for speaking *to* each other and render the minorities invisible; in other words, it would strengthen divisions and foster cross-cultural ignorance. This is quite a powerful argument when applied to the musics of different cultures: as the experience of American radio since the 1960s has shown, separation encourages a stereotyping of viewpoints and discourages cross-fertilization of sounds and styles.

Community radio is far from the only development of importance in minority broadcasting. A national black music station has been proposed many times, most recently by a Department of Environment-commissioned report on ways of creating more employment opportunities for black people in the music industry.[45] In 1987, a research company called National Ethnic Research began a major investigation into the spending power and consumer habits of Britain's blacks, aiming to explore the potential of the black media and explode the myth that the ethnic community is too low paid for the market to be viable.[46] Any hope, however, that new national stations might be developed for minority broadcasting, be it to ethnic minorities or minorities of taste and interest, was quashed by Home Secretary Douglas Hurd in January 1988, with the announcement that newly available frequencies would be allocated to the highest bidder and that the new services would have to provide 'a diverse programme service calculated to appeal to a variety of tastes and interests and not limited to a single format'.[47]

Minorities, in the end, are only what the broadcasting institutions delineate them to be: one of the central points of this book is that youth itself has been so defined, and in such a way that certain youth-identified musics have been elevated to a higher cultural plane than others. The paradox of the growth of music radio in Britain since 1967 has been its targeting not at the youth audience but at older age groups, a targeting likely to continue in radio as in other media as the emphasis in consumer marketing changes: the early years of the 1980s have seen fairly dramatic declines in the circulation of teenage publications, the closure of youth-oriented stores like Now, and a marked drop in the purchase of records by young people, while the decline (of 28 per cent) in the teenage population projected for 1984–94, coupled with the likelihood of continuing high levels of youth unemployment, has been enough to prompt fashion manufacturers and the music industry itself to investigate other, in the long term clearly more profitable markets.[48] The successful launch of the compact disc format in Britain and the high levels of sales among the 25 to 35 age-range market has given added impetus to this, in turn influencing Capital Radio to split its frequencies on Sunday and launch its FM service as CFM, a new stream of music programming – sophisticated, rock-based easy-listening music – aimed at precisely this market and boasting full stereo VHF coverage. The first *overt* example in British radio of streaming by demographics, it attracts high profile, up-market advertising (not for nothing has CFM been dubbed the aural equivalent of a Sunday colour supplement), and has an appeal based on a kind of reverse ghettoization: the creation of a new consumer community, emotionally and materially distinct from the mainstream, bound together by a sense of élitism. CFM is the first of many such ventures, and other stations have already used it as a blueprint for similar services: a less-publicized announcement from the Home Office in early 1988 was that ILR stations would be allowed to start separate services on the AM and FM frequencies as a prelude to being *obliged* to under the terms of planned legislation on broadcasting due for 1989. (In September 1988, Piccadilly Radio became the first ILR station to voluntarily split its programming on a full-time basis when, CFM-style, it refashioned its VHF service as a separate album- and compact disc-orientated station under the name of Key 103.) What CFM represents has nothing to do with Bates-like populism or any Peel-like pursuit of the extraordinary, both of which are essentially products of a system of music broadcasting that may, just may, be reaching its twilight years. CFM forms the marketing man's answer to a social fragmentation that is a fact of the times, and it may well be the shape of radio to come.

a new and noticeably more aggressive programming policy aimed at a 25 to 44 age-span, and LBC staff faced a cut in numbers and the imposition of a new policy aimed at making the station 'instantly recognisable . . . lighter, pacier, more varied and altogether more stylish' and which involved the projected displacement of *Rice 'n' Peas* by a 'black soul and news show'.[1] LBC also began a campaign to widen ownership of its IRN operation among the ILR stations it served, apparently in preparation for its planned re-creation as a national news network. Simulcasting, the IBA-enforced practice of broadcasting the same programme services on the medium wave and FM wavelengths, was formally ended in mid-January 1988, thereby enabling existing ILR stations to effectively run two services without applying for a second franchise. In one of the most extraordinary developments, Richard Branson's Virgin group announced plans to 'service' any resulting new rock music services on FM frequencies by offering a complete programming sequence to ILR stations between the hours of 7 p.m. and 6 a.m.[2] All this has occurred against a background of continuing radio piracy, with Laser openly charging for airplay – £65 per play for a spot on an indie show, *The Garage Goodies* – and the London pirate scene becoming increasingly populated by hustlers out to exploit the money-making potential of untaxed advertising revenue and station-promoted live shows.[3] Meanwhile, Radio Luxembourg announced plans for a daytime service in conjunction with Radio Telefis Eireann that would compete directly with BBC Radio 1.

It was, however, the publication of the Green Paper, *Radio: Choices and Opportunities*, which not only marked the elevation of radio to the political agenda but appeared to set the stage for nothing less than a complete overhaul of the existing system. Even the AIRC, which in 1986 submitted its own *Plan for Radio* to the Home Office mapping out its own conception of how a deregulated radio system should be allowed to develop, was stunned by the far-reaching nature of the proposals. 'I didn't believe this administration could be so radical about radio', director Brian West told *Marketing Week*: 'it's exceeded my wildest hopes'.[4] While stopping short of the part-privatization of BBC wavelengths favoured by the majority of the Peacock Committee – the Paper proposed that BBC Radios 1 to 4 remain intact – it suggested that the whole ecology of broadcasting built around those publicly-owned services be altered to fit a scenario analogous with newspaper publishing, in which consumer satisfaction as expressed through patronage would determine a station's survival. Thus BBC radio would be subject to national competition for the first time, from not just one but three commercial networks; ILR would be deregulated and placed under the jurisdiction of an authority other than the IBA; and community radio stations (privately owned neighbourhood stations according to the new definition) would be licensed and overseen in non-interventionist fashion by the same authority. The operators of the new services (to become effective after 1990, when reorganization of the VHF band will make new frequencies available) would own their own transmitters rather than rent them from the new authority. At the heart of the Green Paper lay a vision of privatized, free-market radio in which BBC radio would be retained in its existing state for pragmatic reasons alone – because of the political and constitutional difficulties in changing its 'public service' base of operation, because retaining it as such frees the new operators from obligations that may hinder their economic progress. It is, of course, a quintessentially Thatcherite vision, but one close to Conservative thinking for many years. The creation of a similar operative dichotomy, with the BBC providing public service and the commercial system specializing in entertainment alone, was discussed seriously at Cabinet level soon after the Heath government came to power in 1970 but rejected as too radical.[5] The difference, as the experience of three parliamentary terms has shown, is that the Thatcher government has both the political will and the political strength to put right-wing radicalism into practice.

Hurd's 1988 proposals, which were widely assumed to form the basis of forthcoming legislation, took the Green Paper scenario even further. If enacted, the IBA would have all responsibility for radio, including the provision of transmitters for rental, removed from it; existing ILR stations and new community stations would come under the umbrella of a new Radio Authority with a brief to regulate with a 'lighter touch'; the new Authority would also oversee the licensing of three national radio networks, not on the basis of programme plans (though certain criteria would have to be met) but to the highest bidders. Competitive tender, Hurd insisted, would 'ensure that the public receives the best return for use of a scarce public resource. It is a fair, efficient and transparent procedure, better than the arbitrary allocation of licences in a closed room'.[6] By far the most radical of all the proposed developments, this latter proposal gave the clearest indication yet as to the government's strategy regarding broadcasting as a whole: radio would act as the testing ground for a similarly radical reappraisal of the franchise system under which Independent Television has operated since its inception.

In this context, one can note that the radio proposals follow close on the heels of a number of other broadcasting developments, all artfully facilitated for specific political reasons, notably the launch of cable television under the supervision of a government-appointed authority with no brief to oversee programme content, most of which is either sponsorship-funded and independently-produced or bought-in from abroad. (Bringing all non-BBC radio under the supervision of the Cable Authority was one option put forward in the Green Paper.) The appointment to Chairman of the BBC of Marmaduke Hussey, his only previous broadcasting experience that of chairing the board of an ailing ILR station, Radio West; the removal of Alasdair Milne, a programme-maker, from the director-generalship and his replacement by a more politically acceptable Michael Checkland, a financial administrator; the proposed privatization of BBC Enterprises; the attempts to impose independent production quotas on the BBC and IBA – all point to a finely tuned political strategy built on marginalizing support for the traditional public service concept of broadcasting and bringing all public bodies under the influence, direct or indirect, of the marketplace. Attempts to break the power of the broadcasting unions and to influence media decision-makers by 'independently' mounted court actions or covert support for the court actions of right-wing pressure groups are all part of that strategy. The long-term intention is the obvious one of maintaining

Thatcherite hegemony, reconstituting broadcasting as both a reflection and a product of untainted capitalist values. Not only would such a reconstitution represent the final stage in the commodification of radio, the stations so constituted would demonstrate within their programmes and in the 'efficiency' of their operations (the saleability of programmes internationally being one criterion) that those values work to the apparent benefit of the majority.

All of which has tended to leave the liberal and radical left, not to mention the 'wet' wing of the Conservative Party, bewildered and disorganized. Whatever its underlying Thatcherite thrust, the Green Paper in particular was a work of considerable political skill in that it appeared to provide something to please all schools of thought within radio – the public service lobby with the retention of the BBC in its present form, the community radio lobby (the Community Radio Association's welcome for the document was no less enthusiastic than that of ASIRS) with proposals for same, the AIRC with the ending of IBA control. In the face of this, the defensiveness and sheer lack of imagination in the various political responses to the planned changes has been breathtaking, limited to vague lip-service to the idea of regulated neighbourhood radio and a promise to preserve the BBC and IBA more or less as they are. Such defensiveness is understandable if not supportable: many on the left, as Richard Barbrook has written, 'support the defence of state control and regulation . . . [their] idealism results from the contradiction between the belief in a state-run economy and the reality of living under a Tory government and bourgeois bureaucracy'.[7] In the last resort, in other words, the BBC and IBA may be the only bastions left against Thatcherism, and they should be preserved for that reason alone. Yet to what degree are either the BBC or IBA worth keeping in their present paternalistic form? As Barbrook goes on, public sector broadcasting in no way breaks with capitalist social relations of production, neither do the workforce have a say in its management; the very structures and ideologies of professionalism from which public service broadcasting draws its strength inhibit the public from any involvement in broadcasting at anything more than the mundane level of phone-ins, game shows, question-and-answer discussions or vox-pops in the street. One of the reasons why community radio is looked on ambivalently by the left is that it questions the notion of professionalism and the role of the broadcasting unions in safeguarding it:

> The community radio movement can centre the debate on *who* owns and controls the mass media. Co-operative organisation must be seen as the substitute for both commercial and state capitalism. The technological restructuring of the mass media should not be feared if this can be the opportunity for extending forms of self-management. Above all, state censorship should be resisted in favour of democratic structures within broadcasting. This seems to make the community radio movement a challenge to the established practices of both the Labour Party and the trade unions. The hostility of the Campaign for Press and Broadcasting Freedom to community radio seems to confirm this.[8]

So, too, does the reaction of the NUJ: far from viewing community radio as a possible source of new employment opportunities within broadcasting, the official line is to see such a third tier of radio as 'broadcasting on the cheap', run by tiny staffs on low salaries supplemented by unpaid volunteer help. The ACTT, too, describes community radio in a policy document on the Green Paper in dismissive terms: 'the flowering of hundreds of new local stations, if it ever happens, is likely to be a superficial and temporary phenomenon'.[9]

The left's record on broadcasting innovation has never been a particularly cheering one; certainly the myopia of Labour governments on radio issues – the half-hearted endorsement of the BBC's local radio experiment in 1967, the failure to act on the Annan Committee's proposals for more accountable local broadcasting – encouraged rather than inhibited the commercial lobby at crucial points in its growth. Against this, the Greater London Council did much during its final years to foster debate in the capital concerning community radio, and its involvement would no doubt have extended to direct financial and practical support had not its own life and that of the original community radio experiment been cut short.[10] The GLC model of support is important if community radio is not to be allowed to develop solely on the small business lines envisaged by ASIRS, though the Green Paper suggested that any future legislation would block local councils, as political bodies, from either ownership or a financial stake in community stations: as it tersely states, 'the purpose of the proposals . . . is to provide opportunities for new services and to provide new outlets for expression and communication – not to create political platforms for particular groups or lobbies'.[11] The effect of this, apart from neutralizing any political impact that the stations might have, will be to force stations into a dependence on commercial funding in the form of advertising or sponsorship, which would have its own neutralizing effect on programme content. In the long term, the most important factor in determining the shape of community radio will not be the apparent editorial freedom that the absence of a 'public service' obligation might convey, but rather the criteria according to which licences will be granted and consequent services monitored: here the government is coy, affirming that 'decisions on the pattern of local and community services should be informed by the views of those in the areas concerned' without suggesting any mechanism by which this might be achieved.[12] Although the Green Paper avoided describing community radio as part of a commercial system (the favoured euphemism, as always, was 'independent'), the emphasis on the appeal of new services to advertisers betrayed the real intention: any framework created for the provision of licences is likely to favour community entrepreneurs who will keep the operations on a commercial keel and prevent them from becoming a campaigning focus. This is right in keeping with Conservative strategy on race and the inner city, where the accent is on forming a precarious alliance between private funding and showpiece community projects and on tapping the economic potential of the ethnic communities concerned. As suggested in Chapter 9, the advertising industry is itself beginning to take notice of that potential, and it is instructive that when Leicester Sound applied to split its AM and FM frequencies on three evenings for an experimental period in 1986, it chose to give over its FM band to an all-Asian service: the new programmes attracted hitherto untapped (and first-language) advertising from Asian companies and brought much increased business to a Birmingham-based agency specializing in Asian advertising.

Radio is part of the commercial arena. No public body is more 'commercially' minded than the BBC, if only in the limited sense of its commercial exploitation of its resources: ILR contractors and record companies are forbidden by legislation from mutual investment, but Radio 1 can blatantly promote releases by BBC Records and back the commercial release of session material recorded for John Peel's programme companies on a custom-made label, Strange Fruit. The question is to what degree the commercial impulse should be checked and to what end: too often, talk of the 'dangers' in removing safeguards from broadcasting smacks of a reluctance to let go of the security blanket of paternalism and with it the implicit belief that listeners and viewers need to be protected from themselves. Alternatives are needed, not simply to commercialism *per se* but to the whole 'professional' thrust of both commercial and supposedly public service-based radio: if community radio can help to demystify broadcasting, by making it more accountable and infinitely more accessible, it will be radical indeed.

Quite what specific effect the envisaged new system of stations would have on the shape of music radio is debatable. I commented in Chapter 9 on the unlikelihood of the various copyright bodies agreeing to a lower scale of payments than that applicable to local radio at the present time: if the differences between deregulated ILR and community radio do become so blurred as to be meaningless – 'there need no longer be a formal distinction between the two kinds of radio', the Paper projects – then the level of costs may turn out to be not only burdensome but prohibitive.[13] There has been little to suggest any willingness on the government's part to change the basis of the copyright law in broadcasting's favour – a perennial AIRC lobbying issue. Community stations may stand the best chance of becoming viable if music, and especially music on record, is not a major feature of their output; if specialist music stations do come into existence, those concentrating on styles or genres which are the speciality of independent, non-PPL affiliated labels, will clearly have a head start over those using the PPL catalogue. An alternative scenario, put forward by some, is that a great increase in new promotional outlets for records may encourage the music industry to relax its demands on payment and its restrictions on needle-time. However, the industry's interest in the promotional importance of the existing local radio system has long been less than fulsome – a fragmented, competitive system of stations covering much smaller areas would be unlikely to inspire much excitement, though the potential is obviously there for close links between community stations and locally-based labels, particularly if the current regulations barring record companies from investing in radio are abandoned.

The interests of the music industry are likely to be far more usefully served by the creation of national services, particularly if two of the three proposed networks aim to capture the audiences currently patronizing Radios 1 and 2. Precisely what programme format national commercial networks should adopt has been taxing members of the AIRC ever since the IBA first announced its intention to stake a claim for a national network in 1980: the general opinion then was that any such service should be news - rather than music-oriented, a national LBC in effect, so as not to attract listeners away from the hard-pressed local stations. The more bullish ILR figures, notably Capital Radio's Managing Director, Nigel Walmsley, spoke out in favour of national commercial radio because it would at last give radio advertising a country-wide platform; others feared that a national network would simply syphon off advertising intended for ILR anyway. The likelihood is that the national networks, as proposed, would indeed be directly competitive with ILR rather than complementary, but the supposition that at least one of them would be wholly music-based (stemming from the perhaps inevitable equation of an all-VHF network with a music service) was quashed by Hurd when the proposals were announced. Touching what at first sight seemed a surprisingly Reithian note, he stated that the new networks would have to provide 'a diverse programme service calculated to appeal to a variety of tastes and interests and not restricted to a single format'. Justifying this later, he insisted that 'any applicant will first have to pass a test of diversity before financial bids are compared. This does not mean a mishmash of boring general stations. It *does* rule out undiluted pop music' (original emphasis).[14] It was this insistence that so puzzled key personnel in the radio and advertising industries, as it seemed to go against both a belief in the free market (if consumers appear to want undiluted pop music, why deny them it?) and the prevailing trend within radio towards targeting *particular* markets with a single programming stream. As Alec Kenny of Saatchi and Saatchi told the *Guardian*, 'I had expected any future development would be designed to provide streaming or specialist programmes. I would not have thought there was any pressing need for more general channels. Perhaps if nobody comes forward with that particular pitch, there will be a general rethink'.[15]

Was Douglas Hurd simply revealing his 'wet' instincts by retaining some semblance of paternalism within the system? A more likely answer was that he was giving a signal to the radio industry that the suggestions hitherto made as to the shape of national radio to come were unacceptable. These suggestions had included a commercial Radio 2-type service, aimed unequivocally at the female consumer; a classical station, suggested by both Richard Francis, former Managing Director of BBC radio and Bill Macdonald, Managing Director of Radio Hallam; a black music network; and a station concentrating on album music ('adult-oriented rock', to use the American phrase) targeted at an affluent 25 to 35 age-range that would attempt to put into national practice many of the lessons learnt from Capital's CFM all-VHF venture.[16] (The latter would have tied in nicely with the direction plotted by the music industry for the 1990s, in which – following the American pattern – singles come to be regarded as no more than samplers for albums, compact discs supersede cassettes and vinyl to become the dominant music format, and the youth market diminishes to the status of a significant but no longer all-important specialist market.) Hurd's assertion that 'it would be a wasted opportunity if we ended up with narrowly focused services having no appeal to many listeners' smacked of populism rather than paternalism, but specialist or demographically-defined programming would also have gone against the principle of commercial competition within radio: the whole idea of having three new networks is that they compete directly with *each other*, which stations aimed at vastly different audiences would not do.[17] Just as important to Hurd's thinking is establishing the new Radio Authority as a *disinterested* body on questions of prioritizing, or effectively arbitrating between, different communities of taste and interest.

But 'independent national radio' remains very much a figment of Home Office imagination: no organized lobby exists for it, and even the advertising industry's enthusiasm, as officially expressed by the Institute of Practitioners in Advertising, is tempered by a fear that three commercially funded networks would fragment the available market. For all the speculation about possible investors in national radio – Virgin Records, Andrew Lloyd Webber's Really Useful Group and Robert Maxwell's Mirror Group Newspapers have been mentioned – only Chalford Communications, in conjunction with Red Rose Radio, had by mid-1988 announced any such intention, and the most concrete proposals as to programme content have come from interested individuals. The most cheerfully radical suggestion (from the Institute of Contemporary Arts) has been for a Channel 4-type network which, like its television counterpart, would effectively 'publish' programmes after commissioning them from independent production companies. There are many other problems to overcome before 'INR' even reaches the drawing board, including the basic question of where the frequencies come from. The Hurd plans would also necessitate removing at least two frequencies from existing BBC services, which might in turn require some rejigging of the latter (Radios 1 and 2 recombining for certain programmes, for example) and, possibly, a diminution in certain aspects of the BBC's public service provision. It is ironic that the one body most committed to the idea of national commercial radio, the IBA, is almost certain to be frozen out of radio altogether.

The government's stated aim is to increase diversity and choice in broadcasting. That the result will simply be more of the same is not a foregone conclusion, though the lesson of unregulated, free-market American radio is just that: pressure for commercial success narrows allowable margins for error, and the outcome is precision-researched formula radio in the shape of similarly programmed stations aimed at increasingly narrow, demographically defined yet highly profitable markets. Music, meanwhile, becomes more and more the universal radio currency, combining (relative) cheapness of programme content with proven audience attractiveness and pure convenience of use: 'we can always supply music', a presenter on BBC Radio Kent told *Radio Times*, 'it's the all-time placebo for everyone'. One does not have to be a fierce believer in Reithian values to deplore such an attitude as demeaning to the music itself, contemptuous of the listener and cynically manipulative, and there is almost a case for believing that the very presence of music – any music – on the air has consistently obscured the potential of radio as a genuinely communicative medium. But it is the context that radio gives popular music which most disappoints and, ultimately, offends – the deliberate placing of music within the general mix of radio output as a kind of emotional policing mechanism, to induce what Raymond Williams once called 'an endlessly mixed, undiscriminating, fundamentally bored reaction . . . an indifferent acceptance'.[18] A beguiling if romantic notion is that radio has a responsibility not only to stimulate but to encourage the independence of thought and taste out of which cultural and intellectual diversity grows: as John Peel puts it, 'the discovery that there is *something else* may be the first appetite you develop that is distinctly your own'.[19] But it is probably true that in mass-mediated culture, listeners and consumers can never constitute their own tastes; the choices are limited in the first place, all manner of pressures bear down to limit not only the diversity but the availability of cultural products. Peel's policy – Reithian to the last! – is to widen that availability, but even here the presenter/producer/programmer is still acting as mediator, giving preference to items of his own selection. Setting up a pluralistic system of radio, whether public service based or commercially run, will not in itself create the conditions under which that discovery of 'something else' may flourish.

# Notes

## Introduction

1. Queen, 'Radio GaGa', EMI QUEEN 1, 1984.
2. John Downing, *The Media Machine*, London, Pluto Press, 1980, p. 161.
3. See bibliography for relevant publication details of the accounts cited here.
4. Capital Radio's FM-only service CFM began on 4 May 1986. As *Broadcast* reported, '[it] will aim for an adventurous and expanded repertoire of high-quality recordings on FM and . . . at an older and more affluent audience than its twin-frequency service has today'. *Broadcast*, 18 April 1986.
5. Home Office Green Paper, *Radio: Choices and Opportunities*, London, HMSO, 27 February 1987.

## Chapter 1

1. Christopher Stone, 'For Gramophone Lovers', *BBC Handbook* 1929, London, BBC, p. 164.
2. Jack Payne, *This is Jack Payne*, London, Sampson, Low & Marston, 1932, p. 56.
3. Ian Whitcomb, *After the Ball*, London, Allen Lane, 1972, p. 110.
4. Raymond Williams, *Television Technology and Cultural Form*, London, Fontana/Collins, 1974, p. 25.
5. See Briggs (1965), Williams (1962), Gallagher (in Gurevitch *et al.* 1982), and Curran and Seaton (1985).
6. For further discussion of mixed programming, see Paddy Scannell and David Cardiff, 'Serving the nation: public service broadcasting before the war', in Bernard Waites, Tony Bennett and Graham Martin (eds), *Popular Culture: Past and Present*, London, Croom Helm, 1982, pp. 185–6.
7. Paddy Scannell, 'Music for the multitude? The dilemmas of the BBC's music policy, 1923–1946', in *Media, Culture and Society*, London, July 1981, pp. 243–60.
8. *BBC Handbook*, 1928, p. 14.
9. *Ibid.*, p. 87.
10. *Ibid.*, p. 70.

11. Simon Frith, 'The pleasures of the hearth: the making of BBC light entertainment', in Tony Bennett *et al.* (eds.) *Formations of Pleasure*, London, Routledge & Kegan Paul, pp. 101–23.
12. *BBC Handbook*, 1928, p. 34.
13. Richard Dyer, *Light Entertainment*, London, British Film Institute, 1973, p. 11.
14. *BBC Handbook*, 1928, p. 34.
15. For an account of these developments, see Whitcomb, pp. 172–9, and Mark Hustwitt, 'Caught in a whirlpool of aching sound: the production of dance music in Britain in the 1920s', in *Popular Music 3: Producers and Markets*, Cambridge, Cambridge University Press, 1983, pp. 7–16.
16. Sid Colin, *And the Bands Played On*, London, Elm Tree Books, 1977, p. 50.
17. For the BBC's early relationship with the Performing Right Society, see Alan Peacock and Ronald Weir, *The Composer in the Market Place*, London, Faber Music, 1975, pp. 62–5.
18. *BBC Handbook*, 1929, p. 204.
19. Quoted in Albert McCarthy, *The Dance Band Era*, London, Spring Books, 1974, p. 49.
20. *Ibid.*
21. Payne, p. 56.
22. *Ibid.*, p. vii.
23. See Colin, pp. 83–95.
24. For an account of musical crazes of the 1920s, see Ronald Pearsall, *Popular Music of the 20s*, Newton Abbott, David & Charles, 1976, Ch. 9 *passim*.
25. Colin, p. 42.
26. Jim Godbolt, *A History of Jazz in Britain, 1919–50*, London, Paladin, 1984, pp. 192–5.
27. Quoted by Gerry Davis in *Too Hot to Handle*, a BBC Radio 4 programme broadcast on 5 August 1986.
28. Scannell, pp. 251–2.
29. Richard Middleton, 'Popular music, class conflict and the music–historical field', in David Horn (ed.) *Popular Music Perspectives 2*, Exeter, IASPM, 1985, p. 39.
30. Maurice Gorham, *Sound and Fury: 21 Years at the BBC*, London, Percival Marshall, 1948, p. 45.
31. *Ibid.*, p. 54.
32. *Ibid.*, p. 52.
33. Frith (*op. cit.*) offers a persuasive analysis of the middlebrow nature of BBC radio programmes at this time.

## Chapter 2

1. For an anecdotal account of early commercial radio, based on an interview with Max Staniforth, see Martin Wainwright, 'The first pirates of the airwaves', *Guardian*, 2 May 1983.
2. This story is told by Roy Plomley in his autobiography, *Days Seemed Longer*, London, Eyre Methuen, 1980, pp. 126–7.
3. Richard Nichols, *Radio Luxembourg: The Station of the Stars*, London, Comet Books, 1983, pp. 9–49, offers a straightforward account of Luxembourg's first decade of operation.
4. See Howard Thomas, *With an Independent Air: Encounters during a Lifetime of*

*Broadcasting*, London, Weidenfeld & Nicolson, 1977, Ch. 3 *passim*, for an insider's account of commercial radio production in the 1930s.

5. Figures quoted in Plomley, p. 125.
6. Charles Stuart (ed.) *The Reith Diaries*, London, Collins, 1975, p. 176.
7. For Eric Maschwitz's role in BBC radio variety, see Derek Parker, *Radio: The Great Years*, Newton Abbott, David & Charles, 1977.
8. See Paddy Scannell and David Cardiff, 'Radio in World War II', Unit 8 of the Open University Popular Culture course, Open University, 1981, pp. 60–7, for a brilliant analysis of the Ryan Report (including extensive excerpts from it) and the thinking informing the establishment of the Forces Programme.
9. *Ibid.*, p. 35.
10. Cited by Gerry Davis in Radio 4 programme *Too Hot to Handle*, broadcast on 5 August 1986.
11. See Asa Briggs, *The War of Words*, Oxford, Oxford University Press, 1970, pp. 579–80.
12. Vera Lynn was herself unaware of these machinations at the time. See her autobiography, *Vocal Refrain*, London, Star Books, 1976, pp. 81–2, for her own impressions of making *Sincerely Yours*. See also Thomas, pp. 94–100, and Briggs, p. 578.
13. *BBC Year Book*, London, BBC, 1945, p. 60.
14. Quoted in Briggs, p. 576.
15. For a full account of these changes, see Briggs, *passim*.
16. 'Programme development', BBC Internal Memorandum, BBC Written Archives, 17 January 1940, quoted by Jean Seaton, 'Social Revolution?' in *Power without Responsibility: The Press and Broadcasting in Britain*, London, Methuen, 1985, p. 188.
17. *Ibid.*
18. *The Reith Diaries*, p. 455.
19. Seaton, *passim*.
20. Maurice Gorham, *Sound and Fury: 21 Years at the BBC*, London, Percival Marshall, 1948, p. 161.
21. *Ibid.*, p. 172.
22. *Ibid.*, p. 173.
23. *Housewives' Choice* began on March 4 1946 and ran until the launch of Radio 2 in 1967, when it assumed the new title of *Family Choice*.
24. Cliff Michelmore and Jean Metcalfe, *Two-Way Story*, London, Elm Tree Books, 1986, p. 50.
25. Davis; see also Michelmore.
26. Asa Briggs, *Sound and Vision*, Oxford, Oxford University Press, 1979, pp. 760–3.
27. *Ibid.*, pp. 756–8.
28. See Mark Hustwitt, 'Caught in a whirlpool of aching sound', in *Popular Music 3*, Cambridge, Cambridge University Press, 1983, pp. 20–5.
29. Official PPL figures quoted on *PPL 50th Anniversary* record, London, PPL, 1984.
30. *Ibid.*
31. Gerald Abraham, 'Star and understudy too', *BBC Year Book*, London, BBC, 1945, p. 59.
32. Briggs, *War of Words*, p. 596–7.
33. PPL.
34. Gorham, p. 171.
35. See Geoffrey Butcher, *Next to a Letter from Home: Major Glenn Miller's Wartime Band*, London, Sphere Books, 1986, Chs. 4 to 6, *passim*.

36. For detail and discussion of the Beveridge proceedings and recommendations, see Briggs, *Sound and Vision*, pp. 299–300, 295–8, 375–88, 908–9, and Seaton pp 193–4.
37. Dick Hebdige, 'Towards a cartography of taste', in Bernard Waites *et al.* (eds.) *Popular Culture: Past and Present*, Beckenham, Croom Helm, 1982, p. 202.
38. Jimmy Young, *J.Y.*, London, Star Books, 1974, p. 100.
39. *Ibid.*, p. 130.
40. George Melly, *Revolt into Style*, Harmondsworth, Penguin, 1970, p. 26.

## Chapter 3

1. See Asa Briggs, *Sound and Vision*, Cambridge, Cambridge University Press, 1979, p. 363.
2. See Ian Whitcomb, *After the Ball*, London, Allen Lane, 1972, p. 115.
3. Pete Murray, *One Day I'll Forget My Trousers*, London, Everest, 1975, p. 89.
4. Richard Nichols, *Radio Luxembourg: The Station of the Stars*, London, Comet, 1983, p. 100.
5. For accounts of British pop music between 1957 and 1963, see the Orbis partwork Ashley Brown (ed.), *The History of Rock*, London, 1982/3, pp. 128–38 and 364–84.
6. Philip K. Eberly, *Music in the Air: America's Changing Tastes in Popular Music 1920–80*, New York, Hastings House, 1982, Ch. 14 *passim*.
7. Eric Maschwitz, *No Chip on My Shoulder*, London, Museum Press, 1957, p. 157.
8. Richard Hoggart, *The Uses of Literacy*, Harmondsworth, Pelican, 1958, pp. 339–40.
9. For a discussion of the implications behind these changes, see Philip Abrams, 'Radio and television', in Denys Thompson (ed.) *Discrimination and Popular Culture*, Harmondsworth, Pelican, 1964, *passim.*
10. For an insider's story of skiffle, see Brian Bird, *Skiffle*, London, Robert Hale, 1958, *passim.*
11. *Ibid.*, p. 96.
12. For an account of British television's treatment of skiffle and rock 'n' roll, see Bob Woffinden, 'Hit or miss?' in Ashley Brown (ed.) *The History of Rock*, London, Orbis, 1982/3, pp. 378–81.
13. *BBC Handbook*, London, BBC, 1957, p. 117.
14. Iain Chambers, *Urban Rhythms*, London, Macmillan, 1985, p. 83.
15. See Stephen Barnard, *Rock: An Illustrated History*, London, Orbis, 1986, pp. 60–9.
16. Eberly, pp. 201–5.
17. *Ibid.*, p. 205.
18. For an account of the ASCAP–BMI dispute, see Stephen Barnard, 'Paying your dues', in Ashley Brown (ed.), *The History of Rock*, London, Orbis, 1983, p. 460.
19. Eberly, pp. 201–5.
20. For PPL measures against the pirates, see Paul Harris, *When Pirates Ruled the Waves*, London, Impulse, 1968, p. 10.
21. *Ibid.*, pp. 65–6.
22. Erik Barnouw, *The History of Broadcasting in the United States*, Vol. 3, New York, Oxford University Press, 1968, pp. 303–4.
23. Quoted in Stuart Henry and Mike Von Joel, *Pirate Radio Then and Now*, Poole, Blandford, 1984, p. 39.
24. See Tony Blackburn, *The Living Legend*, London, Comet, 1985, pp. 45–7, for an account of Radio London's use of its Top Forty chart.
25. Harris, p. 56.

26. Henry and Von Joel, p. 28.
27. Published on 20 December 1966. For reaction at the time, see Harris, Ch. 9 *passim*.
28. Mike Baron, *Independent Radio*, Lavenham, Terence Dalton, 1975, p. 55.
29. Data included in Charlie Gillett, 'Big noise from across the water', paper to the Smithsonian Conference on *The United States in the World*, Washington, DC, 1976.
30. Richard Mabey, *The Pop Process*, London, Hutchinson Educational, 1969, p. 116.
31. Data from *BPI Yearbook 1976*.
32. *Ibid.*
33. Data from *BPI Yearbook 1977*.
34. Henry and Von Joel, pp. 111–13.

## Chapter 4

1. Lord Hill, *Behind the Screen*, London, Sidgwick & Jackson, 1974, p. 127.
2. Quoted in Keith Skues, *Radio Onederland*, Lavenham, Landmark Press, 1968, p. 29.
3. Hill, p. 163.
4. *Ibid.*
5. Lecture by Robin Scott, BBC Concert Hall, 11 October 1967, quoted in Skues, p. 36.
6. See also Melly's more considered reaction to Radio 1 in George Melly, *Revolt into Style*, Harmondsworth, Penguin, 1970, pp. 194–7.
7. Jimmy Young, *J.Y.*, London, Star Books, 1973, p. 165.
8. *Ibid.*, p. 161.
9. See Chapter 7, pp. 118–19.
10. For an account of the origins and philosophy of progressive rock, see Stephen Barnard, *Rock: An Illustrated History*, London, Orbis, Ch. 6 *passim*.
11. Derek Chinnery interview in *Music Week*, 20 April 1974.
12. Quoted in Skues, p. 190.
13. Andrew Weiner, 'From underground to progressive rock', in Jeremy Pascall (ed.), *The Radio One Story of Pop*, London, Phoebus, 1973, pp. 512–16.
14. See Simon Frith, *The Sociology of Rock*, London, Constable, 1978, pp. 103–5.
15. Pete Fowler, 'Skins rule', in *Rock File*, St Albans, Granada, 1972.
16. Quoted in David Rider (ed.), *Happy Birthday Radio 1*, London, Everest, 1977.
17. Unpublished interview with the author, 17 November 1986.
18. Unpublished interview with the author, 24 January 1985.
19. See Tony Blackburn, *The Living Legend*, London, Comet, p. 68.
20. *Happy Birthday Radio 1*, London, Everest, 1977.
21. BBC, *BBC Annual Report and Handbook*, London, BBC Publications, 1985, p. 123.
22. For Radio 1's relationship with PPL over needle-time, see Chapter 6.
23. Nick Higham, interview with Johnny Beerling, *Broadcast*, 25 January 1986.
24. Interview with the author, 24 January 1985.
25. See Chapter 7 for Beerling's playlisting policy, pp. 119–21.
26. Quoted in Jon Savage, 'Pleasing all the people', *Observer*, 19 January 1986.
27. Nick Higham, 'Growing old gracefully', *The Times*, 9 September 1987.
28. Quoted in 'The man at the helm of Radio 2', *Broadcast*, 30 March 1984.
29. Report in *Broadcast*, 26 July 1985.
30. BBC Daily Survey, quoted in 'The man at the helm of Radio 2', *Broadcast*, 30 March 1984.
31. Reported in *Broadcast*, 12 July 1985.
32. Interview with Derek Jameson, *Broadcast*, 30 May 1986.
33. Frances Line interviewed in 'Radio 2 changes its tune', *Broadcast*, 14 March 1986.

34. Quoted in 'Line denies R2 crisis', *Music Week*, 25 January 1986.
35. The BBC's first local radio stations since the 1920s, Radio Leicester and Radio Sheffield, came on air on 8 and 15 November 1967 respectively.
36. Hill, p. 163.
37. The Pilkington Committee envisaged a total of eighty stations in operation by April 1968.
38. Unpublished interview with the author, 23 April 1985.
39. Quoted in Nick Higham, 'Bedfordshire switches on', *Media Week*, 8 March 1985.
40. See Nick Higham, 'BBC appraises central services', *Broadcast*, 24 February 1984.
41. Total expenditure by the BBC on local radio in fiscal year ending 31 March 1984 was £21 million, accounting for 13 per cent of all radio expenditure by the Corporation. BBC *Annual Report and Handbook 1985*, p. 123.
42. Roma Felstein, 'Give the public what it wants?', *Broadcast*, 29 June 1984.
43. Anne Karpf, 'Not airwaving but drowning', *New Statesman*, 1 March 1985.
44. See interview with Robbie Vincent, 'Soul selling', *City Limits*, 22 June 1984, and profile of Tony Blackburn, *Ms London*, 22 July 1985.

## Chapter 5

1. *Television and Radio 1981*, London, IBA, p. 150.
2. Quoted in Andrew Davidson, 'The affluent sociables', *Marketing*, 12 June 1986.
3. The Local Radio Association was founded in 1964, representing ninety groups with commercial backing wanting to establish commercially funded local stations. Its co-founder (with Conservative MP John Gorst) was John Whitney, later Managing Director of Capital Radio and Director-General of the IBA. See the Local Radio Workshop report, *Capital: Local Radio and Private Profit*, London, Comedia, 1983, pp. 7–20, for an account of the origins of the commercial radio lobby in Britain.
4. Lord Hill, *Behind the Screen: The Broadcasting Memoirs of Lord Hill of Luton*, London, Sidgwick & Jackson, 1974, p. 160.
5. Sir Brian Young, 'The paternal tradition in British broadcasting', The Watt Club Lecture 1983. Text published by Heriot-Watt University, Edinburgh, 1983.
6. The IBA's *Notes on Independent Local Radio*, issued in July 1972, set out in the form of questions its requirements regarding the composition of consortia and programme plans.
7. Quoted in Mike Baron, *Independent Radio*, Lavenham, Terence Dalton, 1975, pp. 82–3.
8. Stuart Hall, *Policing the Crisis: Mugging, the State and Law and Order*, London, Macmillan, 1978, pp. 229–30.
9. 'BBC radio could do with some competition, not because it is bad, but because I am sure it will benefit from having a competitor by which to measure at least some part of its performance': Christopher Chataway, quoted in Baron, p. 68. See also Hill, Ch. 20 *passim*.
10. Capital Radio programme plans reproduced in Local Radio Workshop, pp. 112–13.
11. Government White Paper, *An Alternative Service of Broadcasting*, London, HMSO, 29 March 1971.
12. Independent Broadcasting Authority Act 1973, section 1, subsection (1)(d), (1)(e), 23 May 1973.
13. Baron, p. 106.
14. Data compiled from JICRAR figures by Wight Collins Rutherford Scott, quoted in *Marketing Week*, 25 July 1986, p. 51.

15. This agreement was challenged by the ILR stations, represented by the AIRC, in monumentally long-running proceedings before the Performing Right Tribunal. See Chapter 6, p. 106.
16. For the IBA's own affirmative view of ILR history, see Mike Johnson (IBA Senior Radio Officer), 'ILR twelve years on', *Airwaves*, summer 1985, pp. 10–11, and Steve Perkins (IBA Radio Programming Officer), 'All things to all people', *Airwaves*, summer 1986, pp. 16–18.
17. *Television and Radio 1981*, London, Independent Broadcasting Authority, p. 150.
18. Quoted in David Berry, 'Complementary rivals conflict – but only over survey figures', *Broadcast*, 21 June 1985.
19. Interview with the author published as 'Trent: bridging the gap' in *Gongster*, Nottingham University Students Union, 8 March 1977.
20. Baron, p. 102.
21. *Ibid.*, p. 105.
22. Quoted in Tim Brooks, 'A Capital idea', *Media Week*, 19 April 1985.
23. Quoted in 'Capital Radio: Hale and hearty', *Broadcast*, 25 January 1986.
24. For a discussion of the Capital split frequency experiment, see Peter Fiddick, 'Sabbath Day', *Guardian*, 14 April 1986.
25. For background to the appointment, see 'Park shapes a new Capital', *Broadcast*, 11 September 1987.
26. James Curran speaking at an Institute of Contemporary Arts seminar on 'The social effects of advertising', quoted in Alice Rawsthorn, 'Cable advertisers in control', *Marketing*, 6 October 1983.
27. Tony Fish, BBC Radio York, interviewed by the author, 23 April 1985.
28. Figures taken from *Radio: The Atlas*, London Radio Marketing Bureau, 1985, section on Chiltern Radio.
29. William Phillips, 'The Challenge for ILR', *Marketing Week*, 16 November 1984.
30. *Ibid.*
31. Quoted in Alice Rawsthorn, 'Can ILR waive the rules?', *Marketing*, 19 July 1984.
32. Tony Stoller, 'Time for a new rationale to ILR', *Broadcast*, 11 January 1985. See also Stoller, 'Time for a change in local radio', *Broadcast*, 29 June 1984; and Stoller, 'ILR is dead: long live ILR', *Broadcast*, 21 December 1984.
33. For the background to the Oyston takeovers, see Nick Higham, 'Estate agent's new developments', *Media Week*, 24 May 1985, and Gareth David, 'Oyston tunes into market', *Observer*, 11 August 1985.
34. Monthly column by Colin Walters in *Media Week*, 1 March 1985, p. 31.
35. Quoted in 'ILR Controllers against networking', *Broadcast*, 25 May 1984.
36. Jeff Winston, 'Just popping up the local', *Guardian*, 8 October 1984.
37. Tony Stoller, 'Sponsorship: Dobbiroids are back!', *Broadcast*, 27 June 1983.
38. *Ibid.*
39. Alice Rawsthorn, 'Nestlé clinches Chart Show deal', *Marketing*, 11 July 1985.
40. From an unpublished interview with the author, 22 July 1986.
41. See Terence Kelly, 'Has the cavalry arrived?', *Radio Academy News*, January 1987.
42. Tony Stoller, 'What lies behind the odd paradox?', *Marketing Week*, 16 November 1984.
43. See Peter Clark, 'ILR: facing the freesheet threat', *Marketing Week*, 7 September 1984.
44. Nick Higham, 'Waves of optimism', *Broadcast*, 4 September 1987.
45. For example, see William Phillips, 'Radio 1984: famish amid the feast', *Admap*, July/August 1984; Phillips, 'ILR '85: don't fence them in', *Admap*, July/August 1985; Torin Douglas, 'Radio waits for a green light', *Marketing Week*, 14 November

1986; Martin Gillman, 'Will the IBA ever start to help ILR?', *Marketing Week*, 19 July 1985; Morgan Edwards, 'I'm a media planner: I only use radio as an afterthought', *Media Week*, 13 December 1985.
46. See weekly column by William Phillips, *Broadcast*, 26 September 1987.

## Chapter 6

1. Quoted in Roger Wallis, *Big Sounds from Small Peoples*, London, Constable, 1984, p. 242.
2. Quoted in 'Capital Radio: Hale and hearty', *Broadcast*, 25 January 1986.
3. See Erik Barnouw, *The History of Broadcasting in the United States*, vol. 3, New York, Oxford University Press, 1968.
4. Quoted by Tim Blackmore in 'Is there a future for music on the radio?', *Broadcast*, 20 June 1983.
5. For background to the ASCAP-BMI dispute, see Stephen Barnard, 'Paying your dues', in Ashley Brown (ed.), *The History of Rock*, London, Orbis, 1983, p. 460.
6. See Philip K. Eberly, *Music in the Air: America's Changing Tastes in Popular Music, 1920–80*, New York, Hastings Houss, 1982, Ch. 17 *passim*.
7. See interview with Dave Most in Michael Wale, *Vox Pop: Profiles of the Pop Process*, London, Harrap, 1972, p. 287.
8. For Luxembourg's post-1968 history, see Richard Nichols, *Radio Luxembourg: The Station of the Stars*, London, Comet, 1983, pp. 138–89.
9. See Chapter 7, pp. 118–21, for a fuller discussion of the Radio 1 playlist.
10. Interview with Teddy Warrick, *Music Week*, 5 February 1983.
11. For detail on how the BBC-Gallup chart is compiled, see Godfrey Rust, 'Charts: the inside story', *Music Week*, 6 October 1984, and Simon Garfield, *Expensive Habits: The Dark Side of the Record Industry*, London, Faber & Faber, 1986, pp. 122–5.
12. Phil Hardy, *The British Record Industry*, IASPM UK Working Paper, IASPM, 1984, pp. 9–10.
13. See *ibid., passim*; Ray Hammond, *How to Get a Hit Record*, Poole, Javelin, 1985, Ch. 1 *passim*.
14. Hardy, p. 15.
15. Hammond, p. 140.
16. See Hammond, Ch. 6 *passim*.
17. Garfield, Ch. 5 *passim*.
18. See Wallis, pp. 250–2.
19. Rust *op. cit.*
20. For further discussion of the Network Chart, see Chapter 7, pp. 131–2. By mid-1988, because of mounting concern within the industry about the short sales life of hit singles, the BPI was itself considering the introduction of an airplay element to the Gallup chart. Because radio stations tended to stay with a hit longer than its chart life, it was argued, an airplay factor would slow down the rate of descent from the chart. The BBC was reportedly unimpressed by the suggestion. See Robert Sandell, 'Why the Top 10 is on the record industry's hit list', *Sunday Times*, 10 July 1988, and 'Chart debate questions the plastic principle', *Music Week*, 13 August 1988.
21. See Andrew Davidson, 'EMI gets its act together', *Marketing*, 28 February 1985.
22. For a full discussion of the legal aspects of the phonographic performing right in the UK and overseas, see Gavin McFarlane, *Copyright: The Development and Exercise of the Performing Right*, Eastbourne, John Offord Publications, 1980, Ch. 10 *passim*.
23. IBA/PPL agreement, 1972.

24. PRT ruling, 1980.
25. For the conclusions of two of the major protagonists, John Love of PPL and Brian West of the AIRC, on the outcome of the tribunal case, see 'The return of the magnificent seven per cent', *Radio Academy News*, January 1987, reproduced from *International Media Law*, 1987. See same article for a summary of each of the rulings at each stage of the case.
26. This was the argument propounded by Colin Walters, Managing Director of Manchester's Piccadilly Radio, in a keynote speech at the 1985 Music Radio Conference.
27. Quoted in Roma Felstein, 'Copyright: how to place the music', *Broadcast*, 27 January 1984. See also John Morton's article. 'Facing the music', in the same issue.
28. See 'The performer's dimension', *PPL 50th Anniversary* (booklet) London, 1984.
29. Calculated from estimates in the *BPI Yearbook*, 1986. Total retail sales for 1985/6 were £665.3 million, while pre-tax profit was estimated at 6 per cent of sales.
30. For instructive discussions of copyright issues as they affect cable and video, see Charles Levison (ex-Chairman, WEA Records), 'Of myths and music', *Broadcast*, 10 February 1984; Jo Vale, 'Under pressure and still waiting to turn the tables', *Broadcast*, 26 April 1985; Christine Aziz, 'Pop promos: free or not?', *Broadcast*, 31 May 1985.
31. *BPI Yearbook*, 1986, p. 68.
32. See Hardy, p. 23.
33. Nick Higham, 'BBC and ILR have got the needle', *Broadcast*, 15 March 1985.
34. From an interview with David Thomas, Programme Controller, Swansea Sound, 18 February 1985.
35. Figures quoted in William Phillips, 'The challenge for ILR', *Marketing Week*, 16 November 1984.
36. Cited in Roma Felstein, 'Give the public what it wants?', *Broadcast*, 29 June 1984.
37. From an interview with Tony Fish, Programme Controller, BBC Radio York, 23 April 1985.
38. See report, 'IPI opens for trade', in *Music Week*, 11 May 1985.
39. From an unpublished letter to the author from Andrew Clifton, 14 August 1986.
40. Simon Frith, 'Copyright and the music business', *Popular Music* 7 (1), 1988.

## Chapter 7

1. Quoted in an interview by the author published as 'Trent: bridging the gap', *Gongster*, University of Nottingham Students Union, 8 March 1977.
2. For a brief critical discussion of the gatekeeper concept, see Margaret Gallagher, 'Negotiations of control in media organizations and occupations', in *Culture, Society and the Media*, London, Methuen, 1982. For an application of the concept to American radio, see 'The gatekeepers of radio', Ch. 5 of R. Serge Denisoff, *Solid Gold: The Popular Record Industry*, New Brunswick, Transaction, 1975.
3. Johnny Beerling, from an unpublished interview with the author, 17 November 1986.
4. John Downing, *The Media Machine*, London, Pluto Press, 1980, p. 175.
5. Simon Frith, *The Sociology of Rock*, London, Constable, 1978, p. 91.
6. Derek Chinnery, from an unpublished interview with the author, 24 January 1985.
7. *Ibid.*
8. *Ibid.*
9. For a fuller account of the playlisting procedure as it existed at Radio 1 at this time,

see Simon Frith, 'Playing records', in Simon Frith and Charlie Gillett (eds.) *Rock File 3*, St Albans, Granada, 1975, pp. 38–43.

10. For the background to the relaunch of the playlist, see Colin Shearman, 'Why Radio 1 has changed its tunes', *Guardian*, 5 May 1986.

11. See Nick Higham, 'Plugging the Radio 1 disc promo gap', *Broadcast*, 9 October 1987.

12. Author's interview with Johnny Beerling, 17 November 1986.

13. For an account of the Jesus and Mary Chain 'ban', see Mark Cooper, 'The blasphemy of stardom', *Guardian*, 21 July 1986. See also Mike Smith's riposte on the letters page of the *Guardian*, 29 July 1986.

14. Author's interview with Johnny Beerling, 17 November 1986.

15. Dave Laing, *One-Chord Wonders: Power and Meaning in Punk-Rock*, Milton Keynes, Open University Press, 1985.

16. Dick Hebdige, *Subculture: The Meaning of Style*, London, Methuen, 1979.

17. Raymond Williams, 'The growth and role of the mass media', in Carl Gardner (ed.) *Media, Politics and Culture*, London, Macmillan, 1971.

18. Quoted in Mark Williams, 'Signing off', in Ashley Brown (ed.), *The History of Rock*, London, Orbis, 1984, p. 2215.

19. From an unpublished interview with Derek Chinnery, 24 January 1985.

20. Frith, p. 138.

21. Alan Durant, 'Rock revolution or time no-changes: visions of change and continuity in rock music', in Richard Middleton and David Horn (eds.) *Popular Music 5: Continuity and Change*, Cambridge, Cambridge University Press, 1985, pp. 109–11.

22. Tony Hale, 'Mr Music', in *Capital Radio: 10 Years of Music and Madness*, London, Capital Radio, 1983, p. 75.

23. David Lucas, Managing Director of County Sound, quoted in Nick Higham, 'County's efforts to remain sound', *Broadcast*, 27 April 1984.

24. Quoted in 'Battle of the Charts begins', *Music Week*, 15 September 1984.

25. Bob Snyder, quoted in Stephen Barnard, 'Trent Bridging the Gap', *Gongster*, University of Nottingham Students Union, 8 March 1977.

26. Quoted in David Dalton, 'No longer stuck in the groove', *Music Week*, 5 September 1981.

27. Robin Valk, speaking in a session called '18 with a bullet' at 1985 Music Radio Conference, London.

28. David Thomas, interview with the author, 18 February 1985.

### Chapter 8

1. 'Music in ILR: creating the mood', *Television and Radio 1984*, London, IBA, p. 158.

2. Steve Wright, 'Aural purée', *Radio Academy News*, December 1984, p. 16.

3. Derek Bloom, *Marketing*, 6 October 1983.

4. Omnibus survey of 2,000 adults commissioned by the Radio Marketing Bureau, July 1983 and conducted by Research Surveys of Great Britain.

5. Colin Day, Carole Wilkins, Tony Twyman and Graham Woodman, *The Psychology of Radio Listening*, for Capital Radio, August 1983, contained in *The Contribution of Research to Marketing and Advertising Planning*, p. 292.

6. *Ibid.*, p. 309: 'Immediacy, live broadcasting, the continual provision of updated up-to-the-minute information were also unique properties of independent local radio and if these benefits were fully utilised, they are a compelling means of maintaining a favourable image profile.'

7. Tony Fish, interview with the author, 23 April 1985.

8. BBC, *Daily Life in the 1980s*, London, BBC Publications, 1984.
9. Day, Wilkins, Twyman and Woodman, p. 309.
10. Derek Chinnery, interview with the author, 24 January 1985.
11. The Muzak Corporation 'edits all the highs and lows and tensions out of its melodies' (Simon Frith, *The Sociology of Rock*, London, Constable, 1978, p. 132) in providing instrumental music for background use not only in factories but also restaurants, airport lounges, hotels and department stores.
12. Derek Chinnery, interview with the author, 24 January 1985.
13. The inappropriateness of 'drive-time' was pointed out by David Vick of the IBA's research division at the 1985 Music Radio Conference. See report, 'Who is tuning to what and why', *Broadcast*, 15 March 1985.
14. Tony Hale, Head of Music at Capital Radio, speaking at a lecture on 'Music radio in Britain', Queen's Park Library, 6 November 1985.
15. For an analysis of women's magazines in Britain before, during and after the Second World War, see Joy Leman, 'The advice of a real friend: codes of intimacy and oppression in women's magazines 1937–1955', in Helen Baehr (ed.) *Women and Media*, Women's Studies International Quarterly, 3(5), Oxford, Pergamon Press.
16. Ann Oakley, *Housewife*, Harmondsworth, Pelican, 1976, p. 1.
17. Comments heard on Bill Young's mid–morning show on Chiltern Radio, August 1984.
18. Information presented by David Vick at 1985 Music Radio Conference, 1 March 1985.
19. BBC, *Daily Life in the 1980s*.
20. Quoted in Helen Baehr and Michele Ryan, *Shut Up and Listen! Women and Local Radio: A View from the Inside*, London, Comedia, 1984, p. 37.
21. Capital Radio programme plans (extract), reprinted in the Local Radio Workshop, *Nothing Local about It: London's Local Radio*, London, Comedia, 1983.
22. Anne Karpf, 'Women and radio', contained in Helen Baehr (ed.) *Women and Media*, Women's Studies International Quarterly, 3(5), Oxford, Pergamon Press, 1980.
23. Baehr and Ryan, p. 37.
24. *Ibid.*
25. Dave Jamieson, at that time Head of Presentation at Radio Viking on Humberside, writing in *Independent Broadcasting*, winter 1984.
26. Derek Chinnery, interviewed in *Melody Maker*, 15 July 1976.
27. Quoted in Mileva Ross, *Is This Your Life? Images of Women in the Media*, London, Virago, 1977.
28. Johnny Beerling, quoted in 'Pleasing all the people' *Observer*, 19 January 1986.
29. Rosalind Coward, 'Our song', *Female Desire: Women's Sexuality Today*, St Albans, Paladin, 1984, p. 145.
30. Dorothy Hobson, 'Housewives and the mass media', in Stuart Hall *et al.* (eds.) *Culture, Media, Language*, London, Hutchinson, 1980, p. 109.
31. *Sun*, 31 July 1985.
32. Comments heard on mid-morning shows on Chiltern Radio, BBC Radio London and Essex Radio during August 1984.
33. For profiles of Tony Blackburn and accounts of his Radio London show, see Conor Gleason, 'In a blue funk with Blackburn', *Media Week*, 15 March 1985, and Jane Butterworth, 'Black chat', *Ms London*, 22 July 1985.
34. Jimmy Gordon's address to the 1984 Radio Festival, UMIST, Manchester, 3 July 1984.
35. Hobson, p. 108.
36. Karpf, op. cit.

37. Baehr and Ryan, Ch. 7 *passim*.
38. Quoted in Terence Kelly, 'LBC: undiscovered "beauty" of the air', *Broadcast*, 31 October 1986.
39. 'A qualitative research appraisal of the role of the presenter on radio', *IBA Radio Research*, January 1984.
40. Quoted in Karpf, p. 46.
41. The classic 'how to' manuals on disc jockeying careers and basic techniques are *Emperor Rosko's DJ Book*, London, Everest, 1976, and Roy Sheppard, *The DJ Handbook*, London, Corgi, 1986.
42. David Hepworth, 'Redcoats on overdrive: Radio One and the personality factor', *The Rock Yearbook IV*, London, Virgin, 1983, pp. 118–19.
43. For a discussion of the drain of personalities from radio to television, see Nick Higham, 'Radio's loss is TV's gain', *Broadcast*, 4 April 1986.
44. Derek Chinnery, interview with the author, 24 January 1985.
45. Johnny Beerling, 'Radio recruits required', *Music Week*, 5 April 1986.
46. Hepworth, p. 119.
47. Richard Dyer, *Light Entertainment*, BFI Television Monograph, London, BFI, 1973, p. 23.
48. Emperor Rosko, 'The Emperor strikes back', a reply to Beerling's article (see note 45), 19 April 1986.
49. Keith Belcher, 'Dressing down for strip shows', *Broadcast*, 5 July 1985.

## Chapter 9

1. Simon Bates, 'Who's listening?', programme of the 1986 Music Radio Conference, Radio Academy.
2. Speaking in session on specialist music at 1986 Music Radio Conference.

3. Derek Chinnery, interview with the author, 24 January 1985.
4. *Ibid.*
5. British Market Research Bureau, 'The Radio Luxembourg audience', commissioned by Radio Luxembourg, 1983. See summary of the report's main findings in 'Luxembourg surveys evening radio', *Music Week*, 13 August 1983.
6. *Ibid.*
7. Interview with the author, 17 November 1986.
8. Simon Frith, *The Sociology of Rock*, London, Constable, 1978, p. 56. Frith does, however, locate music as a focus of leisure not just in a class context but in that of 'leisure deviancy' – 'people who are deviant not in the way they value music, but in the way they consume it'. See Frith, pp. 56–8.
9. Andrew Weiner, 'From underground to progressive rock', *The Story of Pop*, London, Phoebus, 1973, p. 516.
10. Frith, p. 70.
11. 'London to launch late-night "club" ', *Broadcast*, 23 January 1987.
12. Johnny Beerling, 'Radio recruits required', *Music Week*, 5 April 1986.
13. Johnny Beerling, 'How ads would change the sound of Radio 1', *Broadcast*, 2 May 1986.
14. Derek Chinnery, interview with the author, 24 January 1985.
15. Comment made at session on specialist music at the 1986 Music Radio Conference.
16. Quoted in Roma Felstein, 'What price ethnic programming?', *Broadcast*, 16 March 1984.

17. *Ibid.*
18. Mike Shaft, 'Now we need a black network', *Broadcast*, 29 June 1984.
19. Capital Radio's reapplication for the London (General and Entertainment) local radio contract. See a critique of the application by Nick Higham, 'What's coming next for black Londoners?', *Broadcast*, 11 July 1983.
20. Charlie Gillett, interview with the author, 12 May 1986.
21. Neville Cheetham, *Young People and Local Radio: A Report*, London, National Youth Bureau, 1982.
22. Manpower Services Commission, *Broadcasting and Youth*, London, MSC, Carnouste Gulbenkian Foundation, 1979, pp. 107–8.
23. IBA, *Television and Radio 1986*, London, IBA, 1985, p. 140.
24. David Thomas, interview with the author, 18 February 1985.
25. Unpublished letter to the author, 14 August 1986.
26. For the work of Local Advisory Committees in ILR, see Mike Johnson, 'Public consultation; what's the point?', *Independent Broadcasting*, 32, 18–19.
27. See Brian West, 'Wanted: policy on community radio', *Marketing*, 28 February 1985.
28. Tenth report from the Select Committee on Nationalized Industries, IBA, London, HMSO, 1978, vol. 2, p. 125.
29. For a full inside account of the background to the campaign for community radio in Britain, see Simon Partridge, *Not the BBC/IBA: The Case for Community Radio*, London, Comedia, 1982, *passim*.
30. Lennie Michaels, 'Air on a shoe string', *Time Out*, 29 March 1979.
31. John Hind and Stephen Mosco, *Rebel Radio: The Full Story of British Pirate Radio*, London, Pluto Press, 1985.
32. See Sarah Gibbings, 'Pirates launch a broadside', *Mail on Sunday*, 19 August 1984; 'Pop go the pirates', *Sunday Express Magazine*, 25 November 1984.
33. Vron Ware, 'The station that puts heart into soul', *Guardian*, 8 April, 1985. Peter Fiddick acknowledged that the newspaper had been victim of a hoax in the *Guardian* on 15 April 1985.
34. JICRAR surveys, 1977 and 1984. See 'Pirates over-rated', *Broadcast*, 17 August 1984.
35. For accounts of Greek pirate radio in London, see Philip Kleinman, 'Greek fire scorches the rulebook', *Guardian*, 23 July 1984; Mark Leslie, 'Radio pirate – or Robin Hood?', *Enfield Independent*, 25 July 1984; and Hind and Mosco, pp. 67–72.
36. 'DTI sunset for Sunshine Radio', *Broadcast*, 8 March 1985.
37. Guidelines to applicants, quoted in Nick Higham, 'Neighbourhoods reveal the good taste of radio', *Broadcast*, 13 September 1985.
38. A full list of community radio applicants was published in *Broadcast*, 29 November 1985.
39. Quoted in ' "Racist cry" over Tory community radio axe', *Broadcast*, 4 July 1986.
40. *Radio: Choices and Opportunities*, London, HMSO, February 1987.
41. Colin Walters, 'Why the Home Office must see ILR's point', *Marketing Week*, 6 December 1984.
42. David Thomas, interview with the author, 18 February 1985.
43. 'Needletime breakthrough', *Broadcast*, 5 June 1987.
44. See 'Community radio at union rates?', *Broadcast*, 13 July 1984.
45. Unpublished DoE study by development consultants Urbed. See Rosie Pearson's discussion of the study, 'Young, gifted and jobless', *Independent*, 28 October 1986.
46. 'Researchers to explore black spending power', *Campaign*, 9 January 1987.
47. Quoted in Brian Wenham, 'Mr Hurd's new recipe for radio', *Observer*, 24 January 1988.

48. See John Whitehead, 'The problem of the teenage gap', *Marketing Week*, 25 July 1986, for a discussion of the findings of *Youth Facts '86*, a major commercial research project into marketing and youth (Marketing Direction, 1986).


## Conclusion

1. Nick Higham, 'LBC under analysis', *Broadcast*, 13 February 1987.
2. Branson's service, operative from July 1988, was widely regarded as a testing ground and rehearsal for Virgin's planned entry into national commercial radio. Presenters recruited included Bob Harris, Nicky Horne, Janice Long and television chat show host Jonathan Ross. See 'Virgin woos ILR', *Broadcast*, 11 March 1988; Martin Loat, 'All-night fighters', *Guardian*, 18 July 1988; John Marshall, 'Heat of the Night', *Time Out*, 27 July 1988; and Sid Smith, 'Radio Wars', Q, August 1988.
3. *Music Week*, 21 March 1987. See news story, 'Power and the pirates', *London Daily News*, 3 March 1987.
4. Hilary Robinson, 'Now radio looks at the small print', *Marketing Week*, 6 March 1987.
5. For an account of the Heath government's original plans for radio and television, see Lord Hill, *Behind the Screen: The Broadcasting Memoirs of Lord Hill of Luton*, London, Sidgwick & Jackson, 1974, pp. 160–3.
6. Douglas Hurd, 'A boring mishmash? That's not my plan', *Guardian*, 1 February 1988.
7. Richard Barbrook, 'Community radio in Britain', in *Making Waves: The Politics of Communications*, Radical Science 16, Radical Science Collective, London, Free Association Books, 1985, pp. 56–7.
8. *Ibid.*, pp. 73–4.
9. Quoted in report on 1984 Radio Festival session on community broadcasting, 'Community radio at union rates?', *Broadcast*, 13 July 1984.
10. For an account of the GLC's involvement in community radio, see John Carvel, *Citizen Ken*, London, Chatto & Windus, 1984, pp. 206–11.
11. *Radio: Choices and Opportunities*, London, HMSO, 1987, p. 33.
12. *Ibid.*, p. 36.
13. *Ibid.*, p. 29.
14. Hurd *op. cit.*
15. Quoted in Peter Fiddick, 'Scepticism greets Hurd's proposals for radio', *Guardian*, 21 January 1988.
16. For an account of the various programming possibilities for national commercial radio, see Nick Higham, 'Big names move in for INR', *Broadcast*, 13 March 1987.
17. Hurd *op. cit.*
18. Raymond Williams, *Communications*, London, Chatto & Windus, 1966, p. 106.
19. Quoted in Dave Hill, 'Twenty-five years in an open-necked shirt', *Independent*, 6 January 1987.

# Bibliography

Baehr, Helen, (ed.) (1980) *Women and Media*, Women's Studies International Quarterly, Oxford, 3(1), Oxford, Pergamon Press.

Baehr, Helen, and Ryan, Michéle (1984) *Shut Up and Listen! Women and Local Radio: A View from the Inside*, London, Comedia.

Barnard, Stephen (1986) *Rock: An Illustrated History*, London, Macdonald Orbis.

Barnouw, Erik (1966–68) *The History of Broadcasting in the United States*, vols. 1 to 3, New York, Oxford University Press.

(1975) *Tube of Plenty: The Evolution of American Television*, New York, Oxford University Press.

Baron, Mike (1975) *Independent Radio*, Lavenham, Terence Dalton.

Bennett, Tony. *et al.* (eds.) (1983) *Formations of Pleasure*, London, Routledge & Kegan Paul.

*et al.* (eds.) (1986) *Popular Culture and Social Relations*, Milton Keynes, Open University Press.

Bird, Brian (1958) *Skiffle*, London, Robert Hale.

Blackburn, Tony (1985) *The Living Legend: An Autobiography*, London, Comet.

Booker, Simon (1983) *Inside Capital Radio 194: Ten Years of Music, Magic and Madness*, London, Capital Radio.

Briggs, Asa (1965–79) *The History of Broadcasting in the United Kingdom*, Vols. 1 to 4, Oxford, Oxford University Press.

(1985) *The BBC: The First Fifty Years*, Oxford, Oxford University Press.

Briggs, Susan (1981) *Those Radio Times*, London, Weidenfeld & Nicolson.

Butcher, Geoffrey (1986) *Next to a Letter from Home: Major Glenn Miller's Wartime Band*, London, Sphere.

Carvel, John (1984) *Citizen Ken*, London, Chatto & Windus.

Chambers, Iain (1985) *Urban Rhythms: Pop Music and Popular Culture*, London, Macmillan.

Colin, Sid (1977) *And the Bands Played On*, London, Elm Tree Books.

Coward, Rosalind (1984) *Female Desire: Women's Sexuality Today*, St Albans, Paladin.

Crisell, Andrew (1986) *Understanding Radio*, London, Methuen.

Curran, James and Seaton, Jean (1985) *Power without Responsibility: The Press and Broadcasting in Britain*, London, Methuen.

Denisoff, R. Serge (1975) *Solid Gold: The Popular Record Industry*, New Brunswick, Transaction.

Downing, John (1980) *The Media Machine*, London, Pluto Press.

Dyer, Richard (1973) *Light Entertainment*, London, British Film Institute.

Eberly, Philip K. (1982) *Music in the Air: America's Changing Tastes in Popular Music, 1920–80*, New York, Hastings House.

Frith, Simon (1978) *The Sociology of Rock*, London, Constable.

Gammond, Peter, and Horricks, Raymond (1980) *The Music Goes Round and Round: A Cool Look at the Music Industry*, London, Quartet Books.

Garfield, Simon (1986) *Expensive Habits: The Dark Side of the Record Industry*, London, Faber & Faber.

Gillett, Charlie (1971) *The Sound of the City*, London, Sphere.

Godbolt, Jim (1984) *A History of Jazz in Britain*, London, Paladin.

Gorham, Maurice (1948) *Sound and Fury: 21 Years at the BBC*, London, Percival Marshall.

Gurevitch, Michael *et al.* (eds.) (1982) *Culture, Society and the Media*, London, Methuen.

Hall, Stuart (1978) *Policing the Crisis: Mugging, the State and Law and Order*, London, Macmillan.

—— *et al.* (eds.) (1980) *Culture, Media, Language*, London, Hutchinson.

Hammond, Ray (1985) *How to Get a Hit Record*, London, Javelin Books.

Harris, Paul (1968) *When Pirates Ruled the Waves*, London, Impulse.

Hardy, Phil (1985) *The British Record Industry*, London, IASPM.

Hebdige, Dick (1979) *Subculture: The Meaning of Style*, London, Methuen.

Henry, Stuart, and Von Joel, Mike, (1984) *Pirate Radio: Then and Now*, Poole, Blandford Press.

Hibberd, Stuart (1950) *This is London*, London, Macdonald and Evans.

Hill, Charles (1974) *Behind the Screen: The Broadcasting Memoirs of Lord Hill of Luton*, London, Sidgwick & Jackson.

Hind, John, and Mosco, Stephen (1985) *Rebel Radio: The Full Story of British Pirate Radio*, London, Pluto Press.

Hoggart, Richard (1958) *The Uses of Literacy*, London, Pelican.

Hood, Stuart (1972) *The Mass Media*, London, Macmillan.

Horn, David (ed.) (1985) *Popular Music Perspectives 2: Papers from the Second International Conference on Popular Music Studies*, Exeter, IASPM.

King, Josephine, and Stott, Mary, (eds.) (1977) *Is This Your Life? Images of Women in the Media*, London, Virago.

Langham, Josephine (1986) *Radio Research: The Comprehensive Guide*, London, The Radio Academy.

Lewis, Peter M. (1978) *Whose Media? The Annan Report and After: A Citizen's Guide to Radio and Television*, London, Consumers Association.

Local Radio Workshop (1982) *Nothing Local About It: London's Local Radio*, London, Comedia.

—— (1983) *Capital: Local Radio and Private Profit*, London, Comedia.

Lynn, Vera (1976) *Vocal Refrain*, London, Star Books.

Mabey, Richard (1969) *The Pop Process*, London, Hutchinson Educational.

McCarthy, Albert (1974) *The Dance Band Era*, London, Spring Books.

McFarlane, Gavin (1980) *Copyright: The Development and Exercise of the Performing Right*, Eastbourne, John Offord.

Melly, George (1970) *Revolt into Style*, London, Penguin.

Middleton, Richard, and Horn, David, (eds.) (1981–7) *Popular Music: A Yearbook*, vols. 1 to 5, Cambridge, Cambridge University Press.

Michelmore, Cliff, and Metcalfe, Jean (1986) *Two-Way Story*, London, Elm Tree Books.

Minihan, Janet (1977) *The Nationalization of Culture: The Development of State Subsidies to the Arts in Great Britain*, London, Hamish Hamilton.

Murray, Pete (1975) *One Day I'll Forget My Trousers*, London, Everest.

Nichols, Richard (1983) *Radio Luxembourg: The Station of the Stars*, London, Comet.

Oakley, Ann (1974) *Housewife*, Harmondsworth, Pelican.

Parker, Derek (1977) *Radio: The Great Years*, Newton Abbott, David & Charles.

Partridge, Simon (1982) *Not the BBC/IBA: The case for Community Radio*, London, Comedia.

Payne, Jack (1932) *This is Jack Payne*, London, Sampson, Low and Marston.

Peacock, Alan, and Weir, Ronald (1975) *The Composer in the Market Place*, London, Faber Music.

Pearsall, Ronald (1976) *Popular Music of the 20s*, Newton Abbott, David & Charles.

Pickles, Wilfred (1949) *Between You and Me*, London, Werner Laurie.

Plomley, Roy (1980) *Days Seemed Longer*, London, Eyre Methuen.

Rosko, Emperor (1976) *Emperor Rosko's DJ Book*, London, Everest.

Savile, Jimmy (1975) *Love is an Uphill Thing*, London, Star Books.

Sheppard, Roy (1986) *The DJ's Handbook*, London, Everest.

Skues, Keith (1968) *Radio Onederland*, Lavenham, Landmark Press.

Stuart, Charles (ed.) (1975) *The Reith Diaries*, London, Collins.

Thomas, Howard (1977) *With an Independent Air: Encounters during a Lifetime of Broadcasting*, London, Weidenfeld & Nicolson.

Thompson, Denys (ed.) (1964) *Discrimination and Popular Culture*, London, Pelican.

Tracy, Sheila (1983) *Who's Who on Radio*, Kingswood, World's Work.

Tunstall, Jeremy (1977) *The Media are American: Anglo-American media in the world*, London, Constable.

(1983) *The Media in Britain*, London, Constable.

Waites, Bernard, *et al.* (eds.) (1982) *Popular Culture: Past and Present*, London, Croom Helm.

Wale, Michael (1972) *Vox Pop: Profiles of the Pop Process*, London, Harrap.

Wallis, Roger, and Malm, Krister (1984) *Big Sounds from Small Peoples: The Music Industry in Small Countries*, London, Constable.

Whitcomb, Ian (1972) *After the Ball*, London, Allen Lane.

Williams, Raymond (1966) *Communications*, London, Chatto & Windus.

(1974) *Television: Technology and Cultural Form*, London, Fontana/Collins.

Young, Jimmy (1973) *J.Y.*, London, Star Books.

# Index